The second battlefield

For Jim Sargent

The second battlefield

Women, modernism
and the First World War

Angela K. Smith

Manchester University Press

Manchester and New York

Published by Manchester University Press
Oxford Road, Manchester M13 9NR, UK
and Room 400, 175 Fifth Avenue, New York, NY 10010, USA
www.manchesteruniversitypress.co.uk

Distributed exclusively in the USA by
Palgrave, 175 Fifth Avenue, New York NY 10010, USA

Distributed exclusively in Canada by
UBC Press, University of British Columbia, 2029 West Mall,
Vancouver, BC, Canada V6T 1Z2

British Library Cataloguing-in-Publication Data
A catalogue record for this book is available from the British Library

Library of Congress Cataloging-in-Publication Data
A catalog record for this book is available from the Library of Congress

ISBN 10: 0 7190 5301 3

ISBN 13: 978 0 7190 5301 6

First published 2000 by Manchester University Press

First digital, on-demand edition produced by Lightning Source 2007

Contents

Acknowledgements

This book began as a doctoral thesis and has been nurtured in a number of different environments. I am particularly grateful to Jenny Hartley for her constant advice and encouragement. I would also thank other valuable readers: Trudi Tate, Ann Thompson, Louise Jackson, Nicola Humble, Kim Reynolds and Vesna Pistotnik, and for their useful suggestions, Claire Tylee and Caroline Zilboorg. Thanks are also due to others who supported me through the Roehampton years: Erik Svarny, Claudine Brodin, Jillian Bonner, Helen Poskitt, Sarah Swing, Sue Roderick, Annette Hill, Lisa Sainsbury and Anne Button.

I have also received important advice and encouragement from colleagues and friends at the University of Plymouth. Thanks are due to Tony Lopez, Alan Munton, Mary Brewer, Marion Gibson, Harry Bennett and Laura Salisbury. I am also grateful for the support of my family and friends, John and Maisie Smith, Simon Smith, Sarah Beaman, Deborah Smith, Martin Bradbury for valuable photographic advice and most particularly, as always, Jim Sargent.

The staff at Roehampton Institute Library, the University of Plymouth Library, the Departments of Printed Books and Documents at the Imperial War Museum, the Fawcett Library, London Guildhall University and the Liddle Collection, University of Leeds, have been consistently helpful. Also Matthew Frost and Lauren McAllister for constant good advice.

I am very grateful to Eric and Ginny Stobart for allowing me unlimited access to the papers of Mabel St Clair Stobart; to Giles Pemberton for giving permission to quote from the letters of Eleanora Pemberton; to Evelyn Cleverly OBE for giving permission to quote from the diary of Mary Brown and to Ann Mitchell for giving permission to quote from the diary of Winifred Kenyon.

Every effort has been made to trace copyright owners where applicable, but if any have been omitted please contact the publisher. Apologies are offered to those whom it has proved impossible to identify.

Abbreviations

FANY	First Aid Nursing Yeomanry
NUWSS	National Union of Women's Suffrage Societies
QAIMNSR	Queen Alexandra's Imperial Military Nursing Service Reserve
TFNS	Territorial Forces Nursing Service
VAD	Voluntary Aid Detachment
WAAC	Women's Army Auxiliary Corps
WSPU	Women's Social and Political Union
YWCA	Young Women's Christian Association

Introduction:
the First World War,
modernisms and women

The war is the world, and this cardboard house, eight by nine, behind the trenches, with a roof that leaks and windows that rattle, and an iron stove in the corner, is my home in it. I have lived here ever since I can remember.[1]

In 1914 Mary Borden's field hospital unit entered 'La Zone Interdite', 'the strip of land immediately behind the zone of fire',[2] so named by the French Army because it was out of bounds to all but military personnel. As a military nurse, she was able to cross the geographical boundaries that separated the violent reality of the First World War from civilian society, that relatively safe haven within which most women remained. Borden's work with the medical teams of the French Army took her backwards and forwards along the Western Front throughout the four years of the war, enabling her to observe at first hand the life and death of the battlefield.

But Borden's lifestyle allowed her to cross other boundaries too. An American millionaire married into the British aristocracy, she had moved in Bohemian circles before the outbreak of war and continued to liaise with experimental writers and artists while serving in France.[3] These influences are apparent in *The Forbidden Zone*,[4] which records her experience of the First World War in fictional, non-fictional and poetic fragments. The prose fragments and the poems work to give voice to the silent Poilus (the ordinary soldiers conscripted into the French Army), as well as representing her own voice, as nurse, trying to express her perceptions. The stories, written in the years that followed the war, explore her own responses against a backdrop of hospital life. She employs a wide variety of literary styles, many of which parallel the simultaneously developing modernisms of the early twentieth century. Through this eclecticism, Borden embodies the central thematic concerns of this book: a woman, writing an account of the war, adopting diverse, innovative and modernistic narrative techniques to bring her record to life.

The First World War

Why the First World War? Much has been written about this catalystic conflict in the last years of the twentieth century, suggesting that there are still many unanswered questions. We have trouble coming to terms with the nightmare images of trench warfare perpetuated down the generations by the anguish of Wilfred Owen, the bitterness of Siegfried Sassoon and the detachment of Robert Graves. The haunting voices of the lost continue to reach us through the testimony of the dwindling ranks of survivors.[5] Arguments persist concerning the cause of the war, the motives of the nations involved, even the need to fight at all. In his influential book *The Pity of War*,[6] Niall Ferguson argues against military theorists that, from the British point of view at least, the conflict was avoidable and that the unnecessary economic repercussions remain with us today. Meanwhile the harsh Treaty of Versailles, and the intervening years of isolation and appeasement, lay under the sinister shadow of the century's second great war.[7]

Of course there have been other wars that have promoted social and political debate and inspired literary creativity. The Napoleonic Wars, the Crimea, the American Civil War, the Boer War – the nineteenth century is littered with battlefields. In the final decades, military strategists were able to employ a range of technological weaponry that began to change the face of modern warfare. But the ironclad battleships and trenches of the American conflict were safely located thousands of miles away from the British people, secure in their homeland, the bedrock of empire. Similarly the imperial war in South Africa, as the century closed, left the civilian population at home relatively untouched. However, the First World War could not be so distanced. The guns of the Western Front could be heard across the English Channel. Zeppelins carried out bombing raids along the east coast of Britain. Men were conscripted into combatant or non-combatant service. Women were encouraged to take the places of their men – in the workforce, in industry, on the land. Of the 5,215,162 men who served in the British army, 44.4 per cent were killed or wounded.[8] Very few families escaped unscathed.

The First World War, perhaps the first universal war, is the pivotal theme of this book. It is explored through selections of the writing that it inspired and, further, through the way in which the war experience of the writers influenced their styles and techniques. The book seeks to understand the intrinsic links between warfare and literary development at the beginning of the century. Of course this task is far too large for one study, and I have necessarily had to refine the subject matter, focusing almost entirely on the war writing and experience of women.

I have chosen to concentrate primarily on the work of women for a number of reasons. Despite the fact that there has been significant interest in women's writing of the First World War in recent years,[9] it is still an under-researched area in comparison with the literary representation of men's war experience. So, although the focus on women's writing inevitably excludes some important material, it also opens up fascinating new areas of study which can demonstrate a great deal about gendered life and death experience at the beginning of the century. Because the book examines the writing of women from different areas of society, including some previously unpublished material, it uncovers new representations of the war to contribute to a wider picture.

The search for women's writings of the First World War is, in itself, an important one. Historically the war has been defined as an arena of male dominance, perhaps because many of the most haunting representations of war experience that have survived the intervening decades are built around images of trench warfare. The re-creations presented by Remarque, Sassoon, Barbusse and Graves are so powerful that it is not surprising they have influenced the direction of much historical and literary research.[10] But in reality the trench experience was one encountered by less than half the total population; consequently these texts provide an unrepresentative record of the impact of the war. The current drive to rediscover the wealth of writing produced by women during and after the war, and since then shelved in libraries and archives, rarely to be seen again in print, complements the rich work on war literature carried out in the last decades.[11] It is important to reconsider all types of forgotten fiction, from the sentimental love stories of Berta Ruck,[12] to the pastoral idealism of Sheila Kaye-Smith's *Little England*[13] and the propagandist spy thriller represented in Elizabeth Robins's *The Messenger*.[14] But this book is concerned with the re-establishment of those women who push the boundaries of convention a little further, creating a different kind of female language for the literary representation of war.

Women's writing has very often been excluded from discussions concerning the relationship between modernism and the First World War, perhaps because women are not obvious participants in the popular mythic representations of the war which developed simultaneously with many accepted modernist works. The search for war-generated modernisms in the work of women – some established writers, others completely unknown – has been an exciting one. It could as easily be done through the work of men, crossing gender boundaries once more, but the remit here is women.

The book explores the way in which the heterogeneous nature of women's discourse produced during and after the war can provide an interface between some of the realist literary traditions of the nineteenth century and the more experimental forms of the 1920s. It is divided into two parts. Part I gives attention to non-fiction prose writing, beginning with private and unpublished sources in the form of women's war letters and diaries, working through the transposition of such documents into published versions of personal records. Part II turns to the exploration of fiction, to identify the blossoming of more avant-garde characteristics – modernisms, the roots of which may be located in some of the personal writings and war experiences.

Modernisms

In his book, *Modernisms*, Peter Nicholls sets out 'to provide a conceptual map of the different modernist tendencies'.[15] He challenges the familiar critical assumption of a monolithic modernism, by exploring the 'connections between style, authority and gender which underpinned the various constructions of modernism.'[16] He does so by tracing the roots of modernistic experiment in literature of the nineteenth century from Baudelaire to Melville, moving on through such artistic movements as French Symbolism, Decadence, Futurism, Cubism and Expressionism in the identification of difference. This acknowledgement of 'modernisms' is an important notion, but Nicholls still locates many of these different forces in relation to 'canonical' modernism, that of the 'Men of 1914' – Pound, Eliot, Lewis. Established female modernist writers such as HD (Hilda Doolittle) and Gertrude Stein are termed 'a deliberate and often polemic disturbance within the canonical version'.[17]

Despite early links between HD and Ezra Pound,[18] it seems reasonable to see her work and that of Stein and many other contemporary women as innovatory in its own right, perhaps suggesting that the notion of 'canon' itself is outmoded and needs to be readdressed. As Michael Levenson has argued:

> What once seemed the exclusive affair of 'modern masters', the 'men of 1914' (as Wyndham Lewis called them), now stands revealed as a complex of inventive gestures, daring performances, enacted also by many who were left

out of the account in the early histories of the epoch, histories offered first by the actors themselves and later produced within an academic discourse, willingly guided by the precedents of eminent artists.[19]

Nicholls goes on to examine the 'difference' exhibited by these more prominent female modernists in a useful way. He notes HD's engagement with Freudian psychoanalysis, in contrast with the discomfort expressed by many of her male contemporaries when faced with the ideas of Freud. Marianne DeKoven also stresses the importance of Freud in the development of some female modernisms, in terms of Freud's own research and writings built around women's experience and psychology, of the engagement with issues of psychoanalysis written into texts such as Rebecca West's *The Return of the Soldier*, and in terms of the experiments with female languages carried out by women such as HD, Stein and Dorothy Richardson, which, she suggests, translate through the theoretical work of feminist revisionists such as Luce Irigaray, Julia Kristeva and Helene Cixous.[20] Nicholls discusses Stein, whom he suggests 'invents another version of modernism by circumventing the image altogether and exploring the self-sufficiency of language',[21] an argument which runs parallel with much feminist recasting of notions of modernist enquiry.

These ideas give a brief insight into the current debates surrounding what constitutes modernism, or indeed modernisms. While the image of the 'canon' lingers, it is deeply undermined by the recognition of numerous parallel strands of artistic experimentation, some gendered, many of which are only beginning to be consolidated. This book adds to the debate in two ways. First, it expands ideas of how modernisms may be formulated. Although some of the women discussed in the following chapters are already acknowledged as modernist writers, women such as HD, Katherine Mansfield and, to some extent, May Sinclair and Rebecca West, many are excluded from or unknown to such debates. Second, the book explores the interface between women writing modernisms and the First World War.

Paul Fussell has argued for the 'stylistic traditionalism' of most writing of the First World War, suggesting, 'The roster of major innovative talents who were not involved with the war is long and impressive. It includes Yeats, Woolf, Pound, Eliot, Lawrence and Joyce – that is, the masters of the modern movement'.[22] But this assertion is fundamentally naïve, since the war had a significant impact on everyone who came into contact with it, and this impact is clearly traceable in some of the work of these 'modernist masters'.[23] Furthermore, much of the writing produced as a direct result of the war experience, even that of amateur diarists and letter writers, contains within it elements of stylistic change as these writers strive to find a way to articulate an experience which cannot be easily condensed into conventional language.

By concentrating on the female literary voice I do not want to suggest that a similar argument could not be made for male war writers. The medical testimonies of Georges Duhamel contain many of the modernist characteristics that enhance the hospital stories of Mary Borden and Enid Bagnold; the narrative style of Erich Maria Remarque's *All Quiet on the Western Front* clearly influenced Evadne Price's feminist reworking of the story in *Not So Quiet . . .*; while the poetic language, syntactical unorthodoxy and the non-standard use of punctuation in e. e. cummings's *The Enormous Room* renders the text as deserving of critical reassessment as the work of HD, May Sinclair or Rebecca West.[24]

In *Rich and Strange*, Marianne DeKoven argues that modernist practices evolved to express the radical and revolutionary movements of the early twentieth century. She gives particular attention to the growth of feminism and socialism as ideologies that reject the political doctrines of the nineteenth century. *The second battlefield* interprets the First World War as an equally significant movement, which could demand of its participants new modes of articulation to do justice to the experience of a revolution of such epic proportions.[25] In response, some writers developed various kinds of new or modernist strategies, and some did not. This study focuses upon the former. Formal and stylistic experimentation turns up in unexpected places, and not only in the publications which were *self-consciously* avant-garde.

DeKoven cites a number of characteristics of literary modernism which can be applied to the writing of both women and men as they respond to these associated political and social crises: aesthetic self-consciousness; juxtaposition, montage and fragmentation; paradox, ambiguity and uncertainty; dehumanisation; conscious artifice and the transcendence of familiarity; lack of continuity and crisis. In addition she highlights the way in which modernist forms often include disruptions of hierarchical syntax and other deviations from standard linguistic form.

These characteristics, when filtered through alternative modes of female experience, take on different identities; become female modernisms. Women's participant experience in the First World War, a maelstrom that influenced these inventive processes, opens up the possibilities for the development of further female modernisms. Much of the first section of this book focuses on front-line experience; women who penetrate Mary Borden's 'Forbidden Zone'. These women are able to contribute alternative literary constructions of direct war experience despite, or perhaps because of their alien status. These writings may be termed 'accidental modernisms', created by women who are, in a traditional sense, out of place and time, inadvertently adding to the development of modernisms through their anachronistic location. But arguably, this war, more so than any previous one, became a woman's place, as women from all walks of life were drawn in, both directly and indirectly. This variety of participation is reflected in their written responses.

The women

The beginning of the twentieth century was an exciting time for women. Campaigners for women's rights had been making slow headway in the areas of women's general rights, education and the medical profession since the mid-nineteenth century. Around the turn of the twentieth century there was an acceleration in the campaign for the vote, as many of the numerous suffrage societies amalgamated to create the National Union of Women's Suffrage Societies (NUWSS), closely followed by the formation, by Emmeline Pankhurst and her daughters, of the much more militant Women's Social and Political Union (WSPU).

The unavoidable presence of these movements, either as a result of their peaceful demonstrations or their terrorism respectively, ensured that the issue of women's suffrage was forced on to the political agenda. Prior to 1914, the campaigners for women's rights were frequently thwarted by the argument that since women could not represent their country on the field of battle and thus make the ultimate sacrifice, they could not expect equal citizenship with men.[26] Although some women had found the opportunity to become involved with the action of war during earlier conflicts (the women who worked in the hospitals of the Crimea; Mabel St Clair Stobart and her hospital units in the Balkan Wars in 1912), no previous war had given women the opportunity for the degree of involvement that they were to experience in the First World War. As women got closer to the fighting, so they were able to dismiss the claims that discounted them as citizens; they created the opportunity to construct a heroism which put them on a near equal footing with their male contemporaries.

Much of the first part of this book examines the writing of women who obtained this 'front-line' experience in one form or another, through their private testimonies or their published records. Chapter 1 explores the war through the private diaries of a variety of women, some of whom remained in Britain, others who nursed overseas coming into close contact with the violent reality of the war. These revealing and often poignant records are interesting for many reasons, particularly in terms of the construction of gender histories. But they are also very valuable for the impressions of literary development that they share with the reader. Many of these women borrow from their own literary education as they search for adequate ways to express the things they see and feel. Others adopt less conventional narrative structures as the circumstances of their lives in the firing line make detailed expression impossible. Collectively, these diaries illustrate how some women were involved, albeit inadvertently, in a search for different literary forms triggered by the war experience.

Chapter 2 focuses more specifically on women who operated in the front line. These women used that experience to construct versions of themselves for public consumption in order to promote a cause or idea. Serbian soldier Flora Sandes, the only British woman to see actual military service in the First World War, and hospital unit commandant Mabel St Clair Stobart, both wrote diaries during the war which they later used as the basis for published records. This translation process is an interesting one in literary terms, as well as politically, as the women were able to develop their war experience as a valuable campaigning tool.

Flora Sandes and Mabel Stobart had an unusual amount of direct contact with the actual line of fire. But many women came very close to danger when they worked as nurses or Voluntary Aid Detachments (VADs) in the base and field hospitals of the forbidden zone. Chapter 3 moves entirely into the realm of published responses to the war and examines hospital stories, a genre that is interesting both in terms of content and style. It is here, in the writing of Enid Bagnold, Ellen La Motte and Mary Borden, that some of the 'accidental modernisms' of the First World War begin to emerge more clearly. These are women whose motives for writing are very often political, but whose styles are innovatory and different as they discover the most effective ways to communicate their ideas. The war affects women and affects their writing; the result is explored here as a different kind of modernist enquiry.

The fictional representations explored in the second part of the book take these enquires significantly further. Many established women writers responded to the war in fiction from its earliest days, providing a commentary on the impact of war which is often lively and enlightening. Others, writing later, used their work to reply to the many war narratives by men, which appeared in the decade following the armistice. Chapter 4

concentrates on two of these female responses, tracking gendered interpretations and literary style. Evadne Price's *Not So Quiet... Stepdaughters
of War* is in part a rewriting of Erich Maria Remarque's highly successful
All Quiet on the Western Front, from a woman's point of view. But it is also
more than this, investigating many different types of female experience.
HD's autobiographical novel *Bid Me to Live*[27] begins to raise many questions about the impact of the war on female modernist innovation as she
retells the story of her wartime marriage to Imagist poet Richard
Aldington, a story echoed in his earlier novel *Death of a Hero*.[28]

With the outbreak of the war, many women felt that morally they could
only oppose the conflict. Some felt this for political reasons: the war was
the responsibility of the men who had begun it, not the women who were
excluded from government. Others invoked biological arguments: there
was a belief held by many women that as mothers, the creators of life, any
involvement in the destruction of human life was alien to their nature. Yet
others cited intellectual or artistic reasons, and it is no accident that many
of the writers of fiction that address the issue of pacifism do so through
the medium of the artist. Chapter 5 looks at how established writers like
May Sinclair and Rose Macaulay used their war novels to enter into the
debate about the complex role of the artist in wartime, refuting or endorsing the notion that war means the death of art. Less well known, Rose
Allatini continued the argument in her 1918 novel *Despised and Rejected*
which relates pacifism not only to art but also to other marginalised
sexual, racial and political groups.[29] This discussion of artistic integrity
and commitment, highlighted by the threatening environment of the war,
is reminiscent of many parallel modernist investigations of the interface
between art and life.

Chapter 6 explores the relationship between the war and female modernist practice more directly, through the varied writings of Katherine
Mansfield, Rebecca West and Enid Bagnold. It is here that ideas surrounding the links between women, the First World War and modernisms are
consolidated.

Many of the literary sources for work in this field, both private and
published, have been significantly under-researched. Brief extracts from
the letters of Eleanora Pemberton have been reproduced in *Women's
Letters in Wartime 1450–1945*, edited by Eva Figes.[30] John Masters, in
Fourteen Eighteen,[31] adopts carefully chosen extracts from the diary of
Ethel Bilborough to create his impression of an 'authentic voice of
England in those days'.[32] But his account is unbalanced and makes no
enquiry into the character and motivation of the woman behind the pen.

Most of the primary source materials incorporated here have not been used before, enabling this book to offer an important new contribution to the fields of war, literary and historic study.

For Mary Borden, and many of the other women discussed in the following chapters, the four years of world war were all-encompassing and bitterly personal. The monotony, the repetition of the days combating suffering on the second battlefield of the forbidden zone, became a way of life so powerful, so apparently endless, that the memories of other lives dwindled. Borden wrote, 'The war is the world, and this cardboard house, eight by nine, behind the trenches, with a roof that leaks and windows that rattle, and an iron stove in the corner, is my home in it. I have lived here ever since I can remember'.[33] And the sentiment is echoed by many others: Evadne Price, 'What is to become of us when the killing is over?'[34] and HD, 'The War will never be over'.[35]

It is not new to argue that women were involved in the First World War, nor that they wrote about their experiences. This book seeks to expand our understanding of women's writing about the war. Many of the works I discuss are based upon personal experience; others are based upon hearsay, or fantasy. Women's experience of the First World War, like men's, was complex and diverse, and it produced a startling range of writings. Above all, this book hopes to show that there were many different histories, different kinds of war writing and, indeed, different kinds of modernism. All these writings contribute to our cultural memories of the First World War, and they help us to further understand the development of the twentieth century.

Notes

1 Mary Borden (1929), 'Moonlight', from her *The Forbidden Zone*, London, William Heinemann, pp. 52–3.
2 *Ibid.*, Preface.
3 Borden married General Sir Edward Spears to become Lady Spears. She moved in what later became known as modernist circles in the years before the outbreak of war. She was a friend and patron to Wyndham Lewis. Their relationship developed into an affair in 1915. For further information see Jeffrey Meyers (1980), *The Enemy: A Biography of Wyndham Lewis*, London, Routledge & Kegan Paul.
4 Borden, *The Forbidden Zone*.
5 See for example Peter Vansittart (1998), *Voices from the Great War*, London, Pimlico (first published by Jonathan Cape, 1981) and the oral history records of Lynn MacDonald.

6 Niall Ferguson (1998), *The Pity of War*, London, Allen Lane.

7 The harsh terms of the Treaty of Versailles brought severe problems to the German economy and, arguably, created a breeding ground for fascist politics. The USA withdrew from world politics in the years following the First World War, while the British government adopted a policy of appeasement in an attempt to prevent further war in Europe.

8 See J. M. Winter (1988), *The Experience of World War I*, London, Guild, p. 202.

9 The past few years have seen the growth of scholarly interest in women's writing of the war. See for example: Claire Tylee (1990), *The Great War and Women's Consciousness*, London, Macmillan; Miriam Cooke and Angela Woollacott (eds) (1993), *Gendering War Talk*, Princeton, NJ, Princeton University Press; Helen Cooper, A. A. Munich and S. M. Squier (eds) (1989), *Arms and the Woman: War, Gender, and Literary Representation*, Chapel Hill, NC, and London, University of North Carolina Press; Dorothy Goldman (ed.) (1993), *Women and World War 1: The Written Response*, London, Macmillan; Dorothy Goldman with Jane Gledhill and Judith Hattaway (1995), *Women Writers and the Great War*, New York, Twayne; Margaret Higonnet *et al.* (eds) (1987), *Behind the Lines: Gender in Two World Wars*, New Haven, CT, and London, Yale University Press; Sharon Ouditt (1994), *Fighting Forces, Writing Women*, London, Routledge; Suzanne Raitt and Trudi Tate (eds) (1997), *Women's Fiction and the Great War*, Oxford, Clarendon Press.

10 Most of the major studies of war literature engage primarily with male authors, perpetuating the myth that the trench experience was universal and most significant: Paul Fussell (1977), *The Great War and Modern Memory*, Oxford, Oxford University Press; Bernard Bergonzi (1980), *Heroes' Twilight*, London, Macmillan; George Parfitt (1988), *Fiction of the First World War*, London, Faber & Faber; Eric J. Leed (1981), *No Man's Land: Combat and Identity in World War 1*, Cambridge, Cambridge University Press; Modris Eksteins (1989), *Rites of Spring: The First World War and the Birth of the Modern Age*, New York, Bantam Press. Others like Samuel Hynes (1990), *A War Imagined*, London, Bodley Head are more liberal in the way that they present the experience of war, but such a wide-ranging book does not have the space to carry out much detailed individual exploration.

11 For example: Agnes Cardinal, Dorothy Goldman and Judith Hattaway (1999), *Women's Writing on the First World War*, Oxford, Oxford University Press; Margaret Higgonet (1999), *Lines of Fire: Women Writers of World War 1*, New York, Penguin; Sharon Ouditt (1999), *Women Writers of the First World War – An Annotated Bibliography*, London, Routledge; Claire Tylee (1999), *War Plays by Women*, London, Routledge; Angela K. Smith (2000), *Women's Writing of the First World War: An Anthology*, Manchester, Manchester University Press.

12 Berta Ruck wrote what may be termed women's romantic fiction, which arguably bore little relation to women's actual experience. For example, see B. Ruck (1917), *The Bridge of Kisses*, London, Hodder & Stoughton; or B. Ruck (1919), *The Land Girl's Love Story*, London, Hodder & Stoughton. For further information, see Jane Potter, "'A Great Purifier": The Great War in women's romances and memoirs 1914–1918', in S. Raitt and T. Tate (eds), *Women's Fiction of the Great War*, Oxford, Clarendon Press.

13 Sheila Kaye-Smith (1918), *England*, London, Nisbet. A patriotic study of the effect of war on English rural life in the Romantic tradition of Brooke and Kipling.

14 Elizabeth Robins (1919), *The Messenger*, London, Hodder & Stoughton. A rather sensationalist adventure/spy story which has been compared to the style of John Buchan.

15 Peter Nicholls (1995), *Modernisms: A Literary Guide*, London, Macmillan, Preface.

16 *Ibid.*

17 *Ibid.*, p. 197.

18 They shared a youthful, failed engagement and it was he who famously promoted her as 'H. D. Imagiste'.

19 Michael Levenson (ed.) (1999), 'Introduction', *The Cambridge Companion to Modernism*, Cambridge, Cambridge University Press, pp. 2–3.

20 See Marianne DeKoven, 'Modernism and Gender', in M. Levinson (ed.) (1999), *The Cambridge Companion to Modernism*, Cambridge, Cambridge University Press, pp. 174–93.

21 Nicholls, *Modernisms*, p. 202.

22 Fussell, *The Great War*, pp. 313–14. Fussell's book has been an influential study of the war. Fussell argues that the war was an event of fundamental importance in the shaping of the consciousness of twentieth century culture and ideology. In recent years however, a number of feminist critics have attacked his work because of his failure to acknowledge the existence of women as either writers or participants, thus excluding them from all significance in the development of the century. See for example: Tylee, *The Great War*; Lynne Hanley (1991), *Writing War: Fiction, Gender and Memory*, Amherst, MA, University of Massachusetts Press.

23 For example T. S. Eliot's (1990), 'The Waste Land' in *Selected Poems*, London, Faber & Faber, and D. H. Lawrence's (1986), *Women in Love*, London, Penguin (first published 1920) may be read as responses to the culture of war which surrounded their writing. Similarly Virginia Woolf's (1992), *Jacob's Room*, Oxford and New York, Oxford University Press (first published 1922), her (1976), *Mrs Dalloway*, London, Grafton (first published 1925) and her (1989), *To the Lighthouse*, London, Grafton (first published 1927) may be read with reference to the war.

24 Erich Maria Remarque (1991), *All Quiet On The Western Front*, London,

Picador (first published 1929); Evadne Price (Helen Zenna Smith) (1988) *Not So Quiet... Stepdaughters of War*, London, Virago (first published 1930); E. E. Cummings, (1922) *The Enormous Room*, New York, Boni and Liseright.

25 Marianne DeKoven (1991), *Rich and Strange: Gender, History, Modernism*, Princeton, NJ, Princeton University Press. It should be noted that DeKoven has little to say about the First World War.

26 For further information regarding the war and the campaign for women's suffrage see: Ray Strachey (1989), *The Cause*, London, Virago (first published 1928); Les Garner (1984), *Stepping Stones to Women's Liberty*, London, Heinemann; Sandra Stanley Holton (1986), *Feminism and Democracy: Women's Suffrage and Reform Politics in Britain 1900–1918*, Cambridge, Cambridge University Press; S. S. Holton (1996), *Suffrage Days*, London, Routledge; Maroula Joannou and June Purvis (eds) (1998), *The Women's Suffrage Movement: New Feminist Perspectives*, London and New York, Manchester University Press.

27 Hilda Doolittle (HD) (1984), *Bid Me to Live*, London, Virago (first published 1960).

28 Richard Aldington (1929), *Death of a Hero*, London, Chatto & Windus.

29 Rose Allatini (A. T. Fitzroy) (1988), *Despised and Rejected*, London, GMP (first published 1918).

30 Eva Figes (1994), *Women's Letters in Wartime 1450–1945*, London, Pandora.

31 John Masters (1970), *Fourteen Eighteen*, London, Corgi Books.

32 *Ibid.*, Preface.

33 See note 1 above.

34 Price, *Not So Quiet*.

35 Phrase repeated throughout HD's *Bid Me to Live*.

Part I
Non-fiction

1

The private pen

Private writing of the First World War was very often a clandestine affair because the military authorities made it so. Concern regarding the possible 'leakage of military information'[1] resulted in the publication of a directive by the war office, intended to control the 'contents and dispatch of letters, parcels, etc.'.[2] For the soldiers of the First World War this must have been a painful dictate. It meant, in legal terms, that they were unable to tell their loved ones where they were, what they were doing, if they were well, how they were feeling, or even provide information about other family members or friends. It gave rise to a style of private writing, both in letters and in diaries, built around the empty phrase and the euphemism, entrapped and lifeless within a hollow discourse.

This censorship exacerbated the developing sense of discord between the fighting men and the non-combatants on the home front. This divide ensured that very often the letters received in the trenches seemed as shallow as those posted. Henri Barbusse suggested the futility of these fragile documents in his powerful anti-war novel, *Under Fire*:

> Around the dead flutter letters that have escaped from pockets or cartridge pouches while they were being placed on the ground. Over one of these bits of white paper, whose wings still beat though the mud ensnares them, I stoop slightly and read a sentence – 'My dear Henry, what a fine day it is for your birthday!'[3]

For Barbusse, the letters are as lifeless as the corpses that litter the landscape. The 'still beating' wings emphasise the fragility; delicate creatures which have escaped the security of their pocket homes to be devoured by the same mud that consumes the human dead. The irony of the final line reinforces the hopelessness: it is not a fine day; there will be no more birthdays.

Barbusse suggests that experience cannot be communicated across the divide. The military regulations include vague threats for British soldiers, which operate to further inhibit detailed records.[4] Yet despite these obstacles, the men and women of the First World War kept writing up their experiences as they occurred; filling their diaries and pocketbooks; keeping the postal service busy with their scribblings. These private writings, where they have survived, represent a remarkable primary historical source, despite the best efforts of the censor. They provide a vital tool for understanding the experience of the First World War from both the combatant and the non-combatant point of view.

Many historians have used the private writings of men to illustrate the sometimes turbulent, often boring, life of the trench soldier.[5] But women, too, wrote about their private lives in the form of letters and of diaries, leaving a colourful and varied testimony of the wartime experience. Although extremely valuable from a historical perspective, these documents can often be usefully read as literary texts, despite the imposition of censorship, which was equally as applicable to women writing within the military zone as it was to men. Indeed for women it operated as a kind of double censor as the need to overcome military regulations blended with the opportunity to escape from tight social control of their upbringing. Faced with official restrictions as well as the limitations of their own imaginative or linguistic backgrounds, women composing texts for private consumption often drew on their literary heritage in order to discover a means for authentic self-expression. Where their education failed them, they searched further, often devising new literary techniques in order to articulate their experience adequately.

In her 1929 essay 'Women and Fiction', Virginia Woolf sought to discover a women's history which could explain the development of women's fiction. She turned to the secret history of women's letters and diaries as a means to understanding the development of women's public writing:

> The answer lies at present locked in old diaries, stuffed away in old drawers, half obliterated in the memories of the aged. It is to be found in the lives of the obscure – in those almost unlit corridors of history where the figures of generations of women are so dimly, so fitfully perceived.[6]

Women's experience of the First World War inhabited one such 'almost unlit corridor'. Diaries and letters, long hidden from view, provide a valuable insight both for historical assessments and to indicate the impact of the First World War on literary development. Literary readings of these private texts often bring out a richness that validates these assertions. The

First World War gave many women the opportunity to travel and work in ways that no one could have imagined in the first years of the twentieth century. Many of them wrote about their unusual experiences, providing vital evidence to aid the writing of women's histories and their influence on literary development. As with the private writing of men, women's diaries and letters indicate the conservative culture which produced them while simultaneously illustrating the need for change. Close examination of these texts reveals the traditional influences that helped to shape them, blended with new experimental forms initiated as the women strove to find an appropriate vocabulary to express their new experiences. The result is an exploration of personal consciousness at a time of crisis, which can lead to a fuller picture of the development of women's literature in the long term – not just one narrative, but many.

The link between literature and the writing of the history of the First World War is already well established. This chapter takes this notion further by examining, in more detail, the private writing of a variety of different women as they responded to the war, taking as a starting point an assertion by Paul Fussell from *The Great War and Modern Memory*,[7] that the First World War was literary in a way unmatched by other conflicts. Like men, women experiment with different literary styles as they struggle to find ways adequately to record their experiences, often altering their perspectives in accordance with the tone of the war. The result is a series of shifts, some simple, others more complex, in the way that the writing is structured, often evoking new or different ways of using language, as they revise conventions to find accurate self-expression

The diary has been identified historically as a polyphonic form, articulating a variety of experience,[8] and this seems particularly appropriate when considering the diaries of war. The diaries often blend notions of existing 'feminine' roles with the need to adopt alternative 'masculine' ones in the absence of men. They present war as multi-layered experience in a genre that represents a kind of pastiche of assorted types of writing. It is therefore not surprising to find hints of what might later be identified as experimental writing amongst some of the pages.

In critical terms, women's private writing in the form of diaries and letters may be linked with other forms of women's life-writing such as autobiography. Estelle Jelinek has argued that women's autobiography is often located within the female world of the private, despite their published status.[9] In recent years feminist critics have sought to endorse women's autobiography as an important form of writing,[10] and a related argument can be constructed to suggest women's diaries, too, may hold significant literary value. Similarly, Rebecca Hogan asserts that the diary is an appropriate form for analysis in the field of women's literary studies because it is a specifically feminine mode of discourse.[11] She suggests, 'The diary's valorisation of the detail, its perspective of immersion, its mixing of genres, its principle of inclusiveness, and its expression of intimacy and mutuality all seem to qualify it as a form congenial to women life/writers'.[12]

Critics who are concerned with the importance of the diary as literary text, also speculate regarding the motivation behind the keeping of a diary, and the intended readership, both of which are of particular interest when examining war diaries. Harriet Blodgett considers a variety of motivations ranging from family tradition to self-improvement, through to nostalgia and the need to record experience as a personal souvenir or a record for others.[13] Many of these factors can be applied to the diarists and the letter writers of the war. On 20 January 1915, VAD Winifred Kenyon records that her war diary is a return to a former habit, worrying, 'it is quite impossible to think of writing about everything, so I'm going to write just what occurs to me, and hope that having once started again, I shall keep it up regularly again'.[14] Civilian Ethel Bilborough suggests that her diary will provide a record of the war for posterity, presumably anticipating a readership that moves beyond the personal, while the tiny diary of Mabel St Clair Stobart seems almost certainly to have been written with the notion of a published text in mind, since it provides the basis for *The Flaming Sword in Serbia and Elsewhere*, the political record of her experiences published in 1916.[15] This variety of motives assists in the production of the many different styles, and shall be considered in more detail with the discussion of individual texts.

Personal letters have similarly been equated with women's writing over the centuries, and in wartime the pace of production is considerably accelerated. In the introduction to *Women's Letters in Wartime 1450–1945*, Eva Figes suggests, 'War not only brings separation, which is a necessary prerequisite for writing letters, but, like love, heightens our experience of life. Everything has a new urgency as people are expected to face new dangers, new challenges and unexpected responsibilities'.[16] Women wrote letters to their men at the front, a lifeline home which could be so easily severed as Barbusse suggests. For him, the struggle of the fragile, living letter against the elements of war is a futile one, since nothing can effectively bridge the gap between the home and the battle fronts. Yet some women tried, in their own letters sent from the war zones of Europe as well as from Britain, and these letters often had more than one purpose. Enid Bagnold instructed her mother to keep all the letters she wrote from France, and they later formed the basis of her novel *The Happy Foreigner*.[17]

Eleanora Pemberton, a VAD, anticipated a similar dual purpose for her war correspondence. On 2 November 1914 she wrote, as a postscript to a letter to her parents, 'Finally I should like this letter preserved as I have no time to keep a diary.'[18] Although there may be problems with the idea of letters forming a diary, not the least of which is the issue of military censorship, these letters still illustrate exciting new patterns of literary expression on the part of their writers, as more, better educated women became participants in war than ever before.

Paul Fussell argues:

> By 1914, it was possible for soldiers to be not merely literate but vigorously literate, for the First World War occurred at a special historical moment when two 'liberal' forces were powerfully coinciding in England. On the one hand, the belief in the educative powers of classical and English literature was still extremely strong. On the other, the appeal of popular education and 'self-improvement' was at its peak, and such education was still conceived largely in humanistic terms.[19]

Fussell is interested in the fighting man, but his argument applies equally to women. By 1914 the variety of organisations campaigning for women's rights had been working since the mid-nineteenth century for better education for women, and literature would have made up a substantial part of that education, at least for most middle-class women. Fussell suggests that it is possible to identify many literary influences in the diaries and letters of trench soldiers, particularly officers. But such influences are also clearly delineated in the writings of women who felt the need to record their wartime experiences in a similar way. These influences, blended with alternative, less orthodox literary styles, make the diaries very valuable documents when considering the development of women's writing

The women who chose to write their experience of the war (these do not tend to be working-class women who would not have had either the time, or perhaps the education to do so,[20] although many middle-class women did not write either), like the officers to whom Fussell refers, allow their literary heritage to pervade their writing, even if they do not, themselves, recognise it. Ethel Mary Bilborough, a childless, middle-aged civilian of Chislehurst in Kent, began her diary a few months into the war. She addresses the issues of motivation and content in the opening pages:

July 15th, 1915

This is going to be my war diary. I don't mean its to be political, or literary, or anything of that kind, but it will merely be my own personal impressions, and I shan't even touch on the *fringe* of the vast problem as to what has caused the greatest war that has ever been known in history, or as to what will be likely to terminate it all!

It seems to me that everyone who happens to be alive in such stirring epoch-making times, ought to write *something* of what is going on! Just think how interesting it would be to read years hence! when peace once more reigns supreme, and everything has settled down to its usual torpid routine of dullness(!)[21]

Perhaps it is possible to understand a little of Bilborough's character from the way in which her diary begins. The actual document is extremely neat, tidy and orderly, conforming with the organised way in which she sets out precisely what she is intending to do and why, suggesting a sense of confidence and control. Her apparent concern is for posterity, perhaps hoping to give future generations, or at least her older self, an objective, sincere record of the experience of war from all angles. But the personal nature of this type of narrative makes total objectivity extremely difficult. In fact it quickly becomes clear that the diary is highly political, despite her protestations to the contrary which may be linked to her perception of her status as a woman. Initially, the diary represents a space to articulate her traditionally patriotic views, her criticism of the government and other issues such as her avid condemnation of conscientious objectors. But as the war drags on in its later years, the diary demonstrates a simple shift of Bilborough's perceptions, as she begins to question some of her earlier views. In her autobiography, *Grey Ghosts and Voices* May Wedderburn Cannan wrote, 'Went to war with Rupert Brooke and came home with Siegfried Sassoon'.[22] Although Bilborough never quite reaches Siegfried Sassoon, this statement is indicative of the kind of shift to be found in her diary.

It is also inaccurate to claim that the diary is not literary. Her choice of language is deliberate and self-aware. She describes her personal 'impressions', and 'impressions' is a keyword in the writing of these diaries, indeed, in women's writing of the First World War generally. The sketches in Ellen La Motte's 1919 war record *Backwash of War* are impressionistic in character, and this is exactly the term adopted by Mary Borden to describe her own memories in her war text *The Forbidden Zone*.[23] These are never facts, but interpretations created by the writer, and her choice of language to convey these impressions holds within it many implications for the way in which we, the future generations, may read her and her war.

Ethel Bilborough allows the traditional romantic rhetoric of war to pervade her text. There is something in her glorification that echoes Rupert Brooke and Julian Grenfell. Peacetime is a 'torpid routine of dullness'. It follows then that wartime is 'fresh and thrilling, with an undercurrent of excitement and romance'.[24] She articulates the jingoism of the early months of the war, apparently with complete conviction. She appears to be convinced by the propagandist reporting of the war found in many early newspaper reports: 'The poor brave little Belgium was drawn in, and Germany began to show her fangs.'[25] Her metaphor of the fangs with its biblical implications is effectively simple, suggesting an innate evil in the German enemy, but it is also a reflection of other published propaganda which continued to be produced throughout the war. Contemporary newspapers were filled with reports of German atrocities, and short stories such as those of Rudyard Kipling and Arthur Machen could be adopted for the patriotic cause despite the ambivalence of the authors themselves.[26] But arguably the display of this kind of politics in a private diary has different implications. It is almost as though she is trying to convince herself.

Ethel Bilborough was clearly a woman of some wealth and position. Her husband, a member of Lloyds, worked in the City, and her own position within her direct community was such that she was able to obtain the influence that her strong opinions required. The conservatism of many of her views is evident, perhaps reflecting her status as an upper middle-class, significantly childless, older woman; Bilborough is in the rare position of having no immediate family to lose in this war. She began writing her diary in July 1915; the first entry is particularly long as it has to cover almost a year of the war. Clearly she had come to realise the social and cultural importance of the experience. Her diary is adorned with photographs and newspaper cuttings (many of them her own as she was a regular correspondent to the *Mirror*), and these seem to give the diary a kind of reference book quality; she uses the published material to complement her own ideas and observations, and as a means to justify them.

But some of these views can be very disturbing for the contemporary reader, for example, her attitude towards conscription, which came into force in January 1916. Bilborough attacks the government for being slow to introduce the bill, and for making concessions to those who feel they have a valid reason not to fight. Her opinions are steeped in the rhetoric of propaganda:

March 5th [1916]

Conscription in England has come! One can hardly realise it, things have come about so gradually. Voluntary recruiting did well, but not well enough, and the slackers *had* to be got somehow, so thanks to Lord Derby's scheme all those who wouldn't enlist will be *made* to. But the government have felt their way to this great step very cautiously, very guardedly, and have made absurd concessions relating to men bearing arms who may have 'conscientious' objections to war! and endless exemptions are being made. On these lax lines of course things are not working, & *far* more stringent rules must be enforced if we are to get the necessary men. Naturally every coward and slacker thinks fighting is 'wrong'! and the most ludicrous reasons are being put forward by men who want to get exemption owing to their conscientious (?) scruples! The other day a man who said he was an artist, claimed exemption on the grounds that he 'could not mutilate anything so beautiful as the human form'!!²⁷

Bilborough's own emphasis and use of punctuation reinforces her political views. To her, men appear to be a commodity, part of the machinery of wartime production, reminding us that there is no man in her life who stands to be affected by this legislation. Her language echoes contemporary propaganda, stigmatising those who do not share her opinion. Masters applauds her: 'Mrs Bilborough's fine scorn for the Conchie is very typical of the time, and so is her use of the word "slackers".'²⁸ But his assessment is as limited as hers, attempting to shut out alternative voices. Alternative voices were there nonetheless, like that of Lady Kate Courtney, whose diary is filled with pacifist sentiments.²⁹ And the same 'ludicrous reasons' for exemption, so scorned by Bilborough are very sympathetically portrayed in Rose Allatini's 1918 novel *Despised and Rejected*.³⁰ Bilborough's views might not have been unusual, but they were by no means shared by everyone.

John Masters is selective in his choice of material; 'the authentic voice' must be consistent. But the overall picture that Bilborough presents of herself is not so simplistic. Throughout the diary there is a distinct sense of relief that those who are close to her are not eligible for military service, compounded by her fear for her husband's safety as she watches a dogfight over the City of London:

July 17th, 1917

Overhead there was a swarm of aeroplanes looking like a flight of bees – or butterflies. But the noise! I shall never forget it. There was the peculiar steady drone of the German engines, – loud enough, for they were very low down, and then came a furious banging of the machine guns showing that *our* aeroplanes had attacked the enemy & were doing their best to bring some down. Gracious heavens what next! a wild fight in the air thousands of feet above the earth! – in things like fearful distorted mechanical birds (only with no beauty,) which were circling round each other & engaged in deadly combat; dodging – swerving, diving and soaring, while sometimes they would be lost sight of in a cloud of smoke. There was nothing to be done; I didn't feel like going down to the cellar which people say is the safest place, but I *did* feel sick with anxiety for I knew quite well so many squadrons would *only* be sent over for one purpose, – an attack on London; (the last on June 13th occurred when we were away,) & K's office is in the heart of the city.[31]

The desire to record accurately what she witnesses may help to ease her sense of anxiety for her husband's safety. It may be a kind of self-censorship; the actual detail of the dogfight detracts from the imagined detail of the raid that preys on her mind. Although she begins by seeing the aeroplanes as bees or butterflies, she quickly disassociates such troubling modernity from the forces of nature. These are 'mechanical birds'; it is important that they have no beauty, although she credits them with an agility far more in keeping with real birds than with early flying machines, in an attempt to express the unfamiliar horror of what she is witnessing. Again she uses exaggerated punctuation and stresses as a means of conveying her feelings and ideas, the implicit as well as the explicit. As Bilborough struggles to articulate responses to the wartime scenes that surround her, her private pen constructs an impression of 'self' for us to read and interpret, both in historical and literary terms.

The long-term impact of the war makes Bilborough think, about politics, about society, about herself. The self produced by the diary can be seen to develop as each new event adds another layer to the impressions. The diary holds within it an implied criticism of the government, which becomes more forceful with each tragic occurrence of the war; and events like the sinking of the *Lusitania* (May 1915), and the execution of Edith Cavell (October 1915) move her deeply. The diary presents the impression that her patriotic self-confidence, born out of the society which constructed her, wanes as the war continues, leading her to address issues which further develop the diary self. At the beginning of the war she is worried about the shortage of dog biscuits, by the end it is the suffering of the poor which concerns her, forcing her to confront her own situation of relative well-being.

The early impression of self created by the diary, is that of a woman who articulates the conventional sentiments of the time. By the end of the war, the diary has presented a more thoughtful, perhaps fully rounded self, having confronted, through her writing, much of the hardship of war. She finally seems to question many of those structures that originally helped to form her. The styles that Bilborough adopts when writing her diary illustrate this development. She moves slowly away from the jingoistic rhetoric that shapes the early text (although this never completely disappears), and allows other literary influences to infiltrate her writing, even to some extent, the later war poets who focused on the sorrow and despair created by the war. This enables her to adopt a mood of pathos against which she can present a more comprehensive, although never definitive, impression of middle-class domestic life and experience during the First World War.

Bilborough's diary illustrates how her opinions, and the methods for their expression, alter over a period of time during the war. Other women, whose experience is less marginal, need to find more immediate ways to articulate situations that are alien to their background and upbringing. Those who were away from home when the war broke out adopt alternative literary styles, making their diaries independently interesting. The journal of Daisy Williams, 'Adventures in Germany, May – September 1914' recounts the escape from enemy territory of a young music student.[32] Written retrospectively, the journal begins like a travelogue, and develops into a patriotic diatribe against the German nation and culture, with clear references to the travel literature of the period and anti-German propagandist reporting of the war. For example, here is Williams's response to a café filled with German soldiers and civilians singing patriotic songs, which she enters on her way out of Germany: 'Never, I think, did we feel so acutely as at that moment that we were aliens in a strange land. This loud stamping wild kriegslust was not our way – There was something bestial, sinister in it, that we shrank from.'[33] Again she picks up on the idea of the 'bestial Hun' common in British war propagandist literature and artwork, contrasting it with the notion of English 'reserve'.

Entertainer Rosie Neal, one of a female-only troupe of vocalists, banjo-players and dancers who embarked on a European tour in August 1914, beginning in Hamburg, wrote her account of their experiences in two stages: the first while they remained 'prisoners', the second after they had 'escaped' and returned to Britain.[34] Neal is unsure whether to describe her manuscript as a letter or a story, since it is dedicated to no one specific, yet is constantly addressing an assumed reader. Her prose utilises a variety of styles that might be expected in both genres, from the trivial details of a newsletter, to more dramatic illustrations of their most dangerous moments. It is clear that she intends the account to be read, but there is no indication of by whom.[35]

Even more actively involved in the war were the women who joined the various services. Mary Macleod wrote the following letter to her twin sister in 1918 from the Women's National Land Army camp at Barwick Park, Yeovil in Somerset:

July 13th Letter No 33 to sister Betty

Flanders Nurseries is luxury compared with this place. It would be ripping if it did not rain so much. Land Army boots have arrived, enormous clump-ing army ammunition boots, really not worth the money paid, as they'll be impossible to wear in normal society . . . a wash in cold water 'as far down as possible and as far up as possible' . . . sleeping in a tent . . . there are 7 of us, 5 being 'sweet girl undergraduate hefty types' . . . very Haw, Hawish to begin with. I have to use my holdall as a head raiser and either put my clothes in it as come off or else, put them on top of my feet . . . in night when it rains, streams of water trickle under the sides of tent and wet your mattress . . . we are all feeling fitter than we have done for months. It is 100 yards to the washing marquee and about 300 to the other necessary, from our tent at the end of camp. We belong to a cycling gang, about 1/4 hours ride to the flax . . . it is supposed to be a nine hour day, but you can subtract about two hours for rests, as it has been showery we have extra. Work is moderately strenu-ous . . . had stiff wrists, most people complained of backs and legs. Food is good and should be plentiful, but such a lot of hungry people about 150 to each of four mess tents, and only one dish to serve from, sometimes the first get served scrum for seconds before others have had any . . . undisciplined girls refuse to obey orders. The waste is pretty bad. Some people are faddy and leave piles on their plates then go to Y.W.C.A. [Young Women's Christian Association] and stodge cakes etc. As we are allowed only 1/2lb bread per day it seems unpatriotic . . . do well for butter and cheese, someone heard a Yeovil citizen complaining. Personally enjoying it better than being indoors sewing. The Y.W.C.A. does a lot for us it does seem funny to be using it's hospitality instead of dispensing it.[36]

Macleod adopts a paratactic structure that implies both familiarity as she writes to her sister, and also a type of self-censorship as she carefully constructs a picture of her new life. Her tone is jocular, each negative aspect is quickly contradicted by a positive one; it is almost as the though the night rain and wet mattress are responsible for her new feeling of fitness. Physical discomforts are set against quality and quantity of food. Her use of euphemistic phrases and slang words seems to be representa-tive of shared language codes between the sisters. This assumed mutual understanding allows Macleod's letter to give an effective impression of what the experience of the land girl might have been like because she is able to illustrate both the good and bad aspects of the job. Although she does not dwell on the hardships, they can be identified easily, but the underlying sense of camaraderie as these hardships are shared provides a very balanced account. Although directed at one specific reader, the letter can find an understanding audience with many.

Muriel Thompson, a driver with the First Aid Nursing Yeomanry (FANY) motor ambulance convoy at St Omer in France, recorded what she witnessed in the form of diaries and notes, adopting a very different style.[37] 'Base Notes' is a collection of private fragments of experience, written in her 1918 diary, but independent of the actual diary entries. It seems to be an attempt to re-create an atmosphere rather than any specific event. To do so, she chooses her language and style very carefully:

> Black darkness all around, the smell of the sea & of the rain – first in front a semi-circle of light blown(?) by the ships lamps, showing up the wet sails on the quay, & shining on the deep space below. Twinkling in the distance other lights, & at regular intervals ambulances arriving & stopping by the gangway, while slowly – carefully, four limp forms on stretchers are drawn out one after the other, lowered for a moment to the ground, then raised, & carried on board.
>
> The light shines on the M.O.'s face; his clerk steps to the stretcher, cuts a white label from the patients coat, & calls briskly, 'gunshot wound, left thigh, sir' – 'Ward B,' says the M.O., & the bearers carry on.
>
> Not even the darkness hides the white head on the next stretcher, it shows up startlingly as the lamp light strikes it – no particle of human face is seen – only holes, in a white mask, 'severe burns, sir,' intones the orderly – 'Ward A' is the reply – & another load of bitter human suffering, heroically endured, goes silently away.[38]

Perhaps unconsciously, Thompson's fragments begin to show signs of literary characteristics that will later be called modernist. As she strives to convey the situation she moves away from recounting personal experience, instead evoking sensations through image, light and colour to draw the reader in; the juxtaposition of light and dark silhouettes, the forms of the wounded against a background of weather that can be both smelt and felt. This reinforces their great number and, in turn, their anonymity as they are identified only by the type of wound they have received rather than by any more personal label. Yet the 'white mask' brings with it a kind of personality which cannot be ignored. By hiding the face, Thompson forces the reader to confront the reality behind the bandages using his or her own imagination. Surrounded by the Gothic atmosphere of the night this is particularly sinister; more so, perhaps, because it is not a fiction. Another fragment from the same source reads:

> Afternoon now, a pale lemon-coloured sky with a rose flush, & behind it an ink-black dome of rain clouds driving up – all faces skywards – its worth while to stop & gaze too – a crack avi-man is up, & as you look your heart stops – Sheer against the lemon sky he drops, head first, down, down like a stone – it must be an accident – he can't fall so far on purpose you think – But you are wrong – at the last moment the Belgian ace rights himself, & sails away on the sun like air till he is lost to sight amid the black clouds beyond.

Again Thompson uses colour to create her picture, a lemon sky with a rose flush, ink-black clouds, there is a poetry, an aestheticism, about the description which captures the imagination. The aeroplane is almost like an intruder in the romance of the setting, a drama in the superficial peace of the sky. The airman, dropping down like a stone is reminiscent of Tennyson's 'The Eagle',[39] perhaps hinting at the literary basis of her education. Her non-standard punctuation suggests ellipses, hinting at the stories behind the image. Here the imagination comes into play to allow the reader to complete those stories.

Unlike Bilborough, Macleod and the other women to be considered in this chapter, Thompson does not write of herself in these pieces, but of what surrounds her. She saves personal reflection for her diary. Her involvement in the war, close to the battle front gives her a different kind of insight and she chooses an objective, detached type of prose to convey it. With her primary experiments, she may perhaps be read stylistically as a forerunner to the accidental modernists like Borden and Ellen La Motte who will be discussed in more detail in Chapter 3.

Others actively involved in the war were those women who nursed the wounded or carried out associated hospital work, in Britain or abroad, as professionals or as volunteers.[40] It is these women who produced some of the most interesting war records. Nursing Sister Mary Clarke gives a detailed account of helping the wounded at the Battle of Jutland, June 1916, and the daily routine of a hospital ship, as well as life stationed on Malta.[41] Winifred Kenyon, VAD, kept a diary from January 1915 to November 1918. Her first job was supervising the cooking in a British hospital, but she moved on to be an operating theatre nurse in a hospital near Verdun, returning to St George's in London in 1918. In 1990, at the age of 98, she assisted her daughter in producing a typed manuscript of the text, adding to and commenting further on her experiences and observations, perhaps confirming that her motive for keeping the diary may have been to provide a record for later generations.[42]

The letters of Eleanora Pemberton make fascinating reading, demonstrating a distinct awareness of literary traditions, and frequent attempts to harness them as she searches for a way to express her experiences. She was an active member of the Red Cross before the war and was included among the first VADs to go to France in the autumn of 1914. She held a variety of different posts during her foreign service, often with considerable responsibility, and clearly found a great deal of enjoyment and personal fulfilment in her work. Yet in the summer of 1917, after a spell of leave, she decided not to return to France, joining the Metropolitan Special Constabulary in London instead.

Her later letters show signs of growing dissatisfaction and homesickness, and it is difficult to ignore the fact that she was an only daughter, unmarried, of ageing Victorian parents. Despite the culture shock of the war, she may have perceived it as her duty to look after her parents, and by 1917 she had been away for three long years. Pemberton never alludes to such feelings in her letters, but Vera Brittain, in her autobiography *Testament of Youth*, articulates what may be a corresponding experience:

> my father's interpretation of my duty was not, I knew only too well, in the least likely to agree with that of the Army, which had always been singularly unmoved by the worries of relatives. What was I to do? I wondered desperately. There was my family, confidently demanding my presence, and here was the offensive, which made every pair of experienced hands worth ten pairs under normal conditions.[43]

While she remained in France, however, Eleanora Pemberton wrote a great many letters to her parents. They echo her literary heritage, focusing significantly on a pastoral or Georgian tradition that seems to hold comfort in a time of trouble. Like many others of her generation, she had certainly read Rupert Brooke, and she borrows his poetic style to express her sense of loss. On 4 June 1915 she writes to her mother, 'How many too of the young & eager crowd of Eton and England's most promising manhood now lie still and cold on a foreign soil' emulating Brooke's patriotic romanticism which captured the imaginations of so many of his contemporaries. In the same letter she adopts further a type of romantic war rhetoric when she talks about the great 'strain of *courage* and *fortitude*' imposed upon them (my emphasis). It is a language that felt more and more out of place as the First World War progressed.

On 29 May 1915 Eleanora Pemberton sent a birthday message to her mother:

My dearest Mum

Here is your birthday coming round again and I must just remind you that I am really sharing it with you – almost sitting at breakfast with you, if only thoughts would materialise. I wonder whether the single red rose just outside the drawing room window has come out in time to greet you as it often has before. I hope so. The roses are out here in all the gardens, also honeysuckle and syringa, and there are heaps of wild flowers in the fields and along the river banks.[44]

Pemberton's language here may perhaps be described as feminine. The warmth of her feeling for her mother exudes from every word and there is a sense that she is attempting to blend their two selves together in a quasi-maternal way which at once alludes to her own homesickness, and empathises with her mother's pain at their separation. Her use of the repeated flower imagery operates in practical terms, to bring them closer together in a shared experience, and on a metaphoric level in its emphasis on growth, beauty and hope, the resurgence of nature against all the odds of war. It also operates as a cultural signpost, illustrating a family who are used to internalising romantic rhetoric, embodied here in the shared consciousness of the symbol of the rose.

Pemberton's use of the rose is particularly interesting. It is more than simply the flower which happens to grow outside her mother's window; it has other wider implications in terms of the literary imagery of war, as well as being a traditional symbol of Englishness, which comfortably justifies its use in Pemberton's birthday message. The image is a popular one. A reported favourite song of the soldiers, *Roses of Picardy*, reiterates the sentiment, 'The roses round the door/Makes me love mother more'.[45] Similarly, Helen Zenna Smith, heroine of Evadne Price's pseudo-autobiographical novel *Not So Quiet . . .*, snatches momentary sleep in her icy 'flea-bag' as she slaves in the hellish world of the ambulance convoy, but dreams of her rose-tinted bedroom at home, 'with its rose-pink satin eiderdown', rose wicker breakfast tray, rose coloured china and her dressing jacket, 'adorned with ribbon roses the exact colour of my eiderdown';[46] a rose-womb to substitute for the 'flea-bag' womb.

With this reading, the rose is safe; a symbol synonymous with Pemberton's desire to be at home with her mother. But it may also be read as having a more sinister meaning. The rose had also become a metaphor for battle scars and wounds since many soldiers had noticed the physical similarities between a newly healed wound and a red or pink rose.[47] This alternative meaning gives an added depth to the pain of the mother and daughter, separated by the war.

An emphasis on the pastoral was common in the writing of the First World War, perhaps the best known example being Edmund Blunden's record, *Undertones of War*.[48] Winifred Kenyon uses a sense of the pastoral as a device to suggest security in her diary:

Sunday May 9 [1915]

After the service, Gow, L.J. and I took our tea and went away up over the canal, through the green green grass, blue sky overhead and a delicious breeze and we three lay down under an apple tree in full bloom, and felt at peace with all the world. It's extraordinary how one can feel so perfectly happy in spite of everything.[49]

Perhaps this represents a brave face, and it has the effect of sounding more like a holiday picnic in old England than an afternoon off from a hospital in a war zone.

Pemberton also uses Arcadian images in an attempt to reduce the divide between herself and her English home. On 9 April 1916 she writes of the joys of riding out in the country in a borrowed horse and trap. Again her letter is filled with descriptions of the abundance of spring flowers, but her implied message, the desire for home, is more clearly insinuated:

It was a perfectly *lovely* day and so *very* nice driving about all the hedges are quite green and the trees are just bursting – the convalescent horses are all out at grass and the banks in many places are covered with cowslips and scented violets blue & white (that word is violets not rabbits!) I drive! the others, except one, are not Jehus which is better for me as I enjoy it. In many places the winding lanes with little farmsteads perched on top of steep banks reminded me very vividly of dear Devonshire but there are no moors or heather, only some *very* pretty rolling meadow and orchard land. I am just longing to see the apple blossom which must be a perfect sight in another month or so.[50]

The place described, the countryside around Gournay, although beautiful, is a poor substitute for 'dear Devonshire' and it is questionable whether it is really French apple blossom that she is 'longing' to see. Like so many other literary soldiers, Pemberton uses the pastoral imagery of France to recreate for herself the pastoral reality of England; a physical manifestation of 'Blighty'.[51]

But not all her correspondence is quite so intimate. An early letter (2 November 1914), written prior to the army order regarding postal censorship, illustrates a dramatic shift as Pemberton attempts to find a different language in order to convey the horrors of the wounded in a more effective way. In the following passage, she experiments with other literary influences, trying to find an authentic way to express her political views as well as her emotional response:

> it brought *war* home to one in a way that nothing else, short of the actual battlefield could. The horrible, horrible side of war which sent us these travesties of the fine strong husbands, fathers, lovers, sons who had gone forth so proudly how short a time ago. When you turn down the blanket to wash an arm and find no arm only a soaking bandage that once was white, or you go to feed 'no. 14' and find that he has only half a face and cannot swallow but tries to speak & you strain to understand. It fills you with a fury against the devillish ingenuity which conceived the perfection of the weapons which have caused this devastation and a loathing of the man who set loose these fiends of hell.[52]

In this passage, Pemberton shows the other side of patriotism, juxtaposing the marching heroes with the stationary wounded; and they are 'husbands, fathers, lovers, sons', representing the private and the personal transformed into the public and the uniform. And it is absence that provides her with the power to express the horror with authenticity. When going to wash an arm she finds 'no arm', just a bloodstained bandage, the contrast of the colours operating to reinforce the shock. This is not the stark white bandage rolled by patriotic Bilborough-like matrons in village halls, but a real bandage soiled by a product of the battlefield. More emotive still is the presence of 'no. 14', the man with only half a face. He has no identity; he is a number, all that is left of the dehumanised fathers, lovers and sons. He is a symbol of the reality for the faceless millions who will be lost on the Western Front, captured in Pemberton's precise although not graphic description. But these fragments of images are strong enough to drive home her point, and it is in passages such as this that her language takes on a more experimental tone. Her letter contains stylistic similarities to the musings of Muriel Thompson, representing a dislocation which corresponds with what will later be seen as modernist; new forms which were developed to present the horrors of this war even in private writing.

But there are more traditional literary influences too. As Pemberton goes on to talk about the machinery of war to her parents, she uses more evocative and at times, distinctly religious language. She is in a 'fury' against this 'devillish ingenuity'; she talks of 'devastation', 'loathing' and 'fiends of hell', in a style reminiscent, for example, of the opening books of *Paradise Lost*. Anger is a dominant emotion, colouring every word for her unprotected parents; they have three sons in this war too. Perhaps fortunately for them, less so for us, when Pemberton's letters became subject to the newly established censor, they are filled with more hopeful sentiments; positive thinking about her brothers' experiences and her own 'happy' existence: 'It is an amazingly pleasant peaceful life! It is almost like living at home & it is hard to believe that there is a war raging.'[53]

There are few instances in the diary of Nursing Sister Mary Brown when it is possible to forget that there is a war raging.[54] Her legacy takes the form of three battered notebooks filled with ink blots, dried flowers and scribbled entries; experiences hastily recorded after many exhausting hours caring for wounded soldiers very close to the front line. Brown was a nurse on a hospital ship from May to September 1915, serving in the Dardanelles and participating in the evacuation of Gallipoli. This put her in the rare position of being a woman under fire. As a result, her diary is of particular historical value, but it also illustrates the influence of immediate danger on the literary make up of the writing.

The literary allusion which fills the letters of Eleanora Pemberton is absent from the diary of Mary Brown. Instead the diary presents her as a reporter, witnessing the unspeakable and recording it in a way that helps her and her prospective readers to deal with the implications. Brown's words are somehow less personal than those of Pemberton, her VAD counterpart, presenting a different kind of shift away from convention. Officially she addresses no one but herself, but of herself she does not speak. Her language is more neutral, often lacking expressions of deep personal feeling, unlike Pemberton's. Although flowers fall from Brown's pages there are none in her text, and it is hard for the reader to imagine her asking her mother to write her a 'cuddly' letter to counteract homesickness.[55] Her tone is often factual and flat, despite the dramatic nature of the events she is able to record, and only rarely is her narrative penetrated by a glimmer of emotion. But it is here that she betrays herself. It is often what Brown does not say that can be most revealing in both historic and literary terms.

Mary Brown was one of eight daughters, and upon her own entry into wedlock, (which did not take place until 1934), she became the only one to marry. Consequently, it is possible to surmise that she could have been relatively free of those domestic responsibilities that held so many Edwardian women captive. A qualified nurse from 1912, she joined Queen Alexandra's Imperial Military Nursing Service Reserve, (QAIMNSR), and worked abroad throughout the war, serving first on the hospital ship, with later service in India and Mesopotamia. After the armistice she became a nursing sister for the Anglo-Iranian Oil Company (later BP), and continued to live and work abroad until after the Second World War.

Mary Brown seems to have witnessed a great deal, and this diverse range of experience may have inspired her to record the things she saw, creating a historical record, perhaps for herself, perhaps for others. In *Battling for News*, Anne Sebba suggests, 'Given my personal definition of a reporter as someone who has witnessed an event which they then describe, and perhaps also analyse for others, women have been acting as eye-witnesses, describing horrific and vivid scenes from life, for several centuries'.[56] Brown fits comfortably into this definition, and by viewing her as an on-the-spot reporter it may be possible to identify why she chose to structure her diary in the way she did. The distance and impersonality is occasionally punctuated by a smattering of opinion and analysis, presenting a convincing picture to the future reader, even if none was anticipated at the time of writing.

Despite the British Army's ruling that women should not be allowed in the firing line, during her time in the Dardanelles, Mary Brown was often at the mercy of the Turkish guns. Unlike most women, she was in a position to be an eyewitness to the fighting, yet much of her reportage is purely descriptive, avoiding any preoccupation with personal or emotional response derived from her unusual circumstances. She reports facts, and the reactions of others to those facts:

H S Devanha Dec 16th Thursday [1915]

Anzac. What a noisy night it has been last night. Machine guns firing, rifle fire & monitors firing quite near us.

We took on another crowd to-day. I have now 50. 10 more & I will be full. We have now Australians.

They brought us the sad news that they are evacuating Anzac. I suppose they have come to the conclusion that they will never make any head way, but its awful when one thinks of the lives that have been lost in this one place – over 30,000. The Australians are all very sad about it, they say they don't want to leave Anzac. All their best friends are buried there & they hate the idea of the Turks walking over it.

The hospital on the beach was blown up by the Turks yesterday. There were 16 patients in it. I think all were killed.[57]

Here her own feelings are subordinated to those of the Australian soldiers, the primary players on this stage, always taking precedence over the secondary serving women, putting women like Brown into a kind of no

man's land, between the worlds of combatant and non-combatant; arguably an appropriate position for an objective observer. Characteristically,
the final comment concerning the destruction of the hospital is recorded
without judgement.

When Brown does focus on her own experience, it tends to be in a
direct and informative way, rather than an emotional response:

> Jan 2nd 1916 [Basa, Mesopotamia? – the diary is unclear about exact loca-
> tion]
>
> This is active service & no mistake, brown sugar tinned milk & tinned fish,
> bread & butter not too nice but we must get used to it.
>
> Had my bath in my canvas bath & slept in my camp bed, the night was
> frighteningly cold, I had 7 layers of blanket & a hot bag & still felt cold, the
> mornings & evenings are *very* cold, we interviewed the matron & I am to be
> night Super for to-night to relieve Sister for a night off then I am to relieve
> the others.
>
> The ground is very flat, nothing to be seen but date palms & grey sand,
> we are just on the river bank & the port is opposite the hospital, we see all
> the Hospital ships that come up. They load here & then go back to Bombay,
> the larger vessels cannot come up as the water is too shallow . . .
>
> Our huts are guarded by an armed sentry all night; it makes one feel safe
> when you go to bed knowing there is a man with a fixed bayonet outside
> your door.[58]

Brown concentrates on physical details. As with Mary Macleod it is possible to get a clear sense of what the experience might have been like, but
her focus shifts quickly away from herself to describe her surroundings
and situation, ensuring that the emphasis remains objective.

There may be a number of explanations for Brown's adoption of these
narrative styles. Perhaps she is unable, as a young Edwardian woman, to
locate within her vocabulary of the acceptable, a suitable language to
render her emotional experience authentically. It may be a type of self-
censorship designed to avoid direct confrontation with realities too
horrific to bare. Or possibly she is, as a reporter, trying to protect herself
by avoiding collision with the military authorities. As Anne Sebba suggests, 'Following the introduction of the Defence of the Realm Act (1914),
British War correspondents found themselves used to promote the official
line and gagged as never before'.[59] Hence, she may be adopting another
form of self-censorship, perhaps never saying what she really thinks. By
keeping a diary in the front line she is already in breach of Army
Regulations. Perhaps she is trying to keep to a minimum her 'leakage of
military information'.

On 18 December 1915 Brown witnessed a huge fire on the beach, apparently started by the Turks to light up the positions of the retreating Allies as they prepare to leave Anzac Cove in the final evacuation:

> Matron woke us up about 1.30 am to look at the huge fire on shore & what a big blaze it was, it lit up the whole beach for miles.
> We thought it was our men burning up the stores they were not able to take away, the fire blazed for hours & was still smoking at 5.30 am.
> We discovered from some patients that, the stores were set on fire by a spy, to light up our positions & to show up the ships waiting to take off the men etc. Isn't it wicked.[60]

Her descriptive diary entry ends with a rare judgement: 'Isn't it wicked.' The horror of the deception finally provokes her to comment. But generally she seems to want to keep herself and her values out of the diary. This self-censorship allows her to raise only the most fundamental questions in a world dominated by the Christian paradox of the patriotic honour of national destruction.

However, there are occasions when Brown's diary becomes a revealing document through this very censorship; her own deliberate omissions. One of her richer diary entries provides a useful illustration:

> H. S. Devanha Monday 9th Aug [1915]
>
> Anzac. I was on deck at 5 a.m. The guns woke me up then, the Tanks were doing their *morning hate* it was a continual Boom Boom & crack crack. The whole morning we watched the fighting through field glasses. We saw about 50 of our men leave this trench and make for the Turks. Some of the battleships beside us kept up a continual fire with big guns. The noise was awful & we could see the shell bursting several fell into the water. During the forenoon, shells fired by the Turks went right over our ship into the sea. What a wild and useless bit of country, so many lives are being lost for . . . before we got breakfast, a boat load of wounded came along side and all day the boats were bringing them over. We dressed nearly 1000 . . . we were at it hard all day, had no time to pay attention to the fighting.
> The whole thing is too ghastly to write about . . .
> We had 640 bad cases on at midnight & we had to send away three boat loads that we had no room for . . . As I am writing this the shells are going whistling over our heads, they don't worry me, the noise of the guns so close worries me more.
> We saw the shells going up & exploding by the hundred tonight.
> I am dead tired, it has been a nerve trying day for everyone.[61]

This passage is interesting on a number of levels. As a historical document its value is clear. A woman in the front line, a place usually closed to women, Brown is able to witness and describe the fighting at first hand. Writing under pressure, she manages to convey the relentlessness of the battle for herself as well as the soldiers, and provides insight into the unique, if terrifying, experience of being a nurse 'in the thick of it'. The extract is at once detailed, and yet vague. It is difficult to grasp the chronology of the events taking place, and this is further hampered by the syntactical structure. Rebecca Hogan argues of the 'feminine' diary:

> Because the diary often treats 'small' details at the same length as 'big' events, experience flows metonymically into the diary; things are put down one after another as they occur to the memory. Only on later rereading do we see or make discriminations about what was 'more' or 'less' important, interesting, significant. Diaries are not so much inclusive because they contain *everything* from a given day, as they are inclusive in the sense that they do not privilege 'amazing' over 'ordinary' events, in terms of scope, space, or selection. So as well as being paratactic on the level of grammar and syntax, diaries are paratactic on the level of full entries and of content too.[62]

Brown's diary entry seems to conform to this in terms of its paratactic structure, and in the confusion, the blending of 'small' and 'big' events stimulates a response to a situation which is too powerful and too human for her to retain the role of the detached narrator that she often appears to strive for. Political and ideological views filter through the smoke. There is a sense of her anxiety at having to send away boats loaded with wounded, an awareness of the nurses' limitations, their inadequacy to deal with a situation that is too big. Earlier in her diary, single sentences illustrate the patriotic conservatism of some of her political ideas:

> 15 May 1915
> We get the news by 'wireless' every day, so we are in touch with England all the time, they are interning all the German's in England & not before time.

> 24 May 1915 – Hotel de Suez Canal
> I don't much care for this hotel there are too many Egyptians staying in it for my taste, of course we don't go near the public rooms at all, just straight to our bedrooms.[63]

As the guns roar around her in the later entry, she responds differently; patriotism gives way to humanitarianism as she questions the practical implications of the fight from a less conformist view point: 'What a wild and useless bit of country, so many lives are being lost for', a problematic situation for a nurse, a preserver of life, to deal with. She does not go on to define what would be a 'useful' bit of country on which to spend English lives; perhaps none exists, or perhaps she cannot find words adequate to define it. After the boatloads of wounded start rolling in, she begins to struggle, 'The whole thing is too ghastly to write about'.

The whole thing is too ghastly to write about. Perhaps, but Mary Brown has undertaken to find a way, and the way that she chooses is interesting from a literary point of view. 'The Tanks were doing their *morning hate*'; her unconventional syntactical use of one word, 'hate', enables her to evoke the sensation of being under ritual, and for her, unprovoked bombardment.[64] It is like a precursor to the chilling Orwellian 'Two Minutes Hate' of *Nineteen Eighty-Four* thirty years later. This is reinforced by the effectively simple, if unsophisticated, onomatopoeic illustrations of booms and cracks. The 'wild and useless' futility of the whole situation, the sheer volume of numbers of the wounded, create visual impressions against the background of the guns; the same guns that turned men into hysterics, and that feature as a chorus in the war literature of men and women alike. Rose Macaulay from 'Picnic: July 1917': 'And life was bound in a still ring,/Drowsy, and quiet, and sweet . . ./When heavily up the south-east wind/The great guns beat'.[65] Enid Bagnold from *A Diary without Dates*: 'those distant guns again to-night . . . Now a lull and now a bombardment; again a lull, and then batter batter, and the windows tremble. Is the lull when *they* go over the top?'[66] Bagnold uses similar literary and onomatopoeic techniques to describe the perpetual noise from her English hospital. It is interesting that Mary Brown, writing under pressure as 'the shells are going whistling' above her, in a position to understand fully the implications of those 'lulls', adopts a similar literary style. She adds a new dimension to the story. Although unpublished, her tale may still qualify for a place in the wider spectrum of women's literature and, when considered, may add a new dimension to the development of that literature. And its fragmented nature, perhaps forced upon her by circumstances beyond her control, calls to mind later modernist innovations rather than traditional literary heredity.

With regard to the treatment of the wounded, the daily facts of her job as a nurse, Mary Brown invariably remains silent. Winifred Kenyon is much less coy, and writes enthusiastically of the anatomical details of operations and the smell of gas gangrene. Similarly, Mary Clarke, allows far more of her personal feelings to pervade her diary, and seems determined to record the full horror of the wounded from the Battle of Jutland, including some information about treatment:

2nd June 1916

... then the bad cases began to come in, poor things it was pitiful to see some of them, with legs off & arms off & some fearfully burnt, face, arms, legs and body ... Some of the poor things hadn't been touched since Wed night when the first fight took place & had only the first picnic dressings on their burns. It must have been agonies taking the dressings off, but few of them made a moan. I never saw such bravery in my life.

3rd June 1916

The smell of burns is awful, one gets almost nauseated some-times, but Dr Iles [?] is using Eucalyptus & olive oil for his, so that is taking away the worst of it. The poor things nearly all had to be fed as nearly all have both hands tied up & masks on their faces, & their poor eyes are so bad in most cases, it takes a long time.[67]

But Mary Brown does not even attempt to speak the unspeakable. What she does not say, however, is revealing. Fleeting references to the number of operations with which she has assisted during the day or the number of wounds dressed under chloroform, hint at the truth, but faced with describing reality she is only vague, 'never will I forget the awful sight of that boat load of shattered humanity, & not a murmur from one of them, several were dying'.[68] The blanks and ellipses seem to constitute an appropriate way of responding to the war; asking the reader's imagination to step in once again, rather than offering graphic descriptions which force the writer to confront the reality of the experience. To this end, Mary Brown's diary might usefully help her *not* to remember; to remember only the facts and not the emotional repercussions of the battle experience.

There are some aspects of the experience of war that these women shared with their male contemporaries in the trenches. For days on end Brown writes in her diary 'nothing doing', conveying the sense of boredom that many trench soldiers identify in their reminiscences. Similarly, Mary Clarke writes: 'I am afraid my diary will be rather monotonous but there is practically nothing to put down, it is a good thing it doesn't interest any one but myself.'[69] The women's role is paradoxical; they are not combatant, but they are not non-combatant either; they have the best and the worst of both worlds; allied with soldiers rather than civilians, yet subordinated to them in the eyes of society, and in their own consciousness. This perspective creates for them a subject position that provides a unique basis for written records; perhaps a kind of bridge between the opposing worlds of the home and the battle front.

Eleanora Pemberton is able to sum up their situation with a witty but precise metaphor in a letter of 21 February 1915. She writes to her parents of her dental problems, the removal of a tooth, and its replacement, an operation performed by a modern American dentist with a revolutionary technique: 'It was a *real* tooth he put in – a Tommy's tooth – out of some shattered jaw, I suppose, so I say I have the most permanent 'souvenir' of the war of anybody!! And although I myself have not been to the front, my tooth has!'[70] The metaphor operates on two levels. In literary terms, the innovative medical practise seems to parallel the linguistic experiments that Pemberton, Brown and the other women are, perhaps unconsciously, forced to make as they strive for self-expression, while grappling with the unorthodox: discordant notes which add a new dimension to the existing structures of their writing. This metaphor creates a significant division between them and women like Ethel Bilborough. On another level, Pemberton appears to be aware of the appropriate symbolism. Part of the dead soldier, now part of her, the tooth allows the two to blend, denying the traditional feminine role of inaction, transcending the army rules which, theoretically, kept women out of the line of fire. They were there in the battle, if not directly in the front line, and had to share with the men many of the dangers that existed within the war zone although outside the trenches.

It is impossible to read these diaries and letters without considering again and again the questions of authorial intent. Do these women write for themselves, or with another audience in mind? Mary Brown's diaries certainly masquerade as a personal record, yet there is little of her person in them, and one wonders whether, if she read them later, she may have found that they omitted the details of her experiences that were most important to her. Much may be read between the lines by an informed reader, but for anyone who did not live through the war, this can be little more than speculation. Although Brown does not exactly soften the reality, she seems to take on the stance of a reporter, perhaps as a device to create an impression of order and control, making the whole thing easier to cope with, both for herself and for any prospective reader.

Self-exposure in a time of crisis can be dangerous, but this did not stop Eleanora Pemberton from revealing more of her feelings in her letters to her parents. The presence of an immediate audience, not to mention those ethereal future readers who may examine her letters as a text, enables her to present her personal responses, censor permitting, almost in the manner of a penitent. Her readers operate on one level as her confessors, and consequently, it seems more likely that she may have managed to capture those important moments of her war for future reference. Already in her thirties when the war broke out, Pemberton's involvement typifies the innovatory nature of the impact of war on Edwardian women's lives. And if, as may be speculated, she eventually succumbed to the pull of her filial responsibilities, she certainly witnessed the generation of younger women who followed her, whose independence was created by the war and who helped to instigate the many changes – literary, historical and political – which followed it: 'Some of the convoy VADs whose acquaintance I am gradually making, are very nice. They are all quite young and all come from High Wycombe, St Andrews, Roedean and such like schools, and are *typically* and *essentially modern*'.[71] While to some extent Pemberton, and most of the other women discussed in this chapter, represent the old world, mortally wounded by the war, these women must surely be symbolic of the next phase, the modernist future.

Virginia Woolf suggested, 'The answer lies at present locked in old diaries, stuffed away in old drawers, half obliterated in the memories of the aged'.[72] This may be the answer to many questions concerning the writing both of women's history and women's fiction. In this instance it reveals the location of some of the roots of women's experimental writing of the First World War. The experience of the conflict inspired many women from many different parts of society to write. Their collected experiences can still be found in their own words, too long hidden away from a society that persists, despite the work of recent feminist scholarship, in subordinating these experiences to those of their male contemporaries who fought in the trenches. As Woolf asserted, these words help to illustrate how difficult it is to distinguish between the fact and the fiction, so close is the link between narratives of literature and of history, thus challenging the traditional interpretations, giving voice to multiple narratives. These narratives enable us to identify the areas, such as diaries and letters, in which fact and fiction can blur. The combination of literary influences and the search for alternative language throws new light on the development of women's writing. It is an innovation that begins with the private pen. It is rather like breaking free from a form of cultural censorship. Despite the dictates of the military authority, women do write, and they write things that their Victorian or Edwardian upbringing could not have prepared them for. The need to find ways to articulate new experiences pushed women to experiment with language and style, presenting a shift away from private narrative modes of the past. And these experiments were only the beginning. Both during and after the war, some women used their personal records of experience as a basis for published texts In my next chapter I shall examine the effect of such a transposition on the language and structure of this writing, paying specific attention to its political, feminist and literary implications.

Notes

1 Army order VII issued by the War Office, 24 July 1916. Held in the Department of Documents, Imperial War Museum.

2 Adjutant General's Branch: General Routine Orders (revision of 29 July 1917 on postal censorship) held in the Department of Documents, Imperial War Museum.

3 Henri Barbusse (1988), *Under Fire*, London, Everyman (first published 1917), p. 147.

4 'Each officer or man who privately transmits information (even to those on whose discretion he may have the most complete reliance) inevitably facilitates the task of the enemy's agents and indirectly sacrifices the lives of his comrades. This fact should be impressed on all officers and men, so that all ranks may co-operate to ensure that the progress of the Army is not imperilled or rendered more costly by the criminal folly of a few individuals, who if discovered will be severely dealt with.' Army order VII issued by the War Office, 24 July 1916. Held in the Department of Documents, Imperial War Museum.

5 See for example: Paul Fussell (1977), *The Great War and Modern Memory*, Oxford, Oxford University Press; Samuel Hynes (1990), *A War Imagined*, London, Bodley Head.

6 Virginia Woolf (1966), 'Women and fiction'. In her *Collected Essays*, vol. 2, London, Hogarth Press (first published in *The Forum*, March 1929), p. 141.

7 Fussell, *The Great War*.

8 'The material in a diary may be the very stuff of life, but the diary functions with the same verbal medium and imaginative impact as literature – modern literature especially, for like such literature, the diary remains very close to life in duplicating the multifaceted nature of personality, as well as life's uncertainties, obscurities, and unanticipated events.' Harriet Blodgett (1988), *Centuries of Female Days: Englishwomen's Private Diaries*, New Brunswick, NJ, Rutgers University Press, p. 7.

9 Estelle Jelinek (1980), *Women's Autobiography*, Bloomington and Indianapolis, IN, Indiana University Press.

10 I refer the reader to, for example, Jelinek, *Women's Autobiography*; Shari Benstock (1988), *The Private Self: Theory and Practice of Women's Autobiographical Writings*, London, Routledge; Liz Stanley (1992), *The Auto/biographical I*, Manchester, Manchester University Press, among others.

11 Rebecca Hogan (1991), 'Engendered Autobiographies: The Diary as Feminine Form', *Prose Studies*, 14 (2), September, pp. 95–107.
12 *Ibid.*, p. 105.
13 Blodgett, *Centuries of Female Days*.
14 Winifred Kenyon, unpublished diary, Department of Documents, Imperial War Museum.
15 Mabel St Clair Stobart (1916), *The Flaming Sword in Serbia and Elsewhere*. London, Hodder & Stoughton.
16 Eva Figes (1994), *Women's Letters in Wartime 1450–1945*, London, Pandora, p. 9.
17 Enid Bagnold (1987), *The Happy Foreigner*, London, Virago (first published 1920).
18 Eleanora Blanshard Pemberton, unpublished letters, Department of Documents, Imperial War Museum.
19 Fussell, *The Great War*, p. 157.
20 For further information on the representation of working-class women during the war see Sharon Ouditt (1996), 'Tommy's Sisters: The Representation of Working Women's Experience', in Hugh Cecil and Peter H. Liddle (eds), *Facing Armageddon*, London, Leo Cooper.
21 Ethel Mary Bilborough, unpublished diary, Department of Documents, Imperial War Museum.
22 May Wedderburn Cannan (1976), *Grey Ghosts and Voices*, Kineton, Roundwood Press, p. 113.
23 Ellen N. La Motte (1919), *Backwash of War*, London, G. P. Puttnam's Sons; Mary Borden (1929), *The Forbidden Zone*, London, William Heinemann.
24 Bilborough, diary, 15 July 1915.
25 *Ibid.*
26 See Peter Buitenhuis (1987), *The Great War of Words: Literature as Propaganda 1914–18 and After*, London, B. T. Batsford.
27 Bilborough, diary, 5 March [1916].
28 John Masters (1970), *Fourteen Eighteen*, London, Corgi Books, p. 43.
29 Lady Kate Courtney, *Extracts from a War Diary*, printed for private circulation, December 1927.
30 Rose Allatini (A. T. Fitzroy) (1988), *Despised and Rejected.* London, GMP (first published 1918).
31 Bilborough, diary, 17 July 1917.
32 Daisy Williams, 'Adventures in Germany, May–September 1914', unpublished journal, Department of Documents, Imperial War Museum.
33 *Ibid.*
34 Rosie Neal, unpublished memoir, Department of Documents, Imperial War Museum.
35 An extract from the journal of Rosie Neal can be found in Angela K. Smith

(2000), *Women's Writing of the First World War: An Anthology*, Manchester, Manchester University Press.

36 Mary Macleod, unpublished memoir and letters, Liddle Collection, Brotherton Library, University of Leeds.

37 Muriel Thompson, 'Base Notes', unpublished diary, Liddle Collection, Brotherton Library, University of Leeds.

38 *Ibid.*, no dates or page references exist. The piece is written in the form of an essay or story at the back of the original manuscript diary.

39 Alfred, Lord Tennyson (1994), *The Works of Alfred Lord Tennyson*, Ware, Wordsworth Editions.

40 See Anne Summers (1988), *Angels and Citizens: British Women as Military Nurses 1854–1914*, London, Routledge, p. 269: 'By 1914 few people thought of military nursing as a man's job. The TFNS (Territorial Force Nursing Service) had been constructed on an all-female basis, and the VAD (Voluntary Aid Detachment) scheme had quickly deleted its original provision for supplementary male hospital staff. At least 32,000 women served as military nurses between 1914 and 1919.'

41 Mary Clarke, unpublished diary, Department of Documents, Imperial War Museum. An extract can be found in Smith, *Women's Writing of the First World War.*

42 Kenyon, diary.

43 Vera Brittain (1992), *Testament of Youth*, London, Virago (first published 1933), pp. 421–2.

44 Pemberton, letters, 29 May 1915.

45 Fussell, *The Great War*, p. 245.

46 Evadne Price (Helen Zenna Smith) (1988), *Not So Quiet . . . Stepdaughters of War*, London, Virago (first published 1930), pp. 85–6.

47 Fussell, *The Great War*, pp. 243–4.

48 Edmund Blunden (1978), *Undertones of War*, London, W. Collins (first published 1928).

49 Kenyon, diary, 9 May [1915].

50 Pemberton, letters, 9 April 1916.

51 The concept of 'Blighty' took on enormous symbolic value for all those serving abroad during the First World War. The word itself, derived from the Hindi *bilayati*, oddly meaning 'foreign land', is ripe with imperialist connotations, but for the soldiers of the First World War it represented all the warmth and comfort of home.

52 Pemberton, letters, 2 November 1914.

53 *Ibid.*, 9 April 1916.

54 Mary Brown, unpublished diary, Department of Documents, Imperial War Museum.

55 Brown, diary, 8 October 1916.

56 Anne Sebba (1994), *Battling for News*, London, Hodder & Stoughton, p. 2.

57 Brown, diary, 16 December [1915].
58 *Ibid.*, 2 January 1916 (my omission).
59 Sebba, *Battling for News*, p. 60.
60 Brown, diary, 18 December 1915.
61 *Ibid.*, 9 August [1915] (my omissions).
62 Hogan, 'Engendered Autobiographies', p. 103.
63 Brown, diary, 15 May 1915; 24 May 1915.
64 For further information about contemporary responses to tanks, a very new weapon in 1915, see Trudi Tate (1998), *Modernism, History and First World War*, Manchester, Manchester University Press.
65 Rose Macaulay (1992), 'Picnic: July 1917', in Catherine Reilly, ed., *Scars upon my Heart*, London, Virago, p. 66.
66 Enid Bagnold (1978), *A Diary Without Dates*, London, Virago (first published 1918), p. 91.
67 Kenyon, diary, 2 June 1916; 3 June 1916.
68 Brown, diary, 7 June 1915.
69 Clarke, diary, 30 June 1916.
70 Pemberton, letters, 21 February 1915.
71 Pemberton, letters, 3 December 1916, my emphasis.
72 Woolf, 'Women and fiction', p. 141.

2

Private to public:
the front-line woman

I am not a writer of books, and I dislike publicity . . . The book has been written solely with a view to showing that women can be of independent service in National Defence.[1]

Many women, from all walks of life, felt the need to record their experiences of the First World War in the form of a diary or a journal. And very often they found themselves quite unprepared for the nature of that experience as the war cast them in roles that differed greatly from any they had previously played. Perhaps it was this difference that inspired some women to use these private testaments as the basis for a more public discourse on the war and women's role within it, both making claim for the war as a universal experience, rather than a distinctly male sphere, and using its rewriting as a forum to discuss the politics of women's lives. While some women, for a variety of reasons, adopted literary styles that were experimental and innovatory as a means of articulating such alien experience (discussed in greater detail in Chapter 3), others took the opportunity to exploit the role they had played, publicising their activities for social and political ends – women like Mabel St Clair Stobart, who, in 1915, at the age of fifty-three, became the first woman in the First World War to lead a field hospital unit to the front line. It is fascinating to examine how such women change their writing as they move from the private to the public sphere, in terms of both structure and content; what can be understood from the things that are left out, as well as the alterations to what is included.

Probably the most famous example of the transposition of a private diary into a public text is that of Vera Brittain's *Testament of Youth*, which, upon its publication in 1933, was considered to be ground-breaking in the way in which it located a woman in the male arena of the war. In 1981, her original diary was published as *Chronicle of Youth*, and it is interesting to note how the text written for publication softens much of the patriotic fervour and romanticism adopted by the younger Brittain in her contemporary record.[2]

But Brittain was neither unique, nor the first woman to adapt her personal writing in this way. In 1915 May Sinclair published an edited version of the diary she kept while working as the secretary for a motor Ambulance Corps in Belgium in the early weeks of the war as *A Journal of Impressions in Belgium*, described by Rebecca West as 'one of the few books of permanent value produced by the war'.[3] Sinclair's text dwells on ideas of the romanticism of war, also alluded to in her war novels, and indicates her own frustration at being a woman of mature years, unable to participate satisfactorily in that romance. She also speaks boldly about the actions of the other women in the corps who see more of what she interprets as 'heroic action' than she is able to herself,[4] offering an early example of a war text promoting the role of women.[5] Social historian Caroline Playne used her war diary, together with a vast collection of published texts, newspapers and other forms of discourse as data for her retrospective studies, *The Neurosis of the Nations* (1925), *Society at War 1914–16* (1931) and *Britain Holds on 1917, 1918* (1933), using the diary as a primary source to produce a less overtly personal type of published material.[6]

In addition, women's diaries have been published in their original, if edited, forms. Volume 1 of *The Diary of Virginia Woolf*,[7] covers the years 1915–19 and provides one famous example. What is interesting about Woolf's diary of this period is how little she mentions the war, which must have invaded her life in Sussex despite her reticence concerning its developments, although this is probably a result of her recurring illness during this period. Its absence gives a different slant to the way in which we read both the diary and the woman.[8] In contrast the *Diaries 1915–18* of Lady Cynthia Asquith, speak of little else, allowing the language of war to infiltrate the pages, colouring domestic issues as well as those which deal specifically with the experience of the conflict: 'had a hellish morning in pursuit of my summer tweeds . . . sharp skirmish with Harrods on telephone about my skirt'.[9] In borrowing military language, Asquith, perhaps unconsciously, seems to be looking for new ways to express her 'home front' experience which is itself distorted by the crisis around her.

More recent years have seen the publication of the edited war diaries of 'ordinary' women, who also played significant roles in the war effort. For example *Little Grey Partridge*,[10] presents the illustrated diary of Ishobel

Ross who served with a Scottish Women's Hospitals unit in Serbia.[11] Similarly the *First World War Papers* of Margaret Fawcett, another member of the Scottish Women's Hospitals, including letters, a diary and a retrospective diary were published in 1993, and illustrate the effect of the rewriting of events for a different audience. It is worth looking at a brief example. The following passage is taken directly from Fawcett's original diary:

Sunday October 22

We got here about 9.30 last night after a somewhat exciting ride; we were all perched on the tops of the carts carrying our equipment, of which we have five. There was a nasty thunderstorm on the way along, but luckily Turner had her mackintosh and ground sheet with her, so that we didn't get wet. We are supposed to have gone within three miles of the firing line, which I can quite believe. We seemed to see the flashes of bursting shells on three sides of us, and the roar of the guns was far more distinct than we had heard before.[12]

On her return from the war, probably in 1919, Margaret Fawcett rewrote her diary, both adding to and abridging the original text.[13] The corresponding entry reads:

Sunday October 22

We arrived at our second camping ground at 9.30 the night before. We had had a most exciting ride. There was a thunderstorm, which lasted most of the time, and rather added to the thrill of things; and all the time the guns were blazing away – we could see the shells bursting on the horizon after dark. During the evening we saw the flames from the burning of the oil-tanks at Constanza – they seemed to reach far up into the sky. The fire lasted, I believe, nearly three days. During the afternoon of the 21st we saw many smaller fires, which we were told, were the villages through which we had passed. Bulbul Mic, we heard, was now our first line of trenches.[14]

While it is not stated why Fawcett chose to create a retrospective diary, in doing so she has changed the emphasis within the text. The original entry is concerned primarily with her own experience and that of her companions. The thunderstorm is 'nasty' and she is grateful to have avoided a soaking. There is an uncertainty about their location, which is at once both exciting and sinister.

In the later version it is a 'most' exciting ride rather than simply 'somewhat' exciting. The thunderstorm now 'adds to the thrill of things', providing an appropriate Gothic setting for their brush with the front line. The bursting shells have been relegated to the horizon, but replaced by 'flames' that represent significant military events, about which she would not have known at the time. The effect of the rewriting is to impress upon the reader the wider significance of the night, giving it more dramatic power than the first draft with its focus on the women sheltering from the rain. Although not published until 1993, it seems likely that Fawcett had a greater audience in mind. The historical context and the rather elevated language operate to change this war experience from a very private to a notably more public one.

Mabel St Clair Stobart always kept the wider significance of the war in mind. She was able to use her experiences in the First World War, captured initially in diary form, then developed into a public text, to promote herself and her political messages in the later war and post-war years. It was Stobart's status as a 'front line' woman that enabled her to construct her public persona, and in so doing, transmit her ideas about the future role of women in society to the greatest possible audience.

In 1916 Mabel St Clair Stobart published *The Flaming Sword in Serbia and Elsewhere*,[15] a lengthy, political account of her early involvement in the war, working with hospital units, first in Belgium, then Serbia. It addresses the problems of setting up and running such units, but most attention is given to the retreat of the Serbian army in the face of the Bulgar invasion in late 1915, and is based on the diary she kept during the flight.[16] Owing to the severe conditions during writing, the diary is minimalist, yet there is a poetry and an experimentalism in the result which is interesting in literary terms. For publication, Stobart transforms the accidental innovations of her diary into a much more structurally conventional text, informed by a different kind of radicalism, chiefly political, but with a variety of messages and meanings encoded within it.

Unlike many women who found new paths in the First World War, Stobart had already gained some experience of front-line warfare. In 1909 she set up the Women's Sick and Wounded Convoy Corps, a military-style operation intended to prove that women could be as valuable as men in times of war.[17] Training on the Dorset cliff tops above her family home at Studland, the troops of women learnt the skills necessary to provide essential medical assistance to an army in time of war. They had their first opportunity to put this training into practice when war broke out in the Balkans in 1912. Stobart and her field hospital unit saw seven weeks of service which no doubt provided useful grounding for their First World War experiences yet to come.

When she returned to England, Stobart put pen to paper and produced her first political treatise, *War and Women*. Here she began to articulate her belief that war is an absolute evil, but that women should not be excluded from military involvement and 'the national religion of patriotism' on grounds of their sex, because they were equally affected by the consequences.[18] In her Proem she argues, 'I am not a writer of books, and I dislike publicity . . . The book has been written solely with a view to showing that women can be of independent service in National Defence'.[19]

Stobart was already a middle-aged woman when she embarked upon her 'military' career. Her life had begun in a fairly conventional manner, born in 1862 into a wealthy family, she married,[20] had two sons and enjoyed a life of active leisure, golfing and fishing, in the later years of the nineteenth century. This pleasurable world fell apart in 1901 when her husband lost his fortune speculating on the South African market and the family moved to the Transvaal to seek a new life as farmers. When they returned to England six years later, having recovered their fortune, the future looked much brighter. However, her husband, who had sailed independently, died on the voyage home, leaving Stobart a widow in need of a new direction.

Clearly a determined and confident woman, who had embraced life in the High Veldt, she was not inclined to sit still for very long. The result was the Women's Convoy Corps and embarkation on the path that would lead her to the front line in Serbia and beyond. When war broke out in 1914, Stobart and her women went immediately to Belgium, intent on giving help where it was needed most. As the German army advanced the unit provided valuable support, but was forced to flee along with the other early volunteers. Stobart herself was captured by the Germans and narrowly escaped being shot as a spy. She was released and returned to England to reassemble her team, this time heading for the Balkans once again, intent on setting up field hospital units around Serbia.

In her choice of destination Stobart was not unique. Other British women who felt they could be of use on the or near the front line had also been drawn to Serbia. The Serbians were happy to accommodate the suffragist Dr Elsie Inglis by employing one of her NUWSS Scottish Women's Hospitals after the British War Office told her '"To go home and keep quiet," and that the commanding officers "did not want to be troubled with hysterical women"'.[21]

Flora Sandes, originally a nurse, joined the Serbian army when she was cut off from her unit, becoming the only Englishwoman to see active military service during the First World War. She makes an interesting comparison with Stobart because she, too, was a front-line woman who used her experience and her ensuing written record to promote her chosen cause during and after the War.

By her own admission Flora Sandes just drifted into being a soldier because there was nowhere else for her to go. Once accepted in the army, she adopted an identical life-style to the male soldiers and, according to her accounts, stopped thinking of herself as a woman. She was not the only female soldier in the Serbian army, and her records draw attention to the presence of a number of peasant women who appear to adapt to the hardships of army life as easily as she. But her status as a British woman made her unique. Her performance on the front line led to her gradual promotion and she eventually reached the rank of lieutenant at the end of the war. She was wounded, and decorated for her bravery.

In 1916 Sandes published an account of her experiences, based on her letters and diaries, *An English Woman-Sergeant in the Serbian Army*.[22] The account is a straightforward rendition of events, giving occasional hints of the hardships she had to endure, but the tone is generally rather jolly and romanticised, making the whole experience sound like fun. It is all simply expressed, built around a moral dichotomy of right and wrong, good and evil. Although it may now appear stylistically problematic, Sandes original book proved useful to her at the time, when she used it as ammunition on early fund-raising tours which she made around Britain during the war, collecting money for the Serbian army – her adopted cause.

The literary style of the text served her well. Rather than presenting the war experience with a brutal realism, as we have come to expect from other, very often male, war texts of the 1920s and 1930s, Sandes draws upon a more clichéd notion of the 'male' myth of the romanticism of war. The fighting is presented as a big adventure, the Serbs, as allies, have right on their side and reference to her own physical involvement in the violence is minimised. She often characterises herself as a visitor or a tourist rather than a combatant – at one point, while coming under fire from the Bulgarians for the first time, she laments the loss of her camera, and her photographic records of the occasion:

> We lay there and fired at them all that day, and I took a lot of photographs which I wanted very much to turn out well; but, alas! during the journey through Albania the films, together with nearly all the others that I took, got wet and spoilt. The firing died down at dark, and we left the firing line and made innumerable camp fires and sat round them. Lieut. Jovitch, the Commander, took me into his company, and I was enrolled on its books, and he seemed to think I might be made a corporal pretty soon if I behaved myself. We were 221 in the Fourth, and were the largest, and, we flattered

ourselves, the smartest, company of the smartest regiment, the first to be ready in marching order in the mornings, and the quickest to have our tents properly pitched and our camp fires going at night . . .

That evening was very different to the previous one. Lieut. Jovitch had a roaring fire of pine logs built in a little hollow, just below what had been our firing line, and he and I and the other two officers of the company sat round it and had out supper of bread and beans, and after that we spread our blankets on spruce boughs round the fire and rolled up in them. It was a most glorious moonlight night, with the ground covered with white hoar frost, and it looked perfectly lovely with all the camp fires twinkling every few yards over the hillside among the pine trees. I lay on my back looking up at the stars, and, when one of them asked me what I was thinking about, I told him that when I was old and decrepit and done for, and had to stay in a house and not go out any more, I should remember my first night with the Fourth Company on the top of Mount Chukus.[23]

The above extracts give a clear example of the style Sandes employs in the early writing. Her heightened exclamation 'alas!' seems to attach more importance to her pictures than to her shooting. There is a laziness about 'We lay there and fired at them all day', which makes it feel almost like an aside, while the camp fires seem to have more of the atmosphere of the Boy Scouts about them, than the front line. Enrolment and promotion are simply a matter of good behaviour.

What comes across very strongly is Sandes's sense of pride in belonging. The camaraderie at the root of many later men's war texts, particularly those that deal with enlisted men such as Remarque's *All Quiet on the Western Front*,[24] is emphasised here. Sandes reinforces this with her romanticised description of the mountaintop at night. The moonlight, the hoarfrost, the twinkling campfires, create an impression of serenity which owes something to the visionary spirituality of Wordsworth. It feels anachronistic and as a result directs our impression of her front-line experience in a positive way.

The book, together with her service history, war wound, decorations and her imposing androgynous appearance,[25] also proved useful after the war, when her search for aid for her adopted country took her as far as Australia. By presenting this image of war, and aligning it with women's experience, Sandes created a new notion of a 'female heroism', complicit with the dictates of masculine military accomplishment. The impact was twofold. On the one hand, Sandes made a striking and ultimately interesting figure in post-war society – singularly able to capture the attention of those whom she wished to coax into parting with their money. At the same time Sandes may have, even perhaps inadvertently, struck a blow for the feminist cause; after all, one of the strongest arguments against women's suffrage was built around the concept that full citizenship was only due to those who could represent their country on the field of battle. Sandes did precisely that.

Julie Wheelwright, who examines Sandes in detail in her book *Amazons and Military Maids*, suggests, 'To Australians in 1920, Lieutenant Sandes appeared as the product of a break down in the rigid pre-war concept that a woman's role should be confined to the domestic sphere',[26] thus reinforcing the notion of Sandes as a valuable image for the Women's Movement. But Wheelwright goes on to argue that Sandes's position was so extreme that she could not have had the genuine impact on society that perhaps some feminists may have sought because, 'Her experiences . . . were painted in vivid, heroic colours, to place her far beyond other women's emulation. Her exceptional qualities were used to question but ultimately to reinforce accepted male and female roles since Flora Sandes would remain as the only exception to the rule'.[27]

Perhaps then, as a significant political figure for any 'women's cause' Sandes was ahead of her time. Even so she still represented a lurking danger, and the image of conventional heroism which she came to embody as a result of her front-line experience, served to make her a visible and valuable figurehead for the post-war Serbian campaign.

In 1927 Flora Sandes published a more complete record of her wartime years, *The Autobiography of a Woman Soldier: A Brief Record of Adventure with the Serbian Army 1916–1919*. Despite the suggestions of the subtitle, it is a much more down-to-earth account of her army life, lacking the romanticism of her earlier book. Indeed, it resembles the more well-known memoirs of male combatants. She comments on the inadequacy of her diary as a base text, indicating how dependent she was on memory, when it came to the writing process:

> As a general rule my diary for each day seems to have consisted only of two or three scrawled pencil lines, noting which companies made connection with ours on our immediate right or left flank, and with whom we had to keep in touch, followed by a remark that the bread (frequently our only ration) had not turned up, or that we got some cold stew . . . The fighting I seem rarely to have commented on, beyond brief mention of the name of some special friend killed, or whether we had or had not, taken a position. Nothing of interest of course could be written down in case one were taken prisoner.[28]

Despite the minimalist nature of Mabel Stobart's diary, she manages to communicate a great deal about her situation and experience, through a variety of impressions created by her use of language. As a result, it is possible to speculate that the diary may have been a more useful tool for her in her later writing, than it proved to be for Flora Sandes. However, Sandes's autobiographical descriptions of specific war experiences such as being wounded, are precisely presented despite the limitations of her diary record:

> I immediately had a feeling as though a house had fallen bodily on the top of me with a crash. Everything went dark, but I was not unconscious for I acutely realised that our platoon was falling back. I heard afterwards that every single one of them had been wounded by that shower of bombs. One had his face split from nose to chin, another an arm broken, but none, except myself, had actually been knocked out.[29]

> The First Aid Dressing Station was the same in which I had been a dresser when I first joined the regiment, and by the time we reached it, blood was dripping through the stretcher. I was about at the end of my tether, but they gave me hot drinks, warmed me up, and then laid me on a table to probe round and find some of the numerous pieces of bomb. I buried my nose in the broad chest of Doctor B—, who was standing at my head, while the other one worked, and frankly yowled for the first time. But he knew better than to sympathise with an overwrought patient, so he lit a cigarette, thrust it between my lips, and told me to 'shut up and remember I was a soldier,' which had far more effect than any amount of petting would have done.[30]

These descriptions contain the same level of violence that can be found in many men's war texts. What comes across in these recollections is a determination not to be defined by her womanhood. Her cries of pain as the doctor dresses her wound are quickly plugged with a cigarette. Any sign of weakness may have uncomfortable associations with femininity that would be inappropriate in a front-line hospital, despite the fact that men, too, were often unable to control themselves when in great pain, as many records by nurses testify.[31]

When the army finally decided it had finished with Flora Sandes, that it no longer needed her as a soldier or a figurehead, she was demobbed along with all her contemporaries. The return to femininity, the removal from the 'front line' was a bitter pill for her to swallow:

(31 October 1922 – Demobbed after 7 years)

> I cannot attempt to describe what it now felt like, trying to get accustomed to a woman's life and a woman's clothes again; and also to ordinary society after having lived entirely [like] a man for so many years.

Turning from a woman into a private soldier proved nothing compared
with turning back again from soldier to ordinary woman. It was like losing
everything at one fell swoop, and trying to find bearings again in another
life and an entirely different world.[32]

Sandes never acknowledges her own heroism as an issue, in either text.
Indeed, in the 1927 autobiography, she rarely acknowledges her womanhood. Nonetheless, it was the heady combination of these things that
enabled her to be politically useful to Serbia during and after the war, even
if her status as a novelty prevented her from having a more lasting social
effect.

Mabel Stobart, however, retained her femininity when she entered the
man's world of the front line. The image that she created of herself in
order to convey her political ideas reinforces this, presenting her as a
heroic anachronism – the 'Lady of the Black Horse'.[33] Reading the typescript of her diary, it is easy to imagine the authoritative figure of Stobart
jotting down fragments on horseback as she picks her way along the
treacherous mountain paths, although it is the situation, rather than
herself, which appears to form the central subject of the narrative.

Stobart's private diary and her published text are very different.[34] This
diary records only the last months of her time in Serbia, 9 October to 28
December 1915, during which time her hospital unit was caught up in the
great Serbian retreat, fleeing across the mountains of Montenegro and
Albania, accompanied by thousands of civilian refugees and defeated soldiers. The document itself measures no more than five inches by three
inches, is written in a tiny, scrawled hand, and is virtually illegible.

But once transcribed, Stobart's diary is as interesting in terms of the
way it is written as in the events it describes. The fragmented style of the
diary is curiously evocative, in places literary in ways which resemble both
the pastiche of the other women's diaries and some of the modernist narrative experiments which had been developing since the last years of the
nineteenth century. This fragmentation of the diary enables her to
employ language in a precise and effective way, presenting a clear image
of a heroic self bathed in a myriad of emotions and responses to the
drama that surrounds her. Perhaps inadvertently, she uses language in a
way that often creates a more effective representation of the same events
which can appear vapid when caught up in some of the didactic bluster-
ing of *The Flaming Sword in Serbia and Elsewhere.*

Rebecca Hogan argues, 'immersion in the horizontal, non-hierarchical
flow of events and details – in other words, radical parataxis – seems to

be one of the striking features of the diary as a form'.[35] She could be describing Stobart's original manuscript. Because of the lack of time, the diary contains only the minimum information, punctuated by ellipses; but the specific nature of her language and the structure of the narrative combine to offer a covert analysis, innately revealing something of the woman as well as her circumstances. One illuminating entry reads:

> Sat Oct 23rd
>
> Sent for Priest fr. Alkali [a Major] to service over dead man. Guns firing. Priest chanting Alleluja solitary over dead. Whilst grave dug. Why Alleluja? Dawn. Bustle of departure, no-one thoughts for dead. Last night ask where is he? Answer 'no-one knows'.[36]

Stobart's diary is written in this kind of shorthand, yet somehow the exclusion of all but the essential language gives it a kind of aesthetic quality, particularly in some of the more poetic passages which will be examined later. Here, the halting, disjointed way that the passage reads seems to add to the solitary nature of the event being described, reinforced by the staccato accompaniment of the guns. The scene is complete. The anonymity of the dead is both acknowledged and questioned. Stobart tells us that he is forgotten even before he is buried, whilst highlighting the bitter irony of the priest's incantation, alleluja – praise the lord; the glory is no glory, the potential hope of the dawn setting, displaced by the real need to move on with haste. Using very few words, Stobart reports the scene. Her narrative style holds analysis innately within the language of her text. We understand her anger even though she stands back from the events to describe them, but no overt judgements are offered. The paratactic structure of the diary offers no single subject position to the reader. The text simply foregrounds a series of contradictory positions and attitudes, implicitly political and more powerful for its denial of emphasis.

Her public rendition of the scene is quite different. In *The Flaming Sword* imagination is very important; a vital tool in the building of this text as a political treatise. How it is used can be illustrated by examining the passage in the published text that corresponds directly to that in the diary:

> Then I stood beside the priest, a few yards behind the scrimmage round the bonfires, whilst he, in his gay embroidered robe, chanted, all out of tune, in the old Slavonic language, which no one now understands, the words of the

Greek Church burial service . . . The groans of the wounded, and the
thunder of the guns, coming ever nearer and nearer, made an effective
accompaniment. The only incongruity was the frequent repetition in the
priest's prayers, of the word 'Alleluja!' Why 'Alleluja!'? I asked myself in the
intervals of my 'Amen' responses, as the scene round those bonfires burnt
itself upon my mind.[37]

The passage is, in a sense diluted by syntax, reading more like a tableau
than the story in the former extract. The central reported event, the
burial, remains, but otherwise the scene is almost unrecognisable. It is no
longer dawn, but in fact evening now. The surrounding bustle is a result
of tending the wounded of the retreat, who are surrounded by bonfires to
provide them with warmth. But in Stobart's representation they are,
figuratively as well as literally, in hell. This reconstruction of the battle
zone as hell links with Stobart's continued usage of biblical language, with
echoes of Milton, which conveys both her social background and her literary heritage. The orchestration of the guns is now enhanced by the
groans of the wounded adding to the atmosphere of the nightmare. The
priest 'all out of tune' acts as a metonym for religious orthodoxy, which
has no place in this underworld. Although no longer solitary, this is a
crowded place filled with noise and movement, he is no match for the
forces of evil which surround him.

The syntactic additions to the original structure of the text strive to fill
in the gaps in meaning which give the diary much of its power. Stobart
attempts to eliminate contradictions and ambiguities, with varying
degrees of success, in order to privilege her anti-war leanings. The narrative becomes more overtly political as it works to construct a position for
the reader that allows identification with this narratorial subject, making
it a much more traditionally structured text.

Although her analytical metaphors are not subtle, Stobart still refrains
from making blatant judgements at this point. Her questioning remains,
to ensure that the reader also questions 'Why 'Alleluja!'?', 'no one now
understands'. *The Flaming Sword* is filled with scenes like this. Stobart
piles on the horror, usually appealing to nothing but humanitarian values
in order to prepare the reader for the solutions, hinted at throughout, and
articulated in her final chapters: men have had their chance to govern and
failed; now it is time for women to intervene.

Stobart's views on the role of women in society do not enter into her
diary; other more basic survival needs like food and transport are inevitably her dominant concerns. Much of the document is given over to the
practical and physical concerns of the flight:

Oct. 18th Monday [1915]

Rough dressing station, opn tent. Straw on ground in another open tent for shelter w'ded. Two lying untransportable. If evacuation comes, sent by transp. & die en route. Amputations etc done in open. Bivouac tents for men. For Commandant & 5 others 1 tent beds all round long table in centre ... During eve & night 102 wounded, 1 dead in cart, another died in night. Many badly wounded straight to us fr. 1st aid doctor nr. battlefield. Kept 50 during night evac. till 11 p.m. & fr. 5 a.m. Brought in ox carts & sometimes high basket sides, no open ends. Lift over top.

Sat. Oct. 30th [1915]

Refugees in shelters of branches by roadside with children & pigs. make fire in tent for meals. Spit 5 chickens for supper.

Tues. Dec. 14th [1915]

Sent Marko on to find room. Got one small one & kitchen to cook food, 2 little refugee girls lost parents on trek left here by officers who gave them lift in kola & cdn't wait. Mother lying ill on mattress on floor nr. good Ammer. stove. Cockrill lost all day but turned up when came to halt. Nightmare getting places for ponies in stables. Others grab them & endless talk, too late for bread but hope tomorrow early. Two ponies left en route (William's) as wdn't go, but picked up another on mountain side when fetching hay. Sleet all day till 2 p.m. & very cold. My pony done, can't ride him, another dead man by roadside. No one's business to bury him.[38]

Her interests never stray far from the problems of the next meal and finding shelter for her fellow travellers. But they are interspersed with observations concerning the plight of those who surround her; both the living and the dead. These juxtapositions make the experience of reading the diary rather like traversing an emotional minefield; the wounded soldiers, refugee children and exhausted animals crowd the pages. But Stobart's tone refuses to beg for sympathy. These are simply reported facts. Later they can be used as emotional triggers to give strength to the arguments that she will formulate for the public good in her published text.

There is also a poetry in the diary which gives it an artistic credibility in its own right. Its physical appearance, the hurried nature of its construction, suggests Stobart's aesthetic spontaneity, and her use of some of the more poetic passages when translating the diary suggests that she was satisfied with the effect created by her original writing, which draws on the language of the Romantic poets to create several scenes. It may be that she already had Wordsworth in mind as she traversed the austere

Montenegrin mountains. A comparison of two corresponding passages will give an indication of how this linguistic style of the diary is adapted in the published text.

> Wed. Nov. 3rd
>
> Daybreak beautiful. Sunrise cloud colours marvellous. Golden clouds ag. dark purple hills with wool like folds of clouds in dist to soften effect. One daring cloud like golden dragon spread out alone in the dark sky. Colours too delicate to call blue or gold or crimson. Glories & beauties everywhere. Is it all meaningless or waiting for us to catch meaning? While was thinking about this, the glories disappeared & I saw the eternal picture of drab dressed weary soldiers splashing with open feet in sloppy mud. Sometimes stumbling & rising without murmur cov. with wet mud.[39]

This record, written hastily as she flees from the advancing army retains the fragmented style of the rest of the diary. But it indicates that Stobart has the time to take in the aesthetic qualities of the world around her, and can find some hope in them. There is also a kind of doubt here, as she questions the meaning of such ephemeral beauty set against the despair that surrounds her. The bleak supersedes the glory allowing the passage to act as a metaphor for her attitude to the war in general.

Stobart was clearly struck by the memory of this sunrise and incorporates it into *The Flaming Sword*, but away from the pressures of the retreat she endows it with a much more specific meaning, burying her implied agnosticism beneath a display of religious faith. The sunrise itself immediately follows a passage during which, riding in the convoy at night, Stobart catches herself questioning, 'where, in all this hell, is God?'.[40]

> And immediately the answer came. As if in purposeful response, the mountains in the east threw off the blackness of the night, and showed rich purple against the lightening sky. Over the mountains rose clouds of gold, and pink, and aerial blue, and as the rays of sunlight shot triumphantly into the sky, white mists, thick and soft, that had lain hidden, became, for a moment of pure joy, bathed in all the rainbow colours; one daring cloud of brilliant gold spread itself in the shape of a great dragon across the dark sky. Glories and beauties everywhere, if we could only catch the meaning.[41]

Again Stobart embellishes in the published text, but the syntactic additions do not increase the effect of the moment in aesthetic terms; it operates more to reduce the vivid simplicity that is captured in the diary. Now the passage has become the articulation of a moment of divine inspiration, expressions like 'threw off the blackness of the night', 'triumphantly' and 'pure joy' alter the meaning of the colourful vision inherited from the diary; this is God showing himself to the faithful. It is a sign for future hope rather than present comfort which Stobart does not seem to find problematic despite its continued juxtaposition against the 'nightmare picture of drab-dressed, mud-stained soldiers, slashing with their sandalled feet in the sloppy mud'.[42] Echoes of the diary blend with the later text to present multiple meanings which do not necessarily sit comfortably together.

This discomfort reveals the ideological paradox of the text, which has become a pastiche of different styles and meanings. Stobart draws on her literary heritage as she borrows stylistically from a variety of sources ranging from the Bible to the Romantic poets. At the same time she does not ignore the innovations of her own diary and the powerful poetry contained in its fragments. But *The Flaming Sword* intentionally covers much more, both chronologically and ideologically, so such a pastiche is, perhaps, inevitable.

The evidence of the 1915 diary suggests that as she battles with the elements of the Serbian winter, she is questioning the deeper implications for a 'civilised' society that allows these events to occur, with a view to developing the arguments set out in her first book. On 3 November she notes, 'Hear endless rumbling of wagons like breaking of raging sea on distant shingly beach. World of shadows & dreariness. Some rain again. Is no one angry for all this?'[43] What she describes is the physical reality which surrounds her and again her language is effective. The simple metaphor of the sea suggests a feeling of universality, that this train of refugees has become somehow eternal as a result of the inhumanity of man. And her anger is inflated by the apparent acceptance of calamity that she sees all around her. The hurried nature of her diary forces her to choose language which allows her to say so much, when there is time for so little. The conventional structure of *The Flaming Sword* enables her to identify what she believes to be the fundamental cause of this multinational catastrophe: militarism. She then goes on to propose a solution.

The spectre of militarism is a fairly common theme in war literature. Henri Barbusse attacks it from a soldier's point of view in the closing pages of *Under Fire*:

> They [militarists] pervert the most admirable of moral principles. How many are the crimes of which they have made virtues merely by dowering them with the word 'national'? They distort even truth itself. For the truth which is eternally the same they substitute each their national truth. So many nations, so many truths; and thus they falsify and twist the truth. All those people are your enemies.[44]

Caroline Playne reiterates the sentiment in *Society at War 1914–16*, articulating the idea around which Stobart's, and other earlier texts, were built: 'On the moral plane, as an ideal, militarism has always been at the furthest pole from feminism.'[45]

Stobart's views on militarism are interesting, and primarily gender based. In her Preface she states:

> I believe that humankind is at the parting of the ways. One way leads to evolution – along spiritual lines – the other to devolution – along lines of materialism; and the sign-post to devolution is militarism. For militarism is a movement of retrogression, which will bring civilisation to a standstill – in a *cul-de-sac*.[46]

Stobart's political argument is built around this notion of 'devolution' which, with its Darwinist implications, is uncomfortably situated alongside her deep religious beliefs which also continually permeate her text, reinforced by her very title. Militarism has come to represent the flaming sword that prevents humankind from reaching the Tree of Life. But Stobart subordinates both of these ideas to her more powerful feminist message.

In her published text the role of women is spelt out as different from that of men, although equal, if not superior, as a result of their semi-divine status as mothers, the givers of life. They are not connected with the militarism that is crushing civilisation: 'I believe that militarism can only be destroyed with the help of Woman. In countries where Woman has least sway, militarism is most dominant. Militarism is maleness run riot.'[47]

This political view complements those presented in much of the pacifist/feminist material produced by dissenting organisations during the First World War.[48] In her essay, 'Women and War' Catherine Marshall wrote 'for war, to women, is pre-eminently an outrage on motherhood and all that motherhood means; the destruction of life and the breaking up of homes is the undoing of women's work as life-givers and home-makers'.[49] Marshall's essentialist arguments are located within a pacifist discourse which associates militarism with patriotism in a way which corroborates with some of the ideas of Hugh Cunningham in his essay 'The Language of Patriotism'.[50] Similarly, in 'Militarism Versus Feminism', C. K. Ogden and Mary Sargant Florence call upon notions of maternity and militarism, more recently discussed by Anna Davin in 'Imperialism and Motherhood'[51] to expose the imprisonment of women in gender roles which endanger society as a whole:

War, and the fear of war, has kept woman in perpetual subjection, making it her chief duty to exhaust all her faculties in the ceaseless production of children that nations might have the warriors needed for aggression or defence. She must not have any real education – for the warrior alone required knowledge and independence.[52]

Following the same line, Stobart develops the argument using the war as a lever to further the progression of women in society and to justify their inclusion politics:

Until woman had obtained some experience of war, she could only express sentiments concerning war; but now she is at liberty to give opinions as to the meaning of war. And in the opinion of woman – at least, of one woman, who is, presumably, representative of some other women – war means – the failure of society.[53]

Stobart had herself stood for election on behalf of Westminster to the London City Council in 1913 without success. Now, as a woman who has experienced the impact of the war during the Serbian retreat, she now feels better qualified to comment. She is able to compete alongside the acknowledged female hero, Flora Sandes, for the right to citizenship even though she has not born arms. And she can see through the jingoistic discourse that is being fed to the nation, labelling much of that, too, as masculine.

Women, then, who give life, cannot collude with those who wilfully set out to destroy it. Here Stobart is articulating a sentiment that continues to appear in pacifist/feminist rhetoric.[54] For Stobart and her contemporaries, the issue cannot be separated from that of basic political rights for women and the close proximity of the suffrage campaign.[55] When she suggests 'Woman has hitherto protected the concrete life of individuals; must she not now, in an enlarged sphere, also protect the abstract life of humankind?'[56] she is echoing the sentiments of other women campaigners. Mary Sheepshanks from *Jus Suffragii*: 'Women must not only use their hands to bind up, they must use their brains to understand the causes of the European frenzy, and their lives must be devoted to putting a stop for ever to such wickedness.'[57] Florence and Ogden: 'Here at last it is clear that the higher ideals and aspirations of women coincide with the future welfare of the whole of humanity.'[58] Stobart's comments differ from these, most significantly because of the nature of her experience; she had seen at first hand the consequences of this 'masculine' orthodoxy, enabling her to write with a different type of power. Her participation in the war gives her a kind of political integrity lending authority to her voice as both writer and speaker. The public image she created of herself actively promoted this privileged position.

Stobart's diary may have been crucial as an aide-memoire in qualifying her to write with such passion on a gender debate that was already raging. The emotional clarity of Stobart's brief record is such that it can re-create events in a way that must have been indispensable when she came to write *The Flaming Sword*. But, equally, the diary is interesting for the fragments which it contains that Stobart consciously chooses not to include in her later text, especially with regard to her own personal heroism. Particularly poignant is a part of her closing entry, 28 December 1915, which even in a private record, she saw fit to place in parenthesis: '(Curious revelation of buried feelings when at Brindisi Commander Eadie said something about soon be "home" now. Off guard & nearly broke down)'.[59] Stobart's desire that this identification of weakness should be suppressed in order to maintain the myth of 'British pluck' feeds the public image which is designed to assist her in her campaigning.

The construction of the public self is strictly controlled. Stobart certainly plays down her personal heroism in *The Flaming Sword* lest it should feed the patriotic myth too well, and overshadow the political/pacifist messages of her text. In her diary she notes, 'Col. G. writes long notes of acknowledgement of my services, & going to have it typed by aft. Tells me I'm to receive Red X decoration, also order of St Sava 3rd class, also Gold Medal for service & recommended for White Eagle order for field hospital work';[60] a fleeting reference to these decorations in *The Flaming Sword* operates to reinforce the heroic image without subordinating the plight of the Serbian people.

The image that lasted, 'the Lady of the Black Horse' was first constructed in countless local and national newspaper reports, commentating on the retreat from Serbia in 1915. Stobart had already attracted media attention for her involvement in the Balkan War and this new publicity built on the established reputation. She was 'An English Heroine in Serbia'[61] and 'Mrs Stobart. An English Heroine Loved and Blessed by all Serbians for all she has done for them'.[62] *The Times* reported on 'Heroic British Nurses in Stricken Serbia'[63] and the *Bristol Evening Times* told the 'Story of a Lady who was made a Major . . . Clad in the garb in which she had crossed the Montenegrin and Albanian mountains' as she was interviewed.[64]

This image is both powerful and interesting. On the one hand it emphasises her femininity; she is 'loved and blessed' for her service to others; 'admirable in her solicitude for the wounded'.[65] These descriptions call to mind the clichéd image of the nurse which had been nurtured by propagandist culture since Florence Nightingale. At the same time there is something distinctly masculine about her. 'A Lady who was made a Major' suggests an inversion of expected gender roles rather reminiscent of Flora Sandes, and emphasises her position of authority as the Commandant of her hospital unit. And always there is the symbol of the black horse: 'the woman on the black horse who figured so prominently during the retirement of the Serbs before the Bulgar invasion'.[66] Stobart, mounted at the head of her troops, seems to pass for a military leader of great significance. The image blends dignity with a conventional representation of heroism which, when applied to a woman, makes a powerful combination. Printed in newspapers everywhere to accompany the story, it was a picture that could capture the imagination of the British public, providing the returning Mabel Stobart with an already receptive audience for both her writing and her public speaking.

One newspaper report, by 'one who knows her' captures the image precisely, contrasting the masculine and feminine to create a balanced, if idealised impression of heroism:

> It is no figure of speech to say that I have never met a braver woman or one of stronger personality in spite of her very feminine charm. She is just the type that wins through, not only by her sheer ability but, by virtue of the confidence she inspires in others.[67]

After her return from Serbia at the end of 1915, Stobart began to publicise her ideas about the war, first through *The Flaming Sword* and complemented by a series of public lectures. After the Americans joined the war in 1917 she embarked upon a lecture tour there in an attempt to inspire the American people to support the war effort. As 'the Lady of the Black Horse' she had evidence both photographic and literary, to show them what it was really like. Despite her belief in the importance of peace and the politics by which it should be maintained, she was convinced that the war needed to be won first. As that very rare creature, a woman who had been in the front line, she had the experience to back up her convictions.

As individuals, women like Mabel St Clair Stobart and Flora Sandes were not in a position to change the world. But their activities in the First World War put them in a position that commanded people to take notice. They had done things in time of war that British women had not previously done. And they had used their unique position to attract attention, to make themselves heard for the causes they believed in, through personal appearance and, with a longer lasting effect, through writing.

Admittedly, their success was limited: As Flora Sandes had hoped, money was raised for Serbia but, eighty years on, the Balkans were being torn apart by another crisis of ethnic conflict. Women did obtain representation in the mechanisms of government, although in the years following the First World War the spectre of militarism went from strength to strength with the rise of fascism in Europe.

However, the diaries and subsequent published texts of the front-line women of the First World War begin to tell their own story, looking for hope in an often hopeless situation. Stobart's diary, like those of the women discussed in Chapter 1, illustrates the way in which the immediate experience of the war influenced her style. By glancing at the tiny pages of Stobart's journal, it is easy to understand how necessity forced her to adopt narrative techniques of a type that some accepted modernists worked for years to attain. The experience made her a poet even before it made her a politician with *The Flaming Sword in Serbia and Elsewhere*, articulating an alternative mode of radical modernity; that of feminist politics. In the next chapter I shall remain in the front line to examine the way in which some women blended these issues within their work, creating, intentionally or otherwise, a published modernist language for the politics of the battlefield in hospital stories of the First World War.

Notes

1 Mabel St Clair Stobart (1913), *War and Women*, London, G. Bell.
2 Vera Brittain (1992), *Testament of Youth*, London, Virago (first published 1933); Vera Brittain (1981), *Chronicle of Youth: War Diary 1913–17*, London, Victor Gollancz.
3 Rebecca West (1983), 'Miss Sinclair's Genius', in Jane Marcus (ed.), *The Young Rebecca*, London, Virago, p. 305.
4 The Ambulance Corps included two women, Mrs Knocker (later Baroness de T'Serclaes) and Mairi Chisholm, who went on to be known as 'the Women of Pervyse' when they broke away from the unit and worked with the Belgian army close to the front line. For more information see Baroness de T'Serclaes and Mairi Chisholm (1916), *The Cellar House at Pervyse: A Tale of Uncommon Things from the Journals and Letters of the Baroness T'Serclaes and Mairi Chisholm*, London, A. & C. Black; Baroness de T'Serclaes (1964), *Flanders and Other Fields*, London, Harrap.
5 For further analysis of this text see Suzanne Raitt (1997), 'Contagious Ecstasy: May Sinclair's War Journals', in Suzanne Raitt and Trudi Tate (eds), *Women's Fiction and the First World War*, Oxford, Clarendon Press.
6 Caroline E. Playne (1925), *The Neuroses of the Nations*, London, George Allen & Unwin; Caroline E. Playne (1931), *Society at War 1914–16*, London,

George Allen & Unwin; Caroline E. Playne (1933), *Britain Holds on 1917, 1918*, London, George Allen & Unwin.

7 Virginia Woolf (1977), *Diary of Virginia Woolf*, vol. 1, *1915–1919*, London, Hogarth Press.

8 For further information, see Karen L. Levenback (1999), *Virginia Woolf and the Great War*, New York, Syracuse University Press.

9 Cynthia Asquith (1968), *Diaries 1915-18*, London, Hutchinson, p. 5.

10 Tess Dixon (ed.) (1988), *The Little Grey Partridge: First World War Diary of Ishobel Ross*, Aberdeen, Aberdeen University Press.

11 For further information on the Scottish Women's Hospitals see Leah Leneman (1994), *In the Service of Life: The Story of Elsie Inglis and the Scottish Women's Hospitals*, Edinburgh, Mercat Press; Audrey Fawcett Cahill (ed.) (1999), *Between The Lines: Letters and Diaries from Elsie Inglis's Russian Unit*, Bishop Auckland, Pentland Press.

12 Audrey Fawcett Cahill (ed.) (1993), *The First World War Papers of Margaret Fawcett*, Pietermaritzburg, Wyllie Desktop Publishing, p. 71.

13 See introduction to Cahill, *First World War Papers*.

14 *Ibid.*, p. 114.

15 Mabel St Clair Stobart (1916), *The Flaming Sword in Serbia and Elsewhere*, London, Hodder & Stoughton.

16 Mabel St Clair Stobart, unpublished diary, Department of Documents, Imperial War Museum.

17 This was a breakaway movement from the FANY, founded two years earlier. For further information, see Anne Summers (1988), *Angels and Citizens*, London, Routledge & Kegan Paul.

18 Stobart, *War and Women*, pp. 138–43.

19 *Ibid.*

20 Born Mabel Ann Boulton, she married St Clair Stobart who died in 1907. In 1912 she married Judge John Greenhalgh who accompanied and supported her through all her wartime activities. However she retained her original name because she had already become well known.

21 Ray Strachey (1989), *The Cause*, London, Virago (first published in 1928), p. 338.

22 Flora Sandes (1916), *An English Woman-Sergeant in the Serbian Army*, London, New York and Toronto, Hodder & Stoughton.

23 *Ibid.*, pp. 138–43.

24 Erich Maria Remarque (1991), *All Quiet on the Western Front*, London, Picador (first published 1929).

25 When Sandes embarked on fund-raising tours representing the Serbian army she always dressed in full uniform, carrying a sword and smoking cigarettes; phallic symbols defining her masculine status. It appeared that she was completely at ease with this image, given her stated discomfort when she was forced to return to wearing women's clothes.

26 Julie Wheelwright (1989), *Amazons and Military Maids*, London, Pandora, p. 105.
27 *Ibid.*
28 Flora Sandes (1927), *The Autobiography of a Woman Soldier: A Brief Record of Adventures with the Serbian Army 1916–1919*, London, H. F. & G. Witherby, p. 20.
29 *Ibid.*, p. 63.
30 *Ibid.*, pp. 67–8.
31 See the writings of Ellen La Motte and Mary Borden discussed in detail in Chapter 3.
32 Sandes, *Autobiography of a Woman Soldier*, p. 220.
33 The painting, *The Lady of the Black Horse* by James Rankin, of Mabel Stobart now hangs in the British Red Cross Archive and Museum.
34 Although other diaries written by Stobart in 1915 have survived, I am concerned here with the one that deals specifically with the retreat from Serbia and was written under 'battle' conditions. This diary is held in the Department of Documents, Imperial War Museum.
35 Rebecca Hogan (1991), 'Engendered Autobiographies: The Diary as a Feminine Form', *Prose Studies*, 14 (2), September, p. 102.
36 Stobart, diary, 23 October 1915.
37 Stobart, *The Flaming Sword*, pp. 158–9.
38 Stobart, diary, 18 October 1915; 30 October 1915; 14 December 1915.
39 Stobart, diary, 3 November 1915.
40 Stobart, *The Flaming Sword*, p. 176.
41 *Ibid.*
42 *Ibid.*, p. 177.
43 Stobart, diary, 3 November 1915.
44 Henri Barbusse (1974), *Under Fire*, London, J. M. Dent.
45 Playne, *Society at War*, p. 126.
46 Stobart, *The Flaming Sword*, Preface.
47 *Ibid.*
48 For an alternative contemporary interpretation of early twentieth-century militarism see Niall Ferguson (1998), *The Pity of War*, London, Allen Lane.
49 Catherine Marshall (1987), 'Women and War', in Margaret Kamester and Jo Vellacott (eds), *Militarism versus Feminism*, London, Virago (first published 1915), pp. 35–42.
50 Hugh Cunningham (1989), 'The Language of Patriotism', in Raphael Samuel (ed.), *Patriotism*, vol. 1, London, Routledge, pp. 57–89.
51 Anna Davin (1989), 'Imperialism and Motherhood', in Raphael Samuel (ed.), *Patriotism*, vol. 1, London, Routledge, pp. 203–35.
52 C. K. Ogden and Mary Sargant Florence (1987), 'Militarism versus Feminism', in Margaret Kamester and Jo Vellacott (eds), *Militarism versus Feminism*, London, Virago (first published 1915), p. 57.

53 Stobart, *The Flaming Sword*, p. 311.
54 For example Lynne Segal (1989), *Is the Future Female?*, London, Virago, examines the polemic which identifies a biological link between women and peace, and its binary opposition, men, masculinity and war, relating it to the activities of the women's peace camp at Greenham Common in the 1980s. Nancy Huston (1986), 'The Matrix of War: Mothers and Heroes', in Susan R. Suleiman (ed.), *The Female Body in Western Culture*, Cambridge, MA, Harvard University Press, while striving to find links between war and motherhood, echoes the ideas of Ogden and Florence, identifying a mythological/anthropological division which suggests that motherhood itself deprives women of their capacity to fight, contrasting mothers with 'virgin warriors' in different cultures and legends.
55 Stobart had not been actively involved in the British suffrage campaign because she had been living abroad during the years of greatest activism, although she did share their beliefs. Perhaps this is why she did not receive support when she stood for election.
56 Stobart, *The Flaming Sword*, p. 316.
57 Mary Sheepshanks (1 November 1914), *Jus Suffragii*, quoted in Sharon Ouditt (1994), *Fighting Forces, Writing Women*, London, Routledge, p. 152.
58 Ogden and Florence, 'Militarism versus Feminism', p. 62.
59 Stobart, diary, 28 December 1915.
60 Stobart, diary, 22 December 1915.
61 *Glasgow Bulletin*, 6 November 1915.
62 *Tatler*, 10 November 1915.
63 *The Times*, 6 November 1915.
64 *Bristol Evening Times*, 30 December 1915.
65 Quoted in a number of different newspapers on the same day including the *Highgate and Hampstead Express* and *The Times*, 6 November 1915.
66 *Bristol Observer*, 13 November 1915.
67 *Evening News*, 5 November 1915.

3

Accidental modernisms:
hospital stories of the First World War

This is the second battlefield. The battle now is going on over the helpless
bodies of these men. It is we who are doing the fighting now, with their real
enemies.[1]

The men and women who made up the medical personnel of the First
World War did not, for the most part, operate in the line of fire. But they
were very often close enough to experience the activity of the front line in
a unique way. The soldiers that they treated, in casualty clearing stations,
in base hospitals, even the hospitals in Britain, had regularly come from
direct action. Their wounds were frequently covered only by the flimsy
battle dressings available to the comrades who had assisted them, despite
the fact that their journey may have taken days. Caked in the mud of the
trenches and of no man's land, their condition on arrival seemed to transform the clinical hospital wards into a kind of second battlefield with the
doctors and nurses becoming the new protagonists in a war against
disease, death and deformity.

Service on 'the second battlefield' brings its own rights and privileges,
and the status of medical personnel held an ambivalence which, in many
cases, enabled them to produce written records from an unusual perspective. They were not soldiers, did not experience actual combat, but were
still exposed to many of its most disturbing results. They were firsthand
witnesses of the carnage, who lived in a position of relative safety a few
miles behind the front line. But the horror of what they saw encouraged
many of them to record it, to create voices for the real victims, who more
often than not went unheard.

For women whose social and cultural background had ill prepared
them for such experience, the position was even more complex than for
the male doctors.[2] Many of the incidents they decided to record defied

expression using conventional language and form. While other private writers turned to their literary heritage to find ways to express the unspeakable, these women sought alternative narrative strategies and non-mimetic linguistic experiments to convey their experience. It is as though the situations that they wished to describe cannot be contained within traditional literary forms. Faced with the inadequacy of the old, they attempted instead to negotiate the new. This hypothesis has been identified, but not explored, by Sharon Ouditt.[3] Similarly, in her essay 'Corpus/Corps/Corpse: Writing the Body in/at War', Jane Marcus makes the following suggestion: 'One might then observe that the fragmentation described as typical of modernist texts has an origin in the writing practice of women nurses and ambulance drivers.'[4] This statement is problematic since it is possible to locate this 'modernist' strategy in pre-war experimental writing. However, these writings, produced under the pressure of the second battlefield, do make a significant contribution to our understanding of the development of a wider field of 'modernisms'; accidental literary innovations on a trajectory parallel to the pathways for experimental design followed by the more established modernist artists.

This chapter examines the work of three women writers, Enid Bagnold, Ellen La Motte and Mary Borden, all of whom were nurses active on 'the second battlefield' in its most practical sense. But there is another, more theoretical way of defining 'the second battlefield' – in literary terms. For each of these, the recording of their experiences marked a debut in the world of 'creative' literature and their texts share many thematic and stylistic traits. Their writing is extremely evocative, but is hardly recognised within the body of war literature. This is the first literary battlefield – establishment and recognition as active and important contributors to the dialogue of war. The second is more radical. Forced by the inadequacy of an old language they, perhaps inadvertently, strive to find a new one. The result, as Marcus and Ouditt have begun to suggest, includes the utilisation of many modernist motifs. It produces a type of women's experimental art triggered directly by the war, rather than by any particular desire to be innovatory. Working within current theoretical notions that allow for the existence of 'modernisms', rather than a single monolithic modernism, it is helpful to locate this writing within the wider innovations of the period.[5] This may be termed 'accidental modernism', and it forms an important link between the experience of the First World War and the emergence of a wider modernist practice. Acceptance within an opened up modernist field would mean victory on the second literary battlefield.

In *Women of the Left Bank,* Shari Benstock offers a reading of modernism

> that defines it specifically as a post-World War 1 phenomenon, that empha-
> sises the role the war played in creating the psychology of despair in which
> the ensuing literary movement would ground itself. This definition takes as
> its controlling metaphor the No Man's Land between the trenches of World
> War 1, viewing the modern world as a landscape in which the past is not
> recoverable and the future offers no hope.[6]

Benstock is looking forward to the literary cultures of the 1920s, and she goes on to discuss the way in which the legacy of the war became central to the creation of modernist thought, and the associated problems for defining a female modernism, given that women were so often excluded from the war.[7] But Benstock's argument works equally well when looking back to much of the literature produced in the war. The metaphor of no man's land can be usefully applied to the woman's domain of the Royal Herbert Hospital at Woolwich where Enid Bagnold worked as a VAD. And Claire Tylee suggests that the forbidden zone, the place forbidden to women but occupied by the hospital units of Ellen La Motte and Mary Borden, represents 'an emotional space as significant as No Man's Land';[8] a kind of no woman's land inhabited by select women. The psychology of despair is prevalent within the confines of these hospitals, the landscape of despair surrounds them, thus providing women with their own arena for war experience.

Many of the modernist characteristics identified earlier, aesthetic self-consciousness, fragmentation, paradox and uncertainty, dehumanisation, sense of crisis and an engagement with issues of sexuality, can be discovered within the nurses' war narratives, as well as experiments with language and form. The very location of their experience, in hospitals literally surrounded by the fragments of human bodies straight from the battlefield, is of vital importance. It represents fragmentation, dehumanisation and crisis in their most fundamental forms. Taking these signposts as a framework, it is possible to locate these texts within the development of modernisms, exploring the interface between war, gender and innovatory writing.

Enid Bagnold's *A Diary without Dates*[9] received a mixed response from contemporary commentators. Lady Cynthia Asquith wrote in her diary on 28 March 1918, 'I read *A Diary Without Dates* – wonderfully gripping, pitiless and true, and so vividly written. [Robert] Nichols says it is the only good English thing of the war – bar Siegfried Sassoon'.[10] Having read

Bagnold's book, she experienced a revived interest in her own war work, and adopted a similar linguistic style whenever writing of it in her own diary. In contrast, Virginia Woolf was much less appreciative. On 29 January 1918 she wrote to Vanessa Bell:

> Did you ever meet a woman called Enid Bagnold – would be clever, and also smart? Who went to Ottoline's parties and now lives at Woolwich and nurses soldiers? 'That disagreeable chit?' Yes that is my opinion too . . . She has written a book, called, as you can imagine, 'A Diary Without Dates', all to prove that she's the most attractive, and popular and exquisite of creatures – all her patients fall in love with her – her feet are the smallest in Middlesex – one night she missed her bus and a soldier was rude to her in the dark – that sort of thing.[11]

Woolf's assessment is uncharacteristically unfair and, the tone of the letter suggests, not particularly objective. But her refusal to review *A Diary without Dates* did not lessen the impact it made upon publication. Fifteen thousand copies were produced and, without hesitation, Bagnold was sacked by the matron of the Royal Herbert Hospital. The reason given was that she had breached military discipline,[12] thus highlighting the political implications of the work. Anne Sebba argues that Bagnold's book represents war reporting 'at its most effective', and cites H.G. Wells as expounding its superior value as a war record in a contemporary review.[13] But Bagnold's representation of the hospital system directly attacked the patriarchal institutions which controlled the war. Consequently it was deemed to be bad for morale, particularly at such a critical time during the war, when the attention of the nation was turned to the final German offensive.

Bagnold's book follows the seasons from autumn through to summer. Otherwise the narrative is constructed from rather disjointed fragments of experience, not only Bagnold's, but also those of the soldiers whom she nurses, linked by self-conscious statements which effectively reposition the claustrophobic world of the hospital within the wider spectrum of human experience: 'I did not mean to forget him, but I forgot him. From birth to death we are alone'.[14] Temporal shifts deny the text any clear sense of chronology as Bagnold moves from encounter to reverie without using any form of linguistic bridge. The only constant is the uniform anonymity of the hospital, which swallows up individuals and manufactures the public face of the war.

It is this public representation which Bagnold sets out to crack, using the structure of her text as a weapon. Her tone is calm and detached. She uses simple statements, truncated sentences to create dramatic effect, describing her vision of hospital life as 'An everlasting dislocation of combinations'.[15] She juxtaposes the desire for communion with the mechanisms of the institution, against the paradoxically liberating isolation of the individual within such structures: 'Let them pile on the rules, invent and insist; yet behind them, beneath them, I have that strong, secret liberty of an institution that runs like the wind in me and lifts my mind like a leaf'.[16] This fragmentation, as a literary form, links the dislocated diary entries of the previous chapters with more public modernist experiments. Bagnold's apparent collusion with the system gives her the security to penetrate the sisterhood of professional nurses, while her status as a VAD gives her a different perspective. From the position of an empathetic outsider she can show that the need for anonymity is paramount, among the nurses as well as the soldiers; the latter are often referred to by number rather than by name. Collectively they construct a protective screen to hold up to the world. The truth about hospital life, about the casualties of war must escape the public gaze.

Bagnold's disclosure of this façade provides the radical content of her *Diary*. Her sister breaks down under the strain and is shipped off to another posting; 'if death becomes cheap it is the watcher, not the dying, who is poisoned'.[17] Her representation of the pain and suffering of the soldiers draws them as innocents, victims of a nameless regime which does not value them, and so kicks out at the makers of war: 'one [soldier] wrote to me: "The only real waste is the waste of metal. The earth will be covered again and again with Us."'[18] Her illustration of the dehumanisation of the same men at the hands of the nurses is similarly damning:

> But we forgot to talk of it to Corrigan. The needle was into his shoulder before he knew why his shirt was held up.
>
> His wrath came like an avalanche; the discipline of two years was forgotten, his Irish tongue loosened. Sister shrugged her shoulders and laughed; I listened to him as I cleaned the syringe. I gathered that it was the indignity that had shocked his sense of individual pride.
>
> 'Treating me like a cow . . '
>
> Corrigan was angry all day; the idea that 'a bloomin' woman should come an shove something into me 'systim' was too much for him. But he forgets himself: there are no individualists now; his 'system' belongs to us.[19]

There is a notion of possession foregrounded here. This idea of the power held by the [female] nurses over the [male] soldiers is one which is developed in other women's hospital stories, particularly those of Mary Borden, and will be discussed in more detail later. Here, the emphasis on the 'indignity' introduces a shift in the balance of power. The bodies of the men belong, not to themselves, but to the women. Bagnold's ambition to be accepted into the sisterhood betrays her, implying a perverse appreciation of this power even while she uses her status as a VAD to disassociate herself from this deviation.[20]

Bagnold was encouraged to write a permanent record of her hospital work by her former lover Prince Antoine Bibesco, who was inspired by the language she used to convey the experience in the letters she wrote to him. For his benefit she transformed these into an illustrated and bound gift entitled *Reflections of a VAD*, before submitting them for publication as *A Diary without Dates*. Bibesco was not misguided. Bagnold's language in this work is particularly interesting, and experimental, both in terms of the way that she challenges literary convention and the way in which she questions accepted ideologies concerning the representation of the war. In addition to illustrating her book with an assortment of vivifying metaphors ('Indeed a sister is a curious creature. She is like a fortress, unassailable, and whose sleeping guns may fire at any minute',[21] she rejects the notions of euphemism which so often coloured testimonies of the war; 'The Sister came out and told me she thought he was 'not up to much.' I think she means he is dying'.[22] And she adapts cliché to inject her *Diary* with an ironic humour; 'It takes all sorts to make a hospital. For instance, the Visitors'.[23]

Bagnold also uses her text to examine the different meanings of language. This is especially prominent when she describes her transfer from the officer's ward to the one which houses the regular soldiers, 'the boys'. Here she questions the way in which the institution of the hospital allocates language, categorising and naming inaccurately: 'I can't think of them like the others do, as 'the boys'; they seem to me full-grown men'.[24] She points out that although popular myth labels them all as 'Tommy', they never refer to each other in this way. To overcome the problem of her own social class she highlights her inability to make the men understand her by constructing it as her own failing:

> I suffer awfully from my language in this ward. I seem to be the only V.A.D. of whom they continually ask, 'What say, nurse?' It isn't that I use long words, but my sentences seem to be inverted.[25]
>
> I should like to have parried with Pinker (only my language is so much more complicated than it ought to be).[26]

Her acknowledgement of different forms of language is quantitative rather than qualitative. She investigates the different ways in which language can be used to express experiences. Often forbidden to speak to the men, she listens to them, collecting their speech patterns to complement her own. The previously quoted example of the incident with Corrigan illustrates this effectively. Bagnold incorporates the actual language of the men into her text, with all its colloquialisms, allowing them to speak for themselves. Having no words to articulate the pain of having his dressing changed, Rees sings: 'It was like this: "Ah . . . ee . . . oo, Sister!" and again: 'Sister . . . oo . . . ee . . . ah!" Then a little scream and his song again.'[27] Others speak in riddles of humour and dialect. She learns to read the meanings behind the monosyllabic utterances of men who have no other words, and then translate them, effectively creating emotional charges beneath the apparent detachment of her narrative: 'Ah, these hurried conversations sandwiched between my duties, when in four sentences the distilled essence of bitterness is dropped into my ear!'[28] Thus she is able to capture and represent the point of view of the voiceless soldier; another reason why her book may not have been very good for morale in 1918.

Bagnold is at pains to point out that issues of sexuality have no place in a British war hospital. Her brief romantic fluttering with 'No. 11.' is immediately quashed by the sisters, whose nun-like appearance desexes them, making them 'safe' in the presence of the men whom they treat. Margaret Higonnet argues:

> The theme of the desexing of both men and women, which recurs in many nurses' texts, concerns not so much sexual potency as the destruction of one's most intimate capacity for relationships with others and of a will to continue – since continuation so often means to go on killing.[29]

Yet this process of desexing is not always universal, as I shall discuss later, and for Bagnold, the hospital can liberate gender relationships in a way unthinkable before the war, allowing them to be constructed without the complications of sex: 'It is wonderful to talk to men affectionately without exciting or implying love. The Utopian dreams of sixteen seem almost to be realised.'[30]. She transforms restrictions into new kinds of freedom, thus supporting her original claim that the hospital can be a liberating place. It gives her the scope to express new truths; to create alternative stories.

A Diary without Dates is not without a sense of crisis in keeping with Benstock's notion of a psychology of despair. An atmosphere of despondence prevails. The constant dehumanisation and infantilisation of the men who pass through the wards invites parallels with that other no man's land a few miles distant across the channel. The anonymous, veiled nurses control this landscape with a mechanisation that reinforces the men's helplessness. They, too, are dehumanised, but endorsed with a power which resembles the maternal as they nurture the men, a perverse embodiment of the power discussed by Mabel Stobart. This is a place of transition located within a journey from one front to another. Identities are lost here as they are among the rats and the barbed wire.

> They know so little about each other, and they don't ask. It is only I who wonder – I, a woman, and therefore of the old, burnt out world. These men watch without curiosity, speak no personalities, form no sets, express no likings, analyse nothing. They are new-born; they have as yet no standards and do not look for any.[31]

As if baptised by the fire of the war, men learn of the old world through the nurses. But Bagnold's assertion that this world is 'burnt out' places a question mark over her own place in the new one that the men must create from the destruction. The divide between the combatant and the non-combatant is opened.[32] Anonymous men pass through, and are forgotten, however hard Bagnold tries to retain the memory.

The physical presence of the war is also constant. The mud and dirt of Flanders has to be removed before treatment can begin. The guns that bombard the trenches are audible at night. The cries and commands from the army training camp next door are enough to send men mad: 'All day long little men training to fill just such another hospital as ours with other little men.'[33] It is like a factory production line; a symbol of impersonal modernity. But the close proximity of the war does nothing to blunt her perception and articulation of experience; her text is sharpened by an immediacy that heightens the tone of desperation giving it a radicalism shared by other contemporary modernisms.

Like Enid Bagnold, Ellen La Motte caused the military authorities some concern when, in 1916, she produced *The Backwash of War*.[34] La Motte was an American nurse, specialising in tuberculosis, who had been working in Paris since 1913. From 1915 onwards she worked in a French military field hospital about ten kilometres behind the front line near Ypres. She had previously published some medical writings, but this was her first work of a more 'creative' type. Her book is comprised of a collection of prose sketches, or fragments, which appeared in the autumn of 1916, and in the United States, ran to several editions before being suppressed in the summer of 1918. It was, again, considered bad for morale; a questioning from the inside, of the patriarchal structures which controlled the war. Interestingly, it did not appear in Britain or France until after the war, when it was no longer deemed capable of harm.[35]

It is clearly La Motte's intention to relate publicly the atrocities of the war that she witnessed daily in the hospital. Her text, like Stobart's *The Flaming Sword*, is political, suggesting hypocrisy in the men who run the war. At the same time, in order to present the experience authentically, she searches to find new modes of expression, alternative literary devices, perhaps accidentally, modernist forms to illustrate the suffering of the ordinary soldiers. To do this she pulls together fragments, independent but not unrelated, which create a collage of hospital life. Her controlling metaphor, that of the sea of war, allowing the 'human wreckage of the battlefield' to collect in its backwater, is retained throughout, and her precise, carefully chosen language creates a mood of subtle despair which penetrates her landscape.

Within the fragments she allows her soldiers to speak with dissenting voices blending the political with linguistic expression. In 'La Patrie Reconnaissante' a dying man hurls abuse at stretcher-bearers, surgeons, nurses and fellow patients. His status as a man with no hope gives him a freedom of speech unavailable to those who must go on, and he is able to articulate the bitterness of many. 'I will shout louder than the guns'[36] he cries symbolically. Because he is doomed, he can utter the unspeakable and confront many of the unspoken truths more usually cloaked by patriotism. In 'Alone' La Motte considers the plight of a fatally wounded soldier brought to the hospital, who dies before anyone has the time to grow to know him or care. His past is veiled, all that matters is his present, which is embedded in a medical language. His wound becomes his identity, filled out by detailed descriptions of his condition and the torturous but futile treatment: 'Rochard died to-day. He had gas gangrene. His thigh, from knee to buttock, was torn out by a piece of German shell. It was an interesting case, because the infection had developed so quickly.'[37] As a man, he has ceased to exist even before his death; he is no more than an 'interesting case'. The anonymity of the hospital expressed in Bagnold's *Diary* is also prevalent here. The nurses have the power to deny him identity although they cannot cure him.

In 'The Surgical Triumph' she repudiates the euphemistic, while attacking a technology which can keep alive fragments of human beings who might prefer death. The surgical triumph in question has lost all his limbs, his eyes, and has had the features of his face rebuilt in a distorted fashion by plastic surgery. It is his father's money that has funded this project, yet the boy can only beg for death. Thus a capitalism versus humanitarianism polemic is explored to the detriment of the reputation of medical science. The narrative appears to take place from the point of view of the father, who, as a 'civilised' man, is unable to comply with his son's request. Yet it is the faceless, almost voiceless son with whom we sympathise, reinforcing the tragedy: 'Antoine looked down upon his wreck of a son that lay before him, and the wreck, not appreciating that he was a surgical triumph, kept sobbing, kept weeping out of his sightless eyes, kept jerking his four stumps in supplication, kept begging in agony'.[38] The irony of La Motte's title is apparent here, for there is nothing triumphant about this scene. As with all the fragments, it is not clear whether they report real or representative incidents, however the understanding that this *could* happen is enough to register the political idea.

The irony found here is echoed in other sketches. Her purpose is to represent events from a different perspective, highlighting the inappropriate nature of established and accepted war language. Higonnet argues that La Motte's 'symbolic otherness', brought about by her status as a nurse who is both an insider and an outsider simultaneously, may have helped her in this task: 'Self-consciousness about the limits of one's own knowledge enables a writer to begin the process of breaking the frame of socially or politically constructed knowledge.'[39] However, La Motte's insider status, her own access to a range of medical or institutional 'knowledge' might be more useful to our understanding of her politics and ideas than any limited notion of 'symbolic otherness'. As an important component of the process, La Motte is better able to indicate problems of official representation, making her perhaps more deviant than an outsider with opinions.

Unlike Bagnold's narrative, in which sexuality is an absolute taboo, La Motte deals head on with the position of women in the war zone and their relations with the men. Nurses may well retain the nun-like inscrutability of the Royal Herbert Hospital, but they are not the only women in the forbidden zone of the military world. In 'Women and Wives', La Motte destroys the myth of a no woman's land, articulating concern about the hypocrisy of male regulations and the problematic status of these other women:

> There are many women at the front. How do they get there, to the Zone of the Armies? On various pretexts – to see sick relatives, in such and such hospitals, or to see other relatives, brothers, uncles, cousins, other peoples' husbands – oh there are many reasons which make it possible for them to come. And always there are the Belgian women, who live in the War Zone, for at

present there is a little strip of Belgium left, and all the civilians have not
been evacuated from the Army Zone. So there are plenty of women, first and
last. Better ones for the officers, naturally, just as the officers' mess is better
quality than that of the common soldiers. But always there are plenty of
women. Never wives, who mean responsibility, but just women, who only
mean distraction and amusement, just as food and wine.[40]

None of the other writers address the issue of women's presence at the
front in so direct a way. La Motte's stance is radical and unorthodox given
her own professional position; the nun-nurse should surely be blind to
such concerns. But again it is her position as an insider that gives her
access to this knowledge. There is a detachment in her tone that emphasises her subtext. In this environment it is 'natural' that women should be
no more than 'distraction and amusement'. There is an implied xenopho-
bia in the attitudes that she illustrates, targeted towards the Belgian
women whose primary use is to be consumed, 'just as food and wine'.
Significantly, wives, who represent the domestic rather than the alien, are
not allowed into the war zone. Only women who are nameless commod-
ities or desexed like the nurses can safely be allowed contact with the
homesick soldiers, for such women cannot upset the delicate military
balance.

La Motte ironically illustrates the 'good' husbands of the hospital,
writing daily to their wives before heading off to visit the girls they keep
in the village. She describes the Belgian women as sexually available but
certain to be abandoned when the war ends highlighting the hypocrisy of
male attitudes. They boost morale in a time of crisis just as their rejection
will boost morale when peace returns. Yet despite an apparent neutrality
in her tone, the women that La Motte describes appear as victims: She tells
us ironically, 'It is rather paradoxical but there are those who can explain
it perfectly'.[41] Her position as one of the anonymous, sexless insiders
enables her to expose the effect of male double standards on an indige-
nous female population – war casualties who attract neither attention nor
sympathy.

La Motte also describes Belgian girls from behind the German lines
'forced' into prostitution to act as spies for the German army. Again, her
irony is bitter:

They are very vile themselves, these Germans. The curious thing is, how well
they understand how to bait a trap for their enemies. In spite of having
nothing in common with them, how well they understand the nature of
those who are fighting in the name of Justice, of Liberty and of
Civilisation.[42]

This is another interpretation of the second battlefield. The enemies here are defined not by nationality but by sex. It is a feminist statement that transcends the overt politics of the war. She redefines conventional language, justice, liberty, civilisation, subverting its meaning in the process. By doing so she raises important questions not only about gender and the ideology behind the war, but also about the way in which this ideology is expressed.

In 'Women and Wives' La Motte states, 'Well there are many people to write you of the noble side, the heroic side, the exalted side of war'.[43] But her project in *The Backwash of War* is different. 'I must write you of what I have seen, the other side, the backwash. They are both true.'[44] It is her aim to reveal the underside of the war, that which is displeasing and undesirable to know, and it is this overtly political angle which prompted the suppression of the book in its time and which adds to its value in terms of modernist interpretations. Like Mabel St Clair Stobart, La Motte strikes out at a 'patriarchal militarism', but the linguistic strategies adopted to delineate this idea move it beyond the relative stylistic traditionalism of *The Flaming Sword*, placing it along side other contemporary modernisms.

La Motte, like many of her modernist contemporaries, displays an aversion to the technology of the war and its subsequent dehumanisation of the troops. In 'The Interval', she describes the repetitive regime of the hospital in such a way that the language itself echoes the mechanised routines of war, bathed in undercurrents of perpetual boredom. 'These old wrecks on the beds'[45] no longer seem human, instead they are more like pieces of mechanical debris. Claire Tylee argues:

> The reduction of human beings to inert objects in the factory system of a field hospital after a battle was expressed by La Motte in a strikingly modern prose of flat repetition . . . The emotionless repetition of the sentences is the correlative of the mechanical process they describe. The soldiers are no longer men. They are heaps, wrecks to be recycled like the scrap metal of wrecked cars.[46]

This device of repetition, echoed in Mary Borden's *The Forbidden Zone*, is particularly effective in reinforcing the monotony of the routine, often a horrific one, and the way in which this monotony operates to grind down emotional reactions: 'This is the day of an attack. Yesterday was the day of an attack. The day before was the day of an attack',[47] yet the effect may stimulate a reader response, a kind of empathy which makes the horror of the war feel more present. Thus the political idea is emphasised.

La Motte's attack on military and patriarchal forces is fairly unrelent-
ing in *The Backwash of War*. Her opening sketch, 'Heroes', first published
in *Atlantic Monthly* in 1915, tells the story of a man who has attempted
suicide by shooting himself in the head. It is the responsibility of the
medical staff to save him in order that he may be shot as an example to
other prospective cowards. The fragment shares many characteristics
with Mary Borden's story 'Rosa', also about an attempted suicide who will
not give up his right to die, and they both make powerful arguments
against the waste of resources and the paradoxical nature of military regulations. But while Borden's 'Rosa' finally succeeds in killing himself by
refusing treatment, in La Motte's version, the tale twists as the pensive
night nurse turns to examine the other men of the ward; those whom
society terms heroes because of the accidental nature of their wounds.
They are by turns selfish, vain, gluttonous and filthy, ordinary men forced
into a heroic role that they cannot fulfil. As a character in a later sketch
('Pour La Patri') suggests, 'I was mobilised against my inclination. Now I
have won the *Medaille Militaire*. My Captain won it for me. He made me
brave. He had a revolver in his hand'.[48] La Motte's 'backwash' challenges
conventional notions of heroism, ultimately questioning the idea of a
noble, heroic side to war.

La Motte's representations of war confront those found in many other
narratives, both in terms of the style she adopts and the politics she articulates. She gives the final word to the French people. In 'An Incident',
angry citizens rage at a distinguished staff officer after his horse-drawn
carriage runs down a delivery boy: 'Had he seen so much suffering *en gros*
that it meant nothing to him *en detail*? Or was this his attitude to all
suffering? Was this the Nation's attitude to the suffering of their sons?'[49]
Her book is an attempt to vindicate those without voice. The pain that she
and others witness in field hospitals seems to have nothing to do with the
accepted rhetoric of war. The truth that she is able to record presents a
different vision of the war, one that is contemporary with it. Ironically,
many of the soldiers themselves could not get this close until long after
the event, hence the interval of a decade before many of their published
stories appeared. La Motte's hospital stories foreground the underside of
war in a public way before it was politically acceptable to do so.

The hospital stories of women are interesting because they locate their
narrators in close proximity to the front line. Although gender politics are
not absent from their pages, as La Motte's 'Women and Wives' demonstrates, stylistically, these tales do not differ greatly from those told by
male medical personnel. It seems as though a major role of hospital

stories of the First World War, many of which were written between 1914 and 1918, was to provoke a response to some previously unspoken bitter truths. As such they also form a genre in which gender has little part to play. The French military doctor, Georges Duhamel, wrote in his collection of hospital fragments, *The New Book of Martyrs*, 'It was written that you should suffer without purpose and without hope. But I will not let all your suffering be lost in the abyss'.[50] The title of his book indicates his line of approach. Because these writers are witnesses to all the horror of war, but are only marginal participants in it, they are able to write of the experience with a clarity often missing from the narratives of soldiers. And there develops a deliberately chosen style which many of them share – distanced, detached, neutral and detailed – as they describe events using a controlled language infused with metaphor.

Duhamel was a poet and a playwright who was also a doctor. In *The New Book of Martyrs*, he uses a framework which matches La Motte's, numerous fragments, each telling the sad tale of one broken individual. These are the 'Memories of the Martyrs', often moving between the present and the past tense, factual, detailed and objective, yet injected with a pathos which seeks to inspire a response from the reader, underlining the sense of crisis around which the text is built. As a male doctor it seems likely that he would have been allowed to interact with the patients in a much more significant way than the female nurses; there is not the need for sexless anonymity in order to preserve moral propriety. For example, his narrator is able to develop enough of a relationship with a patient, amputee Leglise, in 'The Sacrifice', to convince him that he cannot lose the will to live. Yet many of his personal stories are remarkably similar to those of the women. The fragmented nature of the text denies any sense of continuity or cohesion, with discordant shifts in narratorial position as Duhamel tries to imagine the thought patterns of the wounded, as well as observing their struggles.

In 'The Thoughts of Prosper Ruffin', he moves to a first person narrative to reproduce the mental ramblings of a wounded man, transported from ambulance to operating theatre, gradually becoming more and more delirious. Although aware of his own wound and those of the men around him, he is unaware that it is he who cries out in agony. These thoughts are replaced by memories of his wife and his work as a gardener, which become more and more dislocated as he is overwhelmed by the chloroform, losing consciousness to the imaginary peal of Whitsun bells: 'Look, there's Felicie coming down to the washing trough. She pretends not to see me . . . I will steal behind the elder hedge. Felicie! Felicie! I have a piece of a 77 in my kidneys. I like her best in her blue bodice.'[51] Duhamel manages to convey a great deal about his subject through these ruptured thoughts, most significantly the inappropriateness of his presence as a soldier, a man given to the nurturing of life rather than its destruction. The juxtaposition of the domestic with the carnage of the war, a device also utilised in other fragments adds a further dimension to the sense of chaos.[52]

Elsewhere he addresses themes similar to those of La Motte, the sense of the alienation and dehumanisation of the wounded, the inability to penetrate their loneliness, the idea of the wound taking over the identity of the subject and the shock of graphic description. And, like La Motte, he tries to keep himself out of the narrative. It is intended as a tribute to the courage of the innocent caught up in an absurd war perpetrated by the guilty. If he cannot keep the soldiers alive, he can at least preserve the memory of their sacrifice.

Although Enid Bagnold, Ellen La Motte and Georges Duhamel are very modern in the way they chose to represent the experiences that they witnessed and shared, the most aesthetically self-aware collection of hospital stories of the First World War is *The Forbidden Zone* by Mary Borden. Borden was an American millionaire who was able to set up her own hospital unit close to the French lines, in which she worked throughout the war. The text is constructed of fragments of differing lengths, short stories and poems, based on scenes that she witnessed and experienced during the war. There is a greater diversity of style here than in the other texts, and an even stronger sense of Borden's narrators manipulating the reader responses. In her prose fragments carefully chosen images and metaphors give the language a heightened emotional clarity, despite a frequent sense of narratorial distance. *The Forbidden Zone* was not published until 1929, so although some of the sketches were reputedly written during the war, there was time for possible revision, and the five stories in the collection were certainly written in the 1920s. Borden's early connections with 'modernist' circles, particularly through Wyndham Lewis, doubtless influenced the construction of her text.[53] This places Borden more firmly in the post-war culture of despair which, Benstock argues, inspired much of what has come to be seen as modernist writing, and this legacy is apparent in these stories. The modernist nature of some of Borden's First World War writing is slowly being acknowledged,[54] but no critical survey has yet done it justice.

Borden's mixture of fragments includes sketches, short stories and poems. Although this, on one level, echoes her nineteenth-century heritage in terms of the short stories written by women of the *fin de siècle*,[55] it also reflects the work of her modernist contemporaries. T. S. Eliot's *The Waste Land* concludes, 'These fragments I have shored against my ruins',[56] similarly Borden's fragments have to remain fragments in order to be true to her experience. In her Preface she suggests:

> To those who find these impressions confused, I would say that they are fragments of a great confusion. Any attempt to reduce them to order would require artifice on my part and would falsify them. To those on the other hand who find them unbearably plain, I would say that I have blurred the bare horror of facts and softened the reality in spite of myself, not because I wished to do so but because I was incapable of a nearer approach to the truth.[57]

Like the 'impressions' which formed the diaries in previous chapters, these fragments provide the most effective way to articulate the unspeakable, but there is an aesthetic self-consciousness about *The Forbidden Zone* which moves it beyond these earlier writings. Although the sense of immediacy is sometimes diluted, there is an artistry about the text, particularly the later stories, suggesting that, this time, the experimentation may be less accidental.

It is possible, however, to read those fragments written during the war as accidental modernisms. Many use similar narrative techniques to those adopted by Ellen La Motte and George Duhamel, although often Borden's use of language is more sophisticated, and it is clear from the start that the reader must enter the landscape of war in order to share the experience. For Borden, this landscape encompasses more than the front line and the hospital. For her the wounded come in many forms as she takes her subjects from across a no man's land of her own definition. In the opening sketch, 'Belgium', the narrator invites the reader on to the streets of a decimated Belgian town, 'Come, I'll show you' she coaxes, then later, 'Come away, for God's sake – come away'.[58] The effect of this direct address is to draw the reader immediately on to the page, into the derelict country; instantly we are there and vulnerable to share the experiences that will soon be offered. She shows us how *little* we really understand in this claustrophobic place surrounded by foreign armies, decaying machinery and the eternal mud which becomes a symbol for all the desecration, 'Mud; with scraps of iron lying in it and the straggling fragment of a nation, lolling, hanging about in the mud on the edge of disaster'.[59] Our entrance into it prevents us from remaining in the safe position of passive observers; our ignorance is illustrated by our inability to recognise the Belgian king, a drab, uniform soldier just like the others: 'Didn't you see him? He came out of the school-house some time ago and drove away toward the sand-dunes – a big fair man in uniform. You didn't notice? Never mind. Come away'.[60] Actively now, we too must confront the fragments of reality which Borden intends to show us, and we need her as our guide.

As we march through these early vignettes, Borden uses an assortment of literary devices to initiate us into the world of the forbidden zone. In 'The Captive Balloon', Borden presents us with a surreal image, 'an oyster in the sky'[61] hovering over no man's land, an eccentric voyeur gazing at the carnage. In 'Paraphernalia' she lists the medical supplies that fill the hospital, disdainful of their value in the face of death, just as La Motte is sceptical of the value of medical science at times. A similar sentiment is discernible in 'In The Operating Room' which highlights the distance between the wounded soldiers and the medical teams that tend them. This fragment is structured as a play; there is no narrator, simply stage directions and characters – three Surgeons, three Patients and a Nurse. Here the reader becomes the audience, directly witnessing a scene that shows more about war than it tells. The result is a polysemic narrative that allows other voices to penetrate the text in independent forms. Each of the characters has space to exhibit their experiences outside the jurisdiction of an omniscient narrator. By each representing a small part of a wider story with implicit problems of articulation, these single voices unify in an attempt to express the unspeakable.

The Surgeons appear as workers on a production line, an appropriate metaphor in a war that is built around new mechanisation.[62] Their attitudes towards the Patients range from the patronising, through the blunt to the sympathetic; to each other they articulate sober professionalism and artistic pride, but lapse into gossip and food, like any other workers, to relieve the monotony of a repetitive job. The Patients are chosen to represent a cross section; the flesh wound in the arm, whose overt pain is the greatest, the amputee, and the fatal stomach wound whose quiet pleading for water almost seems to go unheard. Through their interchanges, and the impressions of the spectres of other 'cases' waiting at the door, Borden attempts to bring the reader into a situation which might otherwise defy description, limited by a language which is often filled with cliché and euphemism, ill equipped to present the 'truth' behind the experience of the war.

In 'Bombardment' there is another shift in the narrative perspective, as we take a bird's eye view of the bombing of a town. From far above in the

silent stillness of the early morning sky we witness the arrival of an aeroplane, hostile precursor to the attack from the ground, a symbolic messenger from the heavens to betray the people of the earth. We witness the
interchange between the 'insect' that is the aeroplane, and a sleeping
giant, the personified town. Each sound is a dramatic intrusion in the perceptible silence created by the high altitude of the subject position; 'and
presently, as if exorcised by the magic eye of that insect, a cluster of houses
collapsed, while a roar burst from the wounded earth'.[63] The people of the
town, an anonymous multitude like the victims of the war, become
vermin, a 'human hive', as they run in search of safety. But we do not relate
to them. Instead the reader sympathises with the town itself, 'the
wounded earth', which becomes an enormous emblem of suffering
humanity, impotent and helpless in the face of the impersonal mechanisation of this war:

> The face of the city had begun to show a curious change. Scars appeared on
> it like the marks of smallpox and as these thickened on its trim surface, it
> seemed as if it were being attacked by an invisible and gigantic beast, who
> was tearing and gnawing it with claws and teeth. Gashes appeared in its
> streets, long wounds with ragged edges. Helpless, spread out to the heavens,
> it grimaced with mutilated features.[64]

Borden presents us with an image of a wounded body, a recognisable allegory for the pain of war. The magnification of this image, attained by the
personification and the narrative distancing, enables her to imprint its
impact upon the world within her text. This town, left finally in convul-
sions, is employed to symbolise the shattering wider implications of the
war, the enormity of the desecration brought about by the decisions of a
minority, 'a speck in the infinite sky'.[65]

Borden uses allegory and metaphor in several of the fragments to make
her language a powerful and effective weapon for reinforcing the more
political, more radical ideas of the text. As pieces written during the war,
they offer dramatic ways of rendering experience that might be impossible for a combatant to convey. Like Bagnold and La Motte, she explores
different linguistic strategies, different ways of presenting contemporary
voices which might have gone unheard. In 'The Regiment', Borden contrasts within her prose, new ideas of the poetic against a backdrop of flat
repetitive sentences which reiterate the relentless monotony of the war.
The sketch opens with a sensual representation of the pastoral, reminiscent of the escapist ideology of Georgian poetry, 'The smiling country was
enjoying itself. The caress of the wind sent shudders of pleasure through

the corn and a fluttering delight through the trees'.[66] The war is given 'the aspect of a country fair';[67] a counterfeit holiday atmosphere in a duplicitous Arcadian idyll, shimmering with an anachronistic sensuality, suggesting the inadequacy of such language and vision in a time of crisis.

Inevitably it cannot last. The tranquillity is shattered by the regiment, represented as the 'shadow of a snake',[68] linguistically reminiscent of the precision of Imagism as Borden searches for more effective articulation. There are no words wasted here, the regiment is an alien creature invading the landscape, consolidated into a deformed uniformity: 'It was a moving mass of men covered over with the cloth of fatigue. Over them was their suffocating weariness, and under them was the dust of the road'.[69] Equally, it draws upon the past. The image itself could have been borrowed from Stephen Crane's *The Red Badge of Courage*:

> The rushing yellow of the developing day went on behind their backs. When the sunrays at last struck full and mellowingly upon the earth, the youth saw that the landscape was streaked with two long, thin, black columns which disappeared on the brow of a hill in front and rearward vanished in a wood. They were like two serpents crawling from the cavern of the night.[70]

Crane's radical individual interpretation of the experience of the American Civil War made a resounding impact upon publication and in many ways, may be read as a precursor to much modern war fiction.

Borden's intrusive marching mass cuts through the fantasy of the country setting. A collection of identical individuals, dreaming of a home they will never see, they operate as an illustration of the perpetual tedium, the greyness of the war. Phonetically the words accentuate the lethargy of their progress. Claire Tylee suggests that Borden's 'very sentence structure typifies the routine process of the war-machine'.[71] Like Ellen La Motte, she adopts a technique of deliberate and meditative repetition, rhythms which echo the endless marching:

> They were old men . . . Being old men, there was nothing they could not accept; there was nothing they could not endure. They had endured fatigue and cold and hunger and wet. They had endured so long that they had ceased to think about these things . . . They were acclimatised to misery . . . They accepted the war. It was a thing to be endured. They were enduring it . . .
>
> There was only one thing they wanted, and this thing they wanted without hope. They wanted to go home, and they knew they were not going home.[72]

Borden's use of language in this sketch evokes the sensation of the regiment's laborious journey, involving the reader physically in their hopeless situation. What she projects is an essence of the experience of war, not diluted by the patriotism and propaganda of an external media, or the synthetic bravado of the staff officers who wait in the town to be decorated in front of the regiment. The regiment 'pours its darkness' in and then out of the town bringing with it 'the war' and 'truth', in isolation from the artifice of the ceremony, acknowledging only the supremacy of the general and his doctrine of military monotony. A further repetitive incantation accompanies their leaving, bringing the tale full circle as the shadow passes from the landscape.

Borden again presents the conflict between the natural and the unnatural in 'The Beach', which explores a dialogue between a crippled soldier and his wife. The surface level of this exchange occurs in the perfect setting of a summer's day at the beach constituting a similar anachorism to that of 'The Regiment'. But their dialogue is multidimensional as they send a variety of messages both to each other and to the reader. Borden's modernist links are reaffirmed here as she adopts a form of interior monologue to highlight the speech problems of her characters who are verbally inhibited by the physical prominence of his deformity. Their silence provides a new kind of language. Since they cannot speak the unspeakable, she allows them to think it, asking the interminable question common to thousands during and after the war, and again recalling Eliot, 'What shall we do?'[73]

Claire Tylee draws attention to the satirical way that Mary Borden uses language in this piece, suggesting that she plays on colloquialisms like 'gone to pieces' and 'faceless' in the crippled soldier's speech to highlight the anonymity of the wounded.[74] Like Bagnold, she adapts a cliché in order to transform its accepted meaning. The soldier's bitterly ironic dialogue also operates to expose the propagandist metaphor of 'war as a game':

> They've a gala night in our casino whenever there's a battle . . . You never saw such a crowd. They all rush there from the front, you know – the way they do from the race-course . . . Gamblers, of course, down and outs, wrecks – all gone to pieces, parts of 'em missing, you know, tops of their heads gone, or one of their legs . . . Some of them have no faces . . .
>
> All that's needed is a ticket. It's tied to you like a luggage label. It has your name on it in case you don't remember your name. You needn't have a face, but a ticket you must have to get into our casino.[75]

In addition, this metaphor plays on the notions of dehumanisation which were to feed the psychology of despair, the literal fragmentation of the bodies of the men, adding to the overall atmosphere of chaos.

In 'Conspiracy' Borden experiments further with language, in association with the issues of gender often addressed in women's war-writing, as she explores the idea of female control in the wartime hospital touched upon by Enid Bagnold. She uses more anachoristic domestic imagery which is at once claustrophobic and sinister: 'Just as you send your clothes to the laundry and mend them when they come back, so we send our men to the trenches and mend them when they come back again.'[76] Borden's tight control of her language and form echoes the control that these women have over their men. Through her narrative she presents a belligerent power dynamic which destroys the traditional balance. The masculine is subordinated to the feminine, and the whole situation is part of a gender-based conspiracy, 'We conspire against his right to die'.[77]

The nurses run a subversive campaign against the death that will release the men from the suffering caused by those who sent them to war. In so doing, the nurses covertly support the power structures that perpetuate the war, allying themselves with those in control. Borden represents this campaign in physical rather than emotional terms. On one level her narrative style highlights once again the dehumanisation of the wounded; as Claire Tylee indicates: 'Men are as expendable and disposable as any other commodity. They are as lacking in personal identity as the items on a conveyor belt. Lying on their backs on stretchers, they are 'pulled out of the ambulances as loaves of bread are pulled out of the oven'.[78]

But on another level Borden's imagery inverts conventional sexual roles in a way that is oppressive and violent. Not only do the women control a man's body, but they violate it, reinforcing his pain in what can easily be read as metaphoric rape: 'We dig into the yawning mouths of his wounds. Helpless openings, they let us into the secret places of his body. We plunge deep into his body.'[79] At the same time the wounded man adopts a feminine aspect, passively accepting the role which the war assigns to him. By dealing with this inversion, shocking in its violence and intensity, Borden contributes to a continuing debate concerning the gendered power dynamics of the First World War.

The focus of this debate is very often the controversial figure of the nurse featured in First World War texts, as here in 'Conspiracy', where the women appear to be more powerful than the men. In 'Soldier's Heart: Literary Men, Literary Women, and the Great War', Sandra Gilbert argues that the war 'virtually completed the Industrial Revolution's construction of anonymous dehumanised man, that impotent cipher who is frequently thought to be the twentieth century's most characteristic citizen'.[80] And she identifies these traits in many of the modernist 'anti-heroes', suggesting that they are products of a world in which women had become more powerful as the war enabled them to take control of their own lives and the lives of others. The figure of the nurse may be used to symbolise such control. Gilbert goes on to argue:

> in works of both male and female novelists the figure of the nurse ultimately takes on a majesty which hints that she is mistress rather than slave, goddess rather than supplicant. After all when men are immobilised and dehumanised, it is only these women who possess the old (matriarchal) formulas for survival.[81]

She suggests that such role reversals also brought about a release of female libidinal energies and anger which added to the gender anxieties that take form in many of the texts by male modernists.

But there are others who argue against her. In *Behind the Lines: Gender and the Two World Wars*, Margaret and Patrice Higonnet offer a 'double helix' theory, suggesting that although women did become more powerful, as Gilbert asserts, the actual balance of power in society was not altered:

> When the home front is mobilised, women may be allowed to move 'forward' in terms of employment or social policy, yet the battlefront – predominantly a male domain – takes economic and cultural priority. Therefore, while women's objective situation does change, relationships of domination and subordination are retained through the discourses that systematically designate unequal gender relations.[82]

An alternative, but related, view has been put forward by Sharon Ouditt: 'While their *experience* contradicted gendered stereotypes, it was contained within an immediate framework that made strategic use of conservative definitions of femininity, and within a cultural system that showed few signs of revolutionising its patriarchal principles'.[83] Similarly, in 'The Asylums of Antaeus: Women, War, and Madness – Is there a Female Fetishism?', Jane Marcus takes issue with Gilbert's ideas, suggesting that 'World War I in fact wiped out women's culture'.[84] Marcus argues, 'The suffrage movement was the training ground for disciplined V.A.D. nurses and ambulance drivers who served in WWI the state which had molested and imprisoned them',[85] implying that women became *more* subservient when they adopted their wartime roles. Certainly La Motte's 'Women and Wives' presents a very negative picture of women's lack of control of their own destinies, sexual or otherwise. Marcus also accuses Gilbert of reaching her conclusions on the basis of only male writers instead of addressing the issues through the medium of the female text.

Compelling though these arguments may be, there are other ways of approaching this debate through the workings of contemporary texts. For women close to the front line, issues surrounding their own empowerment tend to be subordinated to more urgent moral and political concerns, rooted in the primary experience of the war itself. Mary Borden's fragments can appear to offer conflicting evidence concerning the nature of women's power, particularly in relation to issues of female sexuality. It is possible, if desired, to find evidence in *The Forbidden Zone* to support all these cited arguments. More significantly, however, her work, and that of the other women considered here, illustrates the formulation of a different kind of power, the power to write and to create *through* the war, even if their status within it is illusory. The very existence of the debate in these contemporary books illustrates the empowered status of women as writers, able to find a language to articulate their own experience and that of others, thus hoping to make a lasting statement about the horrors of war which may be widely heard and understood.

For example, in 'The Regiment' the arrival of a nurse at the medal ceremony is described thus, 'She was a beautiful animal dressed as a nun and branded with a red cross'.[86] Borden's sentence is filled with multiple, conflicting implications, a modernist practice of defamiliarisation. The woman in wartime is non-human, an animal, removed from traditional stereotypes in a similar way to the anonymous 'no-men', created by the arbitrary nature of the war. But for a woman this can be liberating instead of destructive, giving her a new kind of power. At the same time her clothes designate traditional womanly purity, the nun dedicated to service and compassion, suggesting submissiveness despite her presence in male territory; yet she is tainted by a red brand which seems to bring her illicit sexuality to the forefront. And her sudden freedom from many of the patriarchal restrictions of the nineteenth century is also accentuated; the town perceptively concludes, ' It must have escaped from its owner who, no doubt, prizes it highly'.[87] She is a new woman hiding behind the trappings of the old, released from captivity by the war, filled with ambiguities and open to multiple readings.[88] What is surely most radical and empowering is that Borden can find the language to say all this in one sentence, allowing the actual status of the woman to remain uncertain.

Returning to 'Conspiracy', *The Forbidden Zone,* deals explicitly with ideas of female power born out of women's involvement with the war. If the women who worked as nurses had been imprisoned before the war, whether literally or metaphorically, they are transformed into gaolers in this fragment, refuting Marcus's arguments. It appears to reinforce, to some extent, Gilbert's ideas concerning the ascendancy of female power as a result of the war. But this too is problematic. The narrator of 'Conspiracy' illustrates a cyclical process, send – return – mend – send, which ought to justify its own end: 'Do you hear? Do you understand? It is all arranged just as it should be.'[89] There is satire buried within this narrative which advocates not only a notion of pacifism, but also a condemnation of any mode of female power gained through the blood of men. The linguistic form of Borden's text instructs the reader to understand and to accept; but her subtext covertly articulates the contrary message, that this cycle is wrong. Even while it acknowledges the existence of female power, and indeed female sexual power as a result of wartime role reversals, the validity of that power is questioned. The way in which it is delineated within the text presents the view that the power to oppress others cannot be justified in feminist, political or military terms, and forms part of Borden's overall anti-war argument. Indeed the whole hierarchical process of power is questioned, through the notion that these women have obtained their position by colluding with the military structures responsible for the cyclical destruction of the soldiers; representatives of the very same power structure that imprisoned women in the feminine ideology of the home. While these ironies form a multi-layered feminist argument, the strongest idea in the fragment does not even concern gender, but humanity, for in this presentation of the carnage there can be no winners. Borden, like her fellow women writers, ultimately utilises formulas of female empowerment, which keep contemporary theorists arguing, as a means to articulate other concerns, specifically, the inhumanity of war. The power to add their voices to the records is all that really counts.

While fighting over the fragmented bodies of the men on this 'second battlefield', these women are in danger of being exposed to another traditional enemy, their own sexuality; that taboo subject often addressed by modernist women writers. Margaret Higonnet suggests that 'A distinctive feature of many women's texts . . . is their asexual linguistic treatment of men's bodies'.[90] Admittedly, fragments of whole bodies may be devoid of sexuality, but there are notable exceptions which belie Higonnet's generalisation. Mary Borden confronts ideas of male physical sexuality, through the eyes of woman in 'Enfant de Malheur'. It is a later story that deals with a number of complex issues and focuses on the witnessing of a spiritual battle, a dying soul in torment brought to peace by the vehemence of prayer. However, the narrator's attention is initially drawn to the Enfant de Malheur, the soul in question, in response to his physical beauty. Using codes more commonly adopted for the construction of female character, his identity is created through his body and illustrated by the tattoos that cover it. His criminality and his depravity, neutralised by his dependent state, seem to operate as further metaphors for the danger of his sexuality, a force to which the nun-like nurses should not be exposed. When he goes to the operating table the nurses are turned out of the room by the surgeons, in part because of his obscene language as he succumbs to the anaesthetic, but by implication, this is also because of the inert vulnerability of his perfect body laid out before voyeuristic eyes. This objectification represents a reversal of conventional gender delineation. Borden's narrator, herself a voyeur, spends considerable time describing the Enfant de Malheur's body in order that the reader too will appreciate the perfection of his limbs:

> He had race, distinction, an exquisite elegance, and, even in his battered state, the savage grace of a panther. Not even his wounds could disfigure him. The long gash in his side made his smooth torso seem incredibly fair and frail. The loss of one leg rendered the other more exquisite with its round polished knee and slim ankle.[91]

The Catholic nurse, Pim, is immune, recognising only another fragment in need of care. Through her the status quo is re-established and the Enfant de Malheur's journey towards absolution may begin, but not before the reader has gained some insight into the physical and sensual reality which is unavoidable in the confined hospital space.

It is this focus on the individual in Borden's later stories which, ironically, accentuates the dehumanising effect of the war. More emotive than the spiritual struggle of the Enfant de Malheur is the loneliness of the man who has lost his sight in 'Blind', a story which Claire Tylee believes to be 'one of the most significant pieces of literature to have come out of that War'[92] Borden's idea is similar to La Motte's in 'Alone', but her narrative method is much more sophisticated. Borden penetrates the consciousness of her nurse/narrator in order to explore the contrasting experiences of the war. Her duty, in a hut packed full of stretchers, is to sort the dead from the dying and she is told to expect 'thirty per cent mortality'.[93] The blind man is just one of many, not a priority, 'There was plenty of time. He would always be blind'.[94] Consequently, he is quickly forgotten despite his subtle beauty.

On one level, Borden's narrator presents the reader with stark, detached and detailed images of the gruesome nature of work in a front-line hospital, highlighted by the integral nonchalance of the staff; the bandage which takes away half of a man's brain when it is removed; the knee, boiled up for an experiment that is almost mistaken for food; these and other sights seem to inspire no unusual emotion in the people forced to deal with them. The narrator states: 'I think that woman, myself, must have been in a trance, or under some horrid spell.'[95] Nicola Beauman argues that the purpose of these details is to prove that wartime women were as heroic as the men they nursed,[96] but her analysis is too simplistic in light of the sophisticated construction of Borden's prose. Sharon Ouditt provides a more persuasive interpretation when she comments on the 'juxtaposition of a flat narrative tone with its hideous subject matter' arguing that 'The events break the frame of what is humanly endurable or capable of being articulated in the language of the well-educated woman'.[97] It is another example of Borden's modernist practice, be it accidental, or perhaps, by 1929, more intentional.

Borden also uses 'Blind' to present experience on a more psychological level using the metaphor of the ebb and flow of the sea, a technique that she also adopts in 'The City in the Desert'. A variation on Ellen La Motte's central metaphor, the artistic effect is to accentuate the enormity of the hospital's task:

> It was my business to create a counter-wave of life, to create the flow against the ebb. It was like a tug of war with the tide . . . The dying men on the floor were drowned men cast up on the beach, and there was the ebb of life pouring away over them, sucking them away, an invisible tide; and my old orderlies, like old sea-salts out of a lifeboat, were working to save them.[98]

This highlights Borden's relentless message, the tragedy of the anonymity of the wounded, helpless against the ubiquitous tide of the war.

Another interesting theme in this story is the exposition of the temporary feeling of invigoration born out of working in the busy hospital, and experiencing the illusion of being in control: 'The hospital was going full steam ahead. I had a sense of great power, exhilaration and excitement.'[99] This emotional response resembles that of Enid Bagnold in *A Diary without Dates*. The two narrators share the buzz of hospital life, but gradually learn that this must be over-shadowed by the experience of the wounded. The hospital is not about them; it is about the patients.

In Borden's story it is the blind man who represents the evidence of this truth and others. Time is out of joint. For him an eternity has past in his dark world while the minutes have flown by for the busy nurse/narrator. Time is distorted by the war in a way that feeds the experiments of modernism[100] echoed in Eliot's cry, 'HURRY UP PLEASE ITS TIME'.[101] In 'Blind', time takes on a different meaning for each protagonist. This is reinforced by a narrative shift to the present tense as the blind man calls out to the nurse in his fear of loneliness. She responds; 'I am startled . . . I cannot tell where the voice comes from. Then I hear it again . . . I had forgotten him'.[102] His isolation locates hers, breaking her trance and opening her eyes to the suffering of the individual in a world where individuals have ceased to count: 'The light poured down on the rows of faces. They gleamed faintly. Four hundred faces were staring at the roof, side by side. The blind man didn't know. He thought he was alone, out in the dark. That was the precipice, that reality.'[103] She finds just enough self-control to lie to him, assuring him that he is not alone, before breaking down herself. Perhaps this represents the paradox at the heart of all these texts. As Bagnold suggests, 'From birth to death we are alone'. It is the dehumanising effect of the war which centralises this truth, forcing the women and men who fight in it to come to terms with their own isolation. It is here that a modernist psychology of despair begins, in the no man's land of the blind.

The writing of these women, Mary Borden, Enid Bagnold and Ellen La Motte, serves to reinforce the notion that primary literary responses to the experience of the First World War produced a variety of different modernisms which run parallel to those of the more established experimental writers. It is interesting to consider that Borden's 1931 novel, *Sarah Gay*,[104] may be used as further evidence of this link between the war and the development of modernisms, specifically in the ways that it *fails* to be innovatory. It relates the story of a married woman who discovers true love while working as a nurse in France, and with it, enough liberating force to reject her old life in favour of a new one, even though this means flying in the face of sexual conventions. However, as soon as the war is over and Borden begins to deal with Sarah's attempt to keep her freedom amid the reactionary backlash of the post-war world, the novel returns to more traditional literary codes and the form of romantic cliché.

Sarah Gay retains some of the sense of uncertainty and loss of security that permeates *The Forbidden Zone* and the other texts considered here, but it never achieves the vivid authenticity that is implied by their respective experiments with language and form. Borden, Bagnold and La Motte adopt many modernist practices usually associated with the more famous writers of the 1920s, those modernists who have received most of the credit for literary innovation. The fragments and impressions that make up these hospital stories represent an intensive search for a way in which to convey experience which appears to be unspeakable. Consequently, it is possible that many of the experiments held within the pages may be accidental. When conventional means of expression are no longer adequate, alternatives must be found if a valuable record is to be kept. But the aesthetic self-consciousness found in *The Forbidden Zone* in particular, implies a literary awareness that deserves some credit. The war perhaps prompted all these women to become writers, because of their active participation on the second battlefield. As new writers, they developed new techniques to articulate publicly what they had witnessed in England and France. The identification of such techniques reinforces the links between the First World War and the development of female forms of experimental writing, emerging female modernisms.

Notes

1 Mary Borden (1929), 'Blind', in her *The Forbidden Zone*, London, Heinemann, p. 147.

2 Sharon Ouditt (1994), *Fighting Forces, Writing Women*, London, Routledge, p. 36. Ouditt argues: 'The complexity and ambiguity of these women's experiences was largely owing to the violent clash between the conservative ideologies that enabled them to get out to the war and the failure of those ideologies to mediate or account for the trauma that later beset them. The fissures in the dominant discourse in some cases created new ways of seeing: in others it did nothing but confirm an increasing sense of alienation' (*ibid.*).

3 Ouditt touches on a number of interesting arguments, without following any of them through as they are peripheral to her own thesis, going on to suggest: 'Many of the novels, autobiographies and sketches published during the war set themselves the task of managing and guiding public response to the traumatic events . . . The texts published in the late 1920s and 1930s, in the boom of war writing and often in response to male war stories, present more ambiguous images of war nurses. Indeed they were often written with the express purpose of revealing the horrific nature of nursing men wounded by a new mechanised and chemical armoury . . . These texts, having begun with an enthusiastic response to the call of their country, typically become dominated by images of alienation, dislocation and even madness – motifs of literary modernism' (*ibid.*, pp. 36–8, my omissions).

4 Jane Marcus (1989), 'Corpus/Corps/Corpse: Writing the Body in/at War', in H. M. Cooper, A. A. Munich and S. M. Squier (eds), *Arms and the Woman: War, Gender and Literary Representation*, London, University of North Carolina Press, p. 129.

5 See Peter Nicholls (1995), *Modernisms: A Literary Guide*, London, Macmillan.

6 Shari Benstock (1987), *Women of the Left Bank*, London, Virago, p. 26.

7 *Ibid.*, p. 28.

8 Claire M. Tylee (1990), *The Great War and Women's Consciousness*, London, Macmillan, p. 98.

9 Enid, Bagnold (1978), *A Diary without Dates*, London, Virago (first published 1918).

10 Cynthia Asquith (1968), *Diaries 1915–18*, London, Hutchinson, p. 425.

11 Virginia Woolf, quoted in Anne Sebba (1986), *Enid Bagnold: The Authorised Biography*, London, Weidenfield & Nicholson, p. 61.

12 Anne Sebba (1994), *Battling For News*, London, Hodder & Stoughton, p. 62.

13 In *Battling For News*, Sebba suggests (p. 62): 'As H. G. Wells wrote, "while the official war histories sleep the eternal sleep in the vaults of the great libraries, probably you have all read one or two such books as Enid Bagnold's Diary Without Dates"'. However, she does not provide any further information as to where the quotation originated.

14 Bagnold, *Diary*, pp. 45–6.

15 *Ibid.*, p. 5.

16 *Ibid.*, p. 17.

17 *Ibid.*, p. 78.

18 *Ibid.*, p. 24.

19 *Ibid.*, p. 86–7.

20 Conflict and antagonism between experienced professional nurses and the new VADs is well documented. Bagnold herself deals with it in *A Diary without Dates*. Also see Vera Brittain (1992), *Testament of Youth*, London, Virago (first published 1933); Irene Rathbone (1988), *We that Were Young*, London, Virago (first published 1932).

21 Bagnold, *Diary*, p. 75.

22 *Ibid.*, p. 7.

23 *Ibid.*, p. 13.

24 *Ibid.*, p. 86.

25 *Ibid.*

26 *Ibid.*, p. 96.

27 *Ibid.*, p. 90.

28 *Ibid.*, p. 125.

29 Margaret Higgonet (1993), 'Not So Quiet in No Woman's Land', in M. Cooke and A. Woollacott, (eds), *Gendering War Talk*, Princeton, NJ, Princeton University Press, p. 215.

30 Bagnold, *Diary*, p. 112.

31 Bagnold, *Diary*, p. 56.

32 This combatant/non-combatant divide is discussed in greater detail in Chapters 4 and 5.

33 Bagnold, *Diary*, p. 127.
34 Ellen N. La Motte (1916), *Backwash of War*, London, G. P. Puttnam's Sons.
35 See Tylee, *The Great War*, p. 94, citing La Motte's own introduction to the 1934 edition of *The Backwash of War*.
36 La Motte, *Backwash of War*, p. 27.
37 *Ibid.*, p. 49.
38 *Ibid.*, p. 155.
39 Higgonet, 'Not So Quiet in No Woman's Land', p. 211.
40 La Motte, *Backwash of War*, pp. 102–3.
41 *Ibid.*, p. 104.
42 *Ibid.*, pp. 110–11.
43 *Ibid.*, p. 105.
44 *Ibid.*
45 *Ibid.*, p. 85.
46 Tylee, *The Great War*, pp. 97–8.
47 La Motte, *Backwash of War*, p. 85.
48 *Ibid.*, p. 125.
49 *Ibid.*, p. 186.
50 Georges Duhamel (1918), *The New Book of Martyrs*, London, William Heinemann, p. 32.
51 *Ibid.*, p. 81.
52 A particularly effective example of the juxtaposition of the domestic with the war experience can be found in Dorothy Canfield (1918), 'The Permissionaire', in her *Home Fires In France*, New York, Henry Holt, pp. 27–59. It is too long to quote here in full.
53 See Jeffrey Meyers (1980), *The Enemy: A Biography of Wyndham Lewis*, London, Routledge & Kegan Paul.
54 See Dorothy Goldman with Jane Gledhill and Judith Hattaway (1995), *Women Writers and the Great War*, New York, Twayne.
55 The short story was a very popular genre for women writing around the turn of the century, and later women writers associated with female modernism. See Elaine Showalter (ed.) (1993), *Daughters of Decadence*, London, Virago; Bronte Adams and Trudi Tate (eds) (1991), *That Kind of Woman*, London, Virago; Lynn Knight (ed.) (1993), *Infinite Riches*, London, Virago.
56 T. S. Eliot (1990), 'The Waste Land', in his *Selected Poems*, London, Faber & Faber (first published 1922).
57 Borden, *The Forbidden Zone*, Preface.
58 *Ibid.*, pp. 2 and 3.
59 *Ibid.*, p. 1.
60 *Ibid.*, p. 4.
61 *Ibid.*, p. 12.
62 See Daniel Pick (1993), *War Machine: The Rationalisation of Slaughter in the Modern Age*, New Haven, CT, and London, Yale University Press.

63 Borden, *The Forbidden Zone*, p. 7.
64 *Ibid.*, p. 9.
65 *Ibid.*, p. 10.
66 *Ibid.*, p. 21.
67 *Ibid.*, p. 22.
68 *Ibid.*, p. 23.
69 *Ibid.*, p. 24.
70 Stephen Crane (1994), *The Red Badge of Courage*, London, Penguin (first published 1895), p. 23.
71 Tylee, *The Great War*, p. 101.
72 Borden, *The Forbidden Zone*, p. 27.
73 *Ibid.*, p. 44; T. S. Eliot, 'The Waste Land'.
74 Tylee, *The Great War*, p. 100.
75 Borden, *The Forbidden Zone*, pp. 46–7.
76 *Ibid.*, p. 117.
77 *Ibid.*, p. 119.
78 Tylee, *The Great War*, p. 101.
79 Borden, *The Forbidden Zone*, p. 120.
80 Sandra M. Gilbert (1983),'Soldier's Heart: Literary Men, Literary Women, and the Great War', *Signs*, 8 (3), Spring, p. 423. The subject of the human cost of the mechanisation of the First World War is considered in more detail in Pick, *War Machine.*
81 Gilbert, 'Soldier's Heart', p. 435.
82 Margaret Higonnet *et al.* (eds) (1987), *Behind the Lines: Gender and the Two World Wars*, New Haven, CT, and London, Yale University Press, p. 6.
83 Ouditt, *Fighting Forces*, p. 84.
84 Jane Marcus (1989), 'The Asylums of Antaeus: Women, War, and Madness – Is there a Feminist Fetishism?', in H. Veeser (ed.), *The New Historicism*, London, Routledge, p. 136.
85 *Ibid.*, p. 146.
86 Borden, *The Forbidden Zone*, p. 34.
87 *Ibid.*, p. 35.
88 See Ouditt, *Fighting Forces*, pp. 19–20, for another reading of this quotation.
89 Borden, *The Forbidden Zone*, p. 122
90 Higgonet, 'Not So Quiet in No Woman's Land', p. 215, my omission.
91 Borden, *The Forbidden Zone*, p. 67.
92 Tylee, *The Great War*, p. 98.
93 Borden, *The Forbidden Zone*, p. 147.
94 *Ibid.*, p. 141.
95 *Ibid.*, p. 151.
96 Nicola Beauman (1983), *A Very Great Profession*, London, Virago, p. 34.
97 Ouditt, *Fighting Forces*, p. 39.
98 Borden, *The Forbidden Zone*, pp. 143–4.

99 *Ibid.*, p. 146
100 See Randall Stevenson (1992), 'Time', in his *Modernist Fiction: An Introduction*, London, Harvester Wheatsheaf, ch. 3.
101 T. S. Eliot, 'The Waste Land', quoted in *ibid.*
102 Borden, *The Forbidden Zone*, pp. 156–7, my omissions.
103 *Ibid.*, p. 158.
104 Mary Borden (1931), *Sarah Gay*, London, William Heinemann.

Part II
Fiction

4

'Living words':
the woman's story

The active part played by women in the Great War requires its woman poet or novelist or dramatist, who will transform the dry sentences of Government reports into living words before the memories of 1914–18 pass into oblivion with the war generation.[1]

How many women's stories of the First World War are still familiar to us at the end of the twentieth century? Writing in 1929 for the *Manchester Guardian*, Vera Brittain was clearly anxious that most would not survive. She feared that historical perceptions of the war would subordinate women's experience, no matter how diverse; that it would be buried by the enormous popular appeal of the numerous and often successful men's war narratives which flooded the commercial market in the late 1920s. Books like Siegfried Sassoon's *Memoirs of a Fox-Hunting Man* (1928), Robert Graves's *Goodbye to All That* (1929), Erich Maria Remarque's *All Quiet on the Western Front* (1929) and Richard Aldington's *Death of a Hero* (1929)[2] all presented the public with a war which was essentially male centred. Furthermore, the experiences which their narratives recount, most commonly focused around the lives of trench soldiers, although presenting a powerful image, do not illustrate the way that the war was lived and fought by the majority of men and women away from the front line.

Yet such was the popularity of these books, that theirs is the impression of the First World War which remains with us as the century comes to a close. The success of novels such as Pat Barker's *Regeneration* trilogy[3] and Sebastian Faulks's *Birdsong* (1993)[4] further reinforce this notion. Although these authors do consider other aspects of war experience in their books, it is the power and horror of the trench sequences which has the greatest impact. And despite the fact that in the last decade scholarly attention has focused more fully on women's experience, the majority of media coverage of the eightieth anniversary of the armistice in 1998 was built around the memories of male veterans and the retelling of familiar stories.

Vera Brittain sought remedy for her anxiety in the publication of her autobiography, *Testament of Youth*, which appeared in 1933, and became an immediate best seller.[5] It argued against what Brittain perceived to be the negative presentation of women in many of the popular men's stories and cast an alternative version of the experience of war for the mass market. Despite being a woman's story, it deals sympathetically with the men's war and laments the combatant/non-combatant divide set up by such varying experience. At the same time, however, Brittain's book, by its very difference, may retrospectively serve to illustrate the extent to which trench-culture has come to dominate the creation of the popular mythology of the war.

But Brittain's concern was, to some extent, misplaced. Women had in fact been producing the 'living words' she called for throughout the war and its aftermath, and continued to do so for many decades, some with great success.[6] As I have argued in the previous chapters, women recorded their own experience both publicly and privately without any need for encouragement, creating a literary and historical dramatisation of the multiple roles of women in wartime. Indeed, many women were able to produce novels and autobiographies built around the subject and experience of the war long before the image-making combatant men of the front line, since trench life was hardly conducive to producing lengthy prose works. However, few of these women's stories, despite their contemporary popularity, still remain in print or feature in the public perception of the First World War as the twenty-first century begins.

Like Brittain, many women told their own stories of the war. These stories deserve re-examination and provide the focus for the second part of this book. Some women responded to male experience in their writing, refracting it to present female versions, stories which can be read across critical boundaries to emphasise the similarities as well as the differences between the men's and the women's war. In this chapter I shall attempt to uncover patterns in the way in which women's stories retell more commonly accepted male war stories, producing interesting results, both in terms of content and ideas, and in terms of structure and style. I shall look first at, Erich Maria Remarque's *All Quiet on the Western Front* and *Not So Quiet . . . Stepdaughters of War* by Evadne Price (aka Helen Zenna Smith), and then at the autobiographical novel *Bid Me to Live* by the poet Hilda

Doolittle, which retells the story of her wartime marriage to Richard Aldington and her simultaneous relationship with D. H. Lawrence, both of which helped to shape the development of her writing.[7] By doing so, I wish to illustrate the way in which women could, by responding to the war writing of men, or by offering alternative versions, help to present a much more fully rounded vision of the experience of the First World War. The woman's story which creates the 'living words' for which Vera Brittain appealed.

Not So Quiet . . .: women answer back

In January 1929 Erich Maria Remarque's novel *All Quiet on the Western Front* heralded the beginning of a new phase in the production of literature of the First World War. Its publication was accompanied by the largest advertising campaign in the history of German publishing and 200,000 copies were sold in the first three weeks.[8] Within the year it had been translated into twenty different languages and had achieved similar success in many other countries, Britain among them. In *Rites of Spring* Modris Eksteins suggests that it was this commercial success, more than anything else, which resulted in the literary 'war boom' of the late 1920s and early 1930s.[9] The commercial motive for producing war literature is particularly interesting here, since it prompted the commissioning of a female response.

Inspired by the success of *All Quiet*, the publisher, Albert Marriot, hit upon the idea of producing a spoof 'female' version, retelling the story from a woman's point of view. He approached popular writer Evadne Price about the project, suggesting the title *All Quaint on the Western Front* (to be penned by Erica Remarque). However when Price read Remarque's novel, the inappropriate nature of Marriot's idea became clear to her. She still accepted the commission, resolving instead to write a response to Remarque's text which was both worthy of the original and representative of the 'truth' about the wartime experience of women working in the front line. She obtained her facts from the diary of Winifred Constance Young (now unfortunately lost), who had served as an ambulance driver in France during the war, but who had apparently had trouble convincing her patriotic family of the real hardships she had faced while on active service.[10]

The result was *Not So Quiet . . . Stepdaughters of War*, a pseudo autobiography written by the fictional Helen Zenna Smith, which spawned several sequels. It operates on a number of levels, both as a female retelling of

Remarque's *All Quiet* and as a powerful women's war text in its own right. Jane Marcus has written a comprehensive essay, 'Corpus/Corps/ Corpse: Writing the Body in/at War', which deals with both texts, first produced as an afterword for the 1988 Feminist Press reprint of *Not So Quiet* . . . .[11] Although I am to some extent indebted to her analysis, her emphasis is placed on the way in which the two authors use war as a means to 'write the body', whereas I intend to compare the two texts with a view to examining the wider issues of how women reply to men's war writing and how this enables their own writing to develop.

Price uses her story as an opportunity to dispel myths about the gendered experience of war that banishes women to the safety of the home country. As I have already suggested, this was a war that touched everybody. Price takes this argument a stage further by implying that the experience of some women could parallel that of the men, even though they did not carry arms, particularly in terms of the physical hardship and degradation of modern warfare. But there are differences too. A close comparison will show how Price replicates both the content and the anti-war politics of Remarque's novel, but by presenting it as female experience, she subtly alters the implications. In addition, she borrows the unusual narrative style of *All Quiet*, infusing it with a different female experience enabling her to create a woman's story compatible with the modernisms identified in earlier chapters.

There are a number of obvious connections between the two novels. Helen Smith's platoon of ambulance drivers parallel the soldiers of Paul Baumer's regiment, some personalities forming more obvious doubles than others. The Commandant, Mrs Bitch, is clearly a female manifestation of Remarque's sadistic Himmelstoss. The larger than life aristocratic Georgina Toshington or Tosh, Smith's dominant and infinitely resourceful comrade, is in many ways a female reconstruction of Baumer's veteran friend Katczinsky (Kat). Other motifs and actions are shared; the ritual of eating, concern over physical comfort, camaraderie and issues of social class provide some examples.

In her examination of how these authors 'write the body' Marcus identifies other dominant physical links from sexuality to defecation, but she does not consider the significant implications of the way in which Price and Remarque treat them very differently. There are also a number of parallel scenes in the two texts, not least the opening one, which in both cases describes the characters in a period of rest. It is perhaps inevitable that these scenes cannot correlate exactly, the different roles of soldiers and ambulance drivers dictate the limitations.

Earlier novels such as May Sinclair's *The Romantic* (1920)[12] had argued
that the heroism of women ambulance drivers could be equated to that of
the soldiers. But Price's representation of these women's lives as gruelling
rather than heroic, illustrates an alternative way of breaking down
difference in gendered experience. Women's service is not as heroic, but
as *unheroic* as men's. Both are victims of a militarist culture. Price destroys
the patriotic myth created by Sinclair and her peers. Her women are no
more heroic than Remarque's schoolboy soldiers, nor do they comply
with the feminine codes which disguise First World War nurses as nuns
and angels. As a result Winifred Young is vindicated and a new 'story' told
to the world.

But how 'true' is Price's story? As always, the concept of 'truth' brings
problems. Jane Marcus appears to read *Not So Quiet* . . . as a completely
authentic representation of experience:

> One assumes that the War Office counted on class codes of honour to keep
> the women from telling or writing what they had seen or heard. *Not So Quiet*
> . . . brilliantly broke the sound barrier about what 'Our splendid Women'
> had really seen and heard and done in the war, offending all of those who
> had blocked their ears.[13]

Similarly, Barbara Hardy appears to trust Price's re-creation of the ambulance drivers experience, '*Not So Quiet* . . . is a great title for a fiction which
shouts home-truths and facts to recruiting committees and politicians'.[14]
But surely these interpretations must be problematic when so much of the
book is borrowed, albeit in adapted form, from *All Quiet on the Western
Front*, a novel which has provoked a great deal of debate concerning the
authenticity of its representation of war.

Although Erich Maria Remarque was conscripted into the army in
1916 and did see front-line action, there is some evidence to suggest that
his own experience of the war was actually much more limited than that
of his central protagonist, despite promotional suggestions to the contrary. Eksteins argues that after an only moderately successful literary
career in the 1920s, Remarque hit on the war as an explanation for both
his own dissatisfaction and that of his entire generation. Consequently
Eksteins concludes, 'Remarque was . . . more interested in explaining away
the emotional imbalance of a generation than in a comprehensive or even
accurate account of the experience and feelings of men in the trenches',[15]
suggesting that many of the metaphors Remarque uses are borrowed
from other war novels that he had previously reviewed.

For example, Eksteins argues, 'Remarque's critics said that at the very

least he misrepresented the physical reality of the war: a man with his legs
or his head blown off could not run, they protested vehemently, referring
to two of the images Remarque had used'.[16] There may be an element of
professional jealousy which could explain why critics felt the need to
expose problems of 'fact' in this fiction, but even so, since it is arguably
the violent brutality of these physical images which creates much of the
political/pacifist impact of the text and, indeed, its longevity, such questions of textual authenticity must alter the way in which *All Quiet* may be
read.

The same is true of *Not So Quiet*.... Indeed, Price even borrows the
same image that caused such criticism of Remarque:

> That man strapped down? ... Oh, merely gone mad ... He may have seen
> a headless body running on and on, with blood spurting from the trunk ...
> There are many things the sitters tell me on our long night rides that could
> have done this.[17]

The sitters – the walking wounded who can sit in the front of the ambulance, every one a potential Paul Baumer – provide evidence which some
critics state, *cannot* be true. Then it becomes easy to extend this questioning to other areas of the novel. Can we continue to assume that the harsh
conditions and punishment duties endured by Helen Smith and company
must be true? If then we identify mostly fiction in this fiction, categorising it with the commerciality of the 'war boom', does that operate to
undermine its status as a war story which transforms 'the dry sentences
of Government reports into living words'. Such an approach is probably
too simplistic. But if we consider *All Quiet* and *Not So Quiet* ... with a
healthy scepticism about the balance of fact to fiction they still provide a
wealth of evidence concerning the different ways men and women tackle
representations of gender in war-writing.

Perhaps Remarque's great success may lie in the idea that he has created
'everyman'. Some later critics think so. Eksteins argues, 'In the tormented
and degraded German front soldier depicted in *All Quiet* – and he could
just as easily have been a Tommy, *poilu*, or doughboy – the public saw its
own shadow and sensed its own anonymity and yearning for security'.[18]
But this is a rather simplistic interpretation. The trench soldier may now
be perceived as the most common male symbol of First World War experience, an image perpetuated by the famous poetry and prose of the
battlefield, including *All Quiet*. But it is problematic because men took
on so many different roles both within the various military services
and as non-combatants, and contemporaries would have understood

this. However, the notion that identification with the boy soldiers may explain a generation of disillusionment, may still have been an appealing one.

Both Marcus and Hardy make the point, by dissecting the name Helen Zenna Smith, that Price has correspondingly created a symbolic 'everywoman'; "'Helen" ironically demythologises, participating in war, not providing its cause; "Zenna" is idiosyncratic; "Smith" is Everywoman'.[19] But Price's 'everywoman' is also awkward because the multiple roles taken by women, and indeed by Helen Smith, during the war make it similarly impossible to create a single category of womanhood.

Remarque's novel implies the virtual obliteration of social class boundaries, one that is not necessarily shared by other male novelists.[20] Perhaps this is a Utopian inaccuracy which reinforces the awkward notion of 'everyman' to which Remarque's reader's might relate. Price's text, on the other hand, actually operates to reinforce ideas of a rigid social class system. Helen Smith can only be an ambulance driver at the front *because* she is from a suitable class. These women must be self-supporting; they pay for the privilege of 'doing their bit' in a form comparable with the men, that is, a way in which they get to experience relative suffering at first hand:

> It astounds me why the powers-that-be at the London headquarters stipulate that refined women of decent education are essential for this ambulance work. Why should they want this class to do the work of strong navvies on the cars, in addition to the work of scullery-maids under conditions no professional scullery-maid would tolerate for a day? Possibly this is because this is the only class that suffers in silence, that scorns to carry tales. We are such cowards. We dare not face being called 'cowards' and 'slackers,' which we certainly shall be if we complain.[21]

Caught up and held within the web of a propagandist ideology, Helen Smith and her comrades suffer precisely because they are *not* 'everywoman', imprisoned by neither military law, like Paul Baumer, nor social need, like working-class women, but by a patriotic fervour which sentences them to hold a unique position in the matrix of war.

In fact Evadne Price transcends this limitation to some extent by allowing Helen Smith to re-create herself within the text and represent an alternative figure of wartime womanhood. Having finally abandoned the ambulance convoy and finished with the war after the deaths of her friends Tosh and the Bug, she is forced to bow to family pressure to return to active service in order to obtain money to pay for her sister's abortion.

But as a final blow for her snobbish family, 'The last claw of the cat before it is put in the sack and drowned!',[22] she signs up as a 'domestic worker' in the Women's Army Auxiliary Corps (WAAC), joining the working-class women who use the war as a means of making a living. Smith, together with her family and friends who between them occupy a diverse range of different jobs, enables Price to create an unromantic vision of an assortment of female roles, allowing different kinds of readers to identify with her women, without adopting the particular definition of one uniform. Not 'everywoman' but many different women with many different stories.

In her later role, Helen Smith becomes an assistant cook in the WAAC, spending her days chopping carrots and onions. But by this time the horrors of her war experience have taken their toll and she is too numb to give much thought to food, the fuel that keeps her going, 'I am a slot machine that never goes out of order. Put so much rations into the slot and I will work so long, play so long, and sleep so long'.[23] Paul Baumer, although a cog in the military machine, never appears to reach this mechanical state, and he and his comrades never lose touch with the sensual pleasures of food. *All Quiet* is punctuated with eating sessions: the opening scene when the ranks are so depleted that each man gets double rations; Paul and Kat cooking the illicit goose; the roast suckling pigs, consumed with a spirit of decadence during a violent bombardment; these feastings assume a status of exaggerated pleasure when juxtaposed against the bland monotony of army food. But it is more than this. There is something ceremonial about this ritualised eating, resulting in a kind of collective communion, a bonding motif which has been used symbolically in war literature since *The Iliad*.[24]

Price retains this symbolic eating in *Not So Quiet . . .*, specifically in the ambulance convoy section of the novel, when the experience of the women is used to form a parallel with the soldiers. But in this text the process of eating becomes distorted and is not so overtly positive. The provisions that keep the women alive as they reject the diet of army rations, are biscuits, chocolate and mugs of hot Bovril, all sent in food parcels from home. Trivialised luxury items, not food to fight on. And shared meals in the women's camp lead not to communion but discord. Price uses the setting of a company breakfast, hard bread and warm tea, to allow her characters to articulate a spirited pacifist argument at the expense of exposing the BF, one of the drivers, as a patriotic fool. Price uses another driver, Edwards, as a distinctly feminist spokeswoman to attack the political structures that created the war:

Enemies? Our enemies aren't the Germans. Our enemies are the politicians we pay to keep us out of the war and who are too damned inefficient to do their jobs properly. After two thousand years of civilisation, this folly happens. It is time women took a hand. The men are failures . . . this war shows that. Women will be the ones to stop war, you'll see. If they can't do anything else, they can refuse to bring children into the world to be maimed and murdered when they grow big enough. Once women buckled on their men's swords. Once they believed in that 'death-or-glory-boys' jingo. But this time they're in it themselves. They're seeing for themselves.[25]

The argument here echoes those of Mabel St Clair Stobart and other feminist campaigners of the war years, linking Price with the radicalism of those earlier texts. It is also significant that one of the powerful political arguments in the novel is given centre stage over a group meal, an occasion which ought perhaps to inspire harmony and provide a respite from the pressures of their harrowing work. The breakfast table is a place for debate and division with the jingoistic BF accused, 'you're the most dangerous type of fool there is. Someone ought to collect women like you in a big hall and drop a bomb . . . wipe you out . . . before you can do any more damage'.[26] The harsh conditions of the convoy supply these well brought up, well-educated young ladies with a breeding ground for dissent, and collective experiences like meals provide the spark which ignites their anger.

Even the illicit farewell party that the women hold for the BF before she returns to England, a scene which parallels the comradely eating tableaux in *All Quiet*, results in a division that ultimately leads to the destruction of their small community. Although all the women contribute to the feast, the food provides a weapon to reinforce personal differences as Tosh uses the event to illustrate her hostility towards Skinny, a lesbian member of the group: 'Tosh deliberately withdraws from the party by turning her back and opening a magazine. The insult is deliberate, as deliberate as earlier when she refused to sample Skinny's potted meat.'[27] Whereas the ordinary soldiers in *All Quiet* find no place for clashes of personality within the ranks, the collection of women cannot embrace such harmony. Personal difference will out. It is difficult to say whether Price is intending to suggest that communities of women cannot exist peacefully in an environment where traditional codes of femininity must be abandoned, or whether the women of *Not So Quiet . . .* operate as a more accurate representation of humanity caged together in intolerable conditions, no longer able to ignore the destructive jingoism responsible for putting them there. Events like ritualised eating, that have symbolic significance in the literature of war, are much more problematic in the woman's text. Price's response raises questions not just about gender, but about the mythologising of war and the conventions of war writing itself.

As Marcus suggests, it is possible to read these two novels as texts which 'write the body' in war and eating is part of that process. The physicality of the texts extends beyond this, and again I would suggest that what is represented as positive in Remarque's novel is generally much more problematic in Price's. The latrine passage in *All Quiet* which describes more spiritual communion, this time over defecation, led to Remarque being described as 'the high priest of the "lavatory school" of war novelists'.[28] Again the communion is absent in *Not So Quiet . . .*; this is not something 'ladies' can share. Instead they just clean up after other people's bodies, most particularly in the cleaning of the ambulances. 'Our ambulance women take entire control of their cars, doing all running repairs and all cleaning.'[29] Helen scoffs at the official representation of 'Our Splendid Women'. Her version is different, presenting bodily functions in the least spiritual way possible:

> The stench that comes out as we open the doors each morning nearly knocks us down. Pools of stale vomit from the poor wretches we have carried the night before, corners the sitters have turned into temporary lavatories for all purposes, blood and mud and vermin and the stale stench of stinking trench feet and gangrenous wounds.[30]

Price's blunt prose offers horrors to shock the reader similar to those found in the hospital stories. Again she fights against an earlier convention that refuses to acknowledge women's awareness of such indiscreet bodily functions. The only advantage of getting punishment duty to clean the WC is the opportunity it affords to spend some time in complete isolation, once more denying the validity of military camaraderie. The emphasis on the negative side of human physicality operates in striking conflict with the archetypes of Edwardian femininity which are employed by the creators of the image, 'Our Splendid Women'. Mary Cadogan and Patricia Craig, who discuss the Helen Zenna Smith novels in their book *Women and Children First*, suggest 'Social realism, the impulse to tell the truth about war service and its aftermath, has given way to emotional melodrama and a crude bid for the reader's attention'.[31] But Price's extremism, if indeed that is what it is, may be justified if we take the view that she could be trying to rewrite women's history by destroying the propagandist myths which maintained that women on the battle front could be protected from the realities of the body in war; realities which would never be condoned by the dominant ideology of their upper- and middle-class Edwardian upbringing. They were exposed to much of the horror, just as the men were. Thus Price shows how the physical activity of the war enforced the destruction of conventional gender roles despite the attempts to maintain them in the public eye.

This attempt to break down gender differentiation is further emphasised by Price's treatment of female sexuality. Instead of representing it as 'different' from the male sexuality in *All Quiet*, she actually gives Helen Smith the same physical needs as Paul Baumer; that is the need for some kind of personal solace which cannot be satisfied in any other way. Paul Baumer finds temporary comfort in the arms of a French peasant:

> But then I feel the lips of the little brunette and press myself against them, my eyes close, I want it all to fall from me, war terror and grossness, in order to awaken young and happy . . . And if I press ever deeper into the arms that embrace me, perhaps a miracle may happen.[32]

In a similar way Helen finds compensation by spending the night with a young officer, Robin, the first man she meets when she returns to England, 'shell-shocked' after the ordeal of the ambulance convoy:

> But it was not only because he was whole and strong-limbed, not only because his body was young and beautiful, not only because his laughing blue eyes reflected my image without the shadow of war rising to blot me out . . . but because I saw him between me and the dance orchestra ending a shadow procession of cruelly maimed men.[33]

For Price, this sexual response to the war is as appropriate for the woman as for the man. By treating women in exactly the same way as men with regard to sex, Price questions the double-standard which has been operational for centuries and in so doing, issues a challenge to accepted codes of morality

Price deals directly with the hypocrisy of the sexual double standard, at one point in the novel giving Tosh a heated monologue:

> Immorality, what a chance! Doesn't it make you sick? Slack as much as you can, drive your bus as cruelly as you like, crash your gears to hell, muck your engine till it's in the mechanic's hands half its time, jolt the guts out of your wounded, shirk as much as you can without actively coming up against the powers-that-be – and you won't be sent home. But one hint of immorality and back you go to England in disgrace as fast as the packet can take you.[34]

Tosh's argument is logical, but ironically it is actually the issue of lesbianism in the ranks which has brought it about; that is the discovery of Skinny's lesbianism, effectively revealed by Tosh herself. Jane Marcus suggests that 'Helen Zenna Smith is writing to clear the volunteers of the charge of lesbianism',[35] specifically in response to the implications of *The Well of Loneliness*[36] which presented the ambulance corps as a place where lesbians could find the freedom to be themselves. The unattractive presentation of Skinny and her 'friend' Frost provides evidence to support this theory, but Tosh's outburst does go some way to temper the charge. The expulsion of these two, although uncomfortable, has a double-edged effect. On one level it is condoned, brought about by Tosh, whose heroic status justifies her actions. But her effective change of heart, illustrated in her defensive oration, allows questions to be raised, if not satisfactorily answered, about this and other forms of sex-based persecution.

When read together, *All Quiet on the Western Front* and *Not So Quiet . . .* begin to break down gender distinctions established in the war writing of both men and women. Marcus argues, 'Both experience war through the body of the other. Paul is feminised by war; Helen is masculinized'.[37] There is some evidence to support this as the static, passive representation of the domestic life of the men in the trenches contrasts with the robust and mobile outdoor existence of the female ambulance drivers.

But I would suggest that it is too simplistic just to read these novels and conclude that the result is a straightforward borrowing of gender roles. That is certainly one reading, but Price does more. She forces her protagonist to live through experiences which are as close to those of men as it is possible for a woman to get, and she responds to each as a woman, rejecting, distorting or clinging to the image of femininity that has shaped her, according to each situation. Certainly by driving an ambulance she is active and mobile in a way that is denied to many of the men, but she is still passive, scared and lacking in control just like the trench soldiers. At the same time she is reluctant to cut her hair for fear of losing her feminine identity until physical discomfort forces her to give way. Price's novel adopts a situation similar to that of *All Quiet* and from within that sphere of wartime experience it questions the conventional role of women. It deconstructs both feminine and masculine codes to identify a universal suffering; a female retelling of the story of a complete generation, not just a generation of men.

One of the most obvious ways in which *Not So Quiet . . .* is a direct response to *All Quiet on the Western Front*, is the way in which Price chooses to emulate Remarque's narrative style. The monologue of Paul

Baumer is perhaps a product with many sources from adventure fiction to newspapers, but also seems to be influenced by contemporary modernist experiments with form. This pastiche creates a new way of writing the war. Eksteins describes it thus:

> The simplicity and power of the theme – war as a demeaning and wholly destructive, indeed nihilistic, force – are made starkly effective by a style that is basic, even brutal. Brief scenes and short crisp sentences, in the first person and in the present tense, create an inescapable and gripping immediacy. There is no delicacy. The language is frequently rough, the images often gruesome.[38]

In order to illustrate the accuracy of this description, it is helpful to examine Remarque's use of language in more detail. The following passage provides a good example of how Baumer's narrative is structured:

> The graveyard is a mass of wreckage. Coffins and corpses lie strewn about. They have been killed once again; but each of them that was flung up saved one of us . . . The man on the ground is a recruit. His hip is covered with blood; he is so exhausted that I feel for my water-bottle where I have rum and tea. Kat restrains my hand and stoops over him . . . If he has been hit in the stomach he oughtn't to drink anything. There's no vomiting, that's a good sign. We lay the hip bare. It is one mass of mincemeat and bone splinters. The joint has been hit. This lad won't walk any more.[39]

In Remarque's nightmare vision the corpses blend with the living dead of the battlefield to present an image of the apocalyptic futility of this war. The abrupt sense of present suffering is multiplied by the youth and innocence of the wounded man. The anatomical precision of Remarque's description repudiates the tradition of euphemism that was often a feature of earlier writing of the battle front.[40] Practicality replaces sentiment, the sympathy of a 'womanly' response is entirely absent, suggesting again that a straight exchange of gender roles is too simplistic a theory. Despite their enforced passive role, these men are not personally feminised by the experience, one which, ultimately, women do not ever share.

In *English Fiction and Drama of the Great War 1918–39*, John Onions comments on the way in which he believes that Price's *Not So Quiet . . .* parodies Remarque's stylistic tactics:

> Open the novel at random and parody threatens to emerge. In fact the novel is a complementary feminist reply to Remarque's story; the style and construction are both pastiche; the narrator like Remarque's, is morally destroyed by war; the final paragraph describes the death of her soul in a tone which echoes clearly the concluding lines of *All Quiet*.[41]

Price deliberately commandeers Remarque's illusory, dispassionate language, but if this is parody, it is without satire, and her female rewriting creates a different variation of literary language. She reduces the feminine motifs of the women's popular fiction upon which she had built her career, blending them with masculine ones to present a female experience of a male world. This gives a new slant to war writing and offers an alternative strand of modernism to sit beside other experimental forms. Her success in presenting female experience through the 'male' language of Remarque enables her to reject the notion that men have a monopoly in the world of warfare:

> The guns are going it with a vengeance. No sleep for the men in the trenches to-night. Poor wretches, are they as cold and unhappy and homesick as I am? I can hardly believe it possible. A distant glow on the sky-line shows clearly through the window, yellow and warm, like London from the outskirts . . . The Front. Now and again there is a distant explosion, the flash quite visible, the explosion quite audible and distinguishable above the guns. A mine or a bomb attack. More killed . . . more wounded . . . more convoys. More hell . . . more bloody, bloody hell.[42]

Smith creates her own primacy, wondering if the men's experience can be as bad as hers. The techniques of a present tense narrative, ellipses, stilted sentences and vivid images of human suffering are also reminiscent of the 'accidental modernisms' of the previous chapter. There is further discord in the juxtaposition of the image of London with the explosions from the front, presenting an uncomfortable feeling of dislocation. The repetition at the end of the passage echoes the literary techniques of Borden and La Motte to create the sensation of the relentlessness of her situation. But Price's location of Smith within a more belligerent environment than the nurses, allows her to bring women's experience into line in a new and exciting way. The breakdown of gender barriers and the exploration of taboos that were a legacy of the female modernist experiments of the intervening post-war years seem to give Price an added freedom as she constructs her text. The result, the combination of older popular forms, a new interpretation of gender experience and an experimental narrative technique, makes a valuable contribution to the development of female modernist practice.

Both *All Quiet* and *Not So Quiet* . . . are influenced by the stylistic innovations of modernism, but are rooted in the literature of popular culture. By appealing to a commercial market, and by dealing explicitly with the war, these novels have been firmly categorised as war literature, outside the recognised modernist movement. But as Eksteins argues:

All Quiet captured for the popular mind some of the same instincts that were being expressed in 'high art.' Proust and Joyce, too, telescoped history into the individual. There is no collective reality, only individual response, only dreams and myths, which have lost their nexus with social convention.[43]

Remarque's novel can be seen as an important contribution of the fragmented voice of the individual, sitting comfortably along side other developing modernisms. It is beginning to be accepted that there is a distinct overlap between modernisms and war fiction, and *All Quiet* is a text which deserves to be re-addressed despite its status as a popular novel.

The same arguments may be applied to *Not So Quiet . . . .* Jane Marcus asserts, 'Evadne Price here shapes a new form of cinematic, dialogic, and dramatic interior monologue for modernism, a very tightly controlled but daring form different from James Joyce, Dorothy Richardson, or Virginia Woolf'.[44] Indeed Price's narrative is, in many ways, much more sophisticated than Remarque's. Although she adopts similar patterns for structuring her language in much of the novel, Price intersperses these with reminders of the feminine, rendered obsolete by Helen Smith's situation. Driving an ambulance full of raving men to hospital, she tries to drown their screams with memories of her coming-out dance, the juxtaposition of images reinforcing the obsolescence of the latter:

> Crawl, crawl, crawl.
> *Did I hear a scream from inside?* I must fix my mind on something . . . What? I know – my coming-out dance. My first grown-up dance frock, a shining frock of sequins and white georgette, high-waisted down to my toes . . . *Did I hear a scream? . . .* Made over a petticoat . . . *don't let them start screaming* . . . a petticoat of satin.[45]

Helen's stream of consciousness emphasises her growing state of panic. The repetition of the crawl sets the pace of the passage. The intrusion of reality into her attempts at self-distraction suggests something of the hysteric, as she tries to piece together the fragments of memory that might save her. The overt femininity of the remembered images renders them inadequate for the task she has set them; an outmoded language which no longer has a valid meaning in the environment of the war. Through scenes like this one, Helen herself is able to offer more than one voice to the text.

At the same time the structure of the narrative allows for the presence of other voices to accompany Helen's. The incorporation of newspapers, articles, imagined dramatic scenarios between the commandant and others, allows many voices to speak from the pages of *Not So Quiet . . .* in a modernist polyphony which accords with Bakhtin's idea of 'heteroglossia'.

Letters play an important part here as in many war stories. Thus Price enables us to hear the war from a number of different angles, both condoned (Helen, her sister Trix, her fiancé Roy Evans-Mawnington) and condemned (Helen's mother and Aunt, Mrs Evans-Mawnington), as she constructs the anti-war ideas which lie at the heart of the text.

And beyond this chorus of other voices there is a subtext of silence. Marcus suggests, 'In the first person narrative dramatic monologue or soliloquy, the ellipses indicate self-interruption and the repression of even more rage than is on the page . . . The punctuation asks the reader to read between the lines, to guess at the unsaid and the unsayable'.[46] Marcus identifies that Price is trying to find an answer to that eternal question; how can the writer articulate the unspeakable. As Remarque has Paul Baumer conclude, 'it is too dangerous for me to put these things into words. I am afraid they might then become gigantic and I be no longer able to master them'.[47] But from within the literary pastiche that makes *Not So Quiet*. . . the more sophisticated text, the multiple voices, coded absences and censored messages provide the reader with clues which suggest how to read the silent subtext which contains the essence of the war.

Evadne Price's 'living words' take many forms and are borrowed from many sources; Erich Maria Remarque and Winifred Young, the languages of patriotism, propaganda and pacifism. The collage that they create speaks for both women and men of her generation: 'And I see us a race apart, we war products . . . feared by the old ones and resented by the young ones . . . a race of men bodily maimed and of women mentally maimed. What is to become of us when the killing is over?'[48] 'What is to become of us when the killing is over?' is sentiment much repeated in war novels.

'The war will never be over.' This persuasive repetition binds together HD's autobiographical novel *Bid Me to Live*. 'The war will never be over'. For HD the war does not end, but instead becomes a kind of foundation upon which she can build her own exploration of the development of her writing. When she desires the men in her life, Richard Aldington and D. H. Lawrence to 'bid her to live', she effectively means bid her to write. But as her novel illustrates, it is only when she can break free and retell their collective story in her own way, that she can produce the 'living words' which will effectively write her war.

Living with words: the war according to HD

HD differs from the other writers I have considered so far in that she has already been critically acclaimed as a modernist writer both for her contribution to Imagist poetry and for her later poetical and prose works. The specificity of Imagism, as defined first by F. S. Flint, then by Ezra Pound, with its ideology of precise representation, like many other modernist avant-garde art forms, flourished during the First World War, and for some writers this may have been an effective way of articulating the wartime experience. But, as Jane Gledhill suggests in her essay 'Impersonality and Amnesia: A Response to World War 1 in the Writings of H.D. and Rebecca West': 'Publicly Imagism had won acclaim as the poetic of the War years, but privately lives were wounded and relationships shattered, and objectivity was far from easy.'[49] When her husband and fellow Imagist poet, Richard Aldington, found it very difficult to write his poetry in the trenches, he consoled himself with the knowledge that HD was continuing their work at home. In fact she was not. HD destroyed many of her wartime poems and turned instead to prose as a means of interpreting the experience that was smashing her life. It was the beginning of her creation of a series of highly complex and experimental, autobiographical prose works which were to span her life.

The Aldington marriage did not survive the war. After the trauma of a stillborn child in 1915, HD was advised to avoid pregnancy (i.e., sexual relations) until the end of the war. Perhaps the combination of her withdrawal and his experience at the front sent Aldington into an affair with another woman, Dorothy Yorke (known as Arabella). HD sought solace in an intensely spiritual/creative, yet physically abortive relationship with D. H. Lawrence, before moving to Cornwall with musicologist Cecil Gray. Her subsequent pregnancy effectively ended her marriage even though Gray deserted her and Aldington took legal and public responsibility for the child. Susan Stanford Friedman suggests, 'These events, most of which were entangled with the war, were so personally traumatic for HD that she wrote and rewrote about them in her prose in an attempt to effect a "writing cure" in the self-analysis of autobiographical fiction'.[50]

First begun in 1918, finished by 1927, *Bid Me to Live* was revised in the 1930s and again significantly after the Second World War when HD reestablished a correspondence with Aldington which lasted until her death (they had divorced in 1937). *Bid Me to Live* was finally published in 1960, over forty years after its commencement. It retells a story already loosely recorded by Richard Aldington in his 1929 novel *Death of a Hero*, which also marked his first attempt at creative prose. For Aldington and HD these events were inextricably linked with their war experience, but both writers consciously chose to reject or distort the structures of their Imagist, past for the literary construction of these memories.

In her version of the story HD moves beyond the restrictions of her Imagist roots and the bitter irony of Aldington's realist prose, even while these forms influence her work. During the war, and Aldington's absence, she shared her writing with D. H. Lawrence, and read his manuscripts. *Bid Me to Live* also tells the story of this relationship, and the subsequent effect that Lawrence had on her work. Peter Firchow identifies that Lawrence's novel *Aaron's Rod* represents another early version of their story,[51] which suggests that it was an important time for all the writers, perhaps because the experiences brought by the war were overwhelming and could not be ignored. Ultimately HD subsumes the literary styles of those who surrounded her to create her own unique modernism. The palimpsest that is *Bid Me to Live* shows how the experience of the war influenced her development as a writer.

Before considering *Bid Me To live* in more detail, it will be useful to make a brief survey of Aldington's *Death of a Hero*, which presents a fictional set of events that bear a remarkable similarity to the traumas of the Aldington marriage. The novel appeared in the wake of *All Quiet on the Western Front*; perhaps part of the mass of war literature that Modris Eksteins suggests jumped on the bandwagon of Remarque's success. But Aldington professes to have first begun his novel immediately after the armistice, at a time when he already knew that his wife had started to experiment with prose as a way of articulating experience. It was too soon; he abandoned it, returning to the project ten years later, 'almost day for day' – that is, *before* the publication of *All Quiet* and its subsequent success. Aldington seems to have been aware that his first attempt at novel writing is flawed; the narrative tone is rather unbalanced, but he emphasises his right to defy convention:

> To me the excuse for the novel is that one can do any damn thing one pleases . . . I am all for disregarding artistic rules of thumb. I dislike standardised arts as much as standardised life. Whether I am guilty of Expressionism or Super-realism or not, I don't know and don't care. I knew what I wanted to say, and said it.[52]

Just as he once flouted the laws of poetry, so he now attempted to build a prose to carry his ideas. The result is a passionately anti-war tract that is, at times, disturbingly misogynist in character.

Death of a Hero tells the story of a painter, George Winterbourne, tracing his history from before his birth to his 'suicide' on the Western Front in November 1918. Winterbourne is never a 'hero' in the conventional sense, particularly in terms of his decision to die. Consequently, the tale carries the same kind of irony as Ellen La Motte's earlier fragment, 'Heroes'. It is divided into three parts with a Prologue in which the unidentified narrator, a 'friend' who met Winterbourne at officer's training camp, summarises the story he is about to tell, beginning satirically by describing the way in which Winterbourne's obnoxious and thoroughly unbelievable family react to the news of his death. The use of this narrator allows Aldington to distance himself from painful events and memories, rather than confronting them head on as HD chooses to do. In parts I and II, the narrator retells the story of George's life up until he goes to France in much greater detail. There is plenty of room for moralising digression, which enables the narrator to spell out his anger at those who allowed the war to happen, and those who perpetuated it as he was fighting. He blames all non-combatant members of society for this, and Winterbourne's wife and mistress, Elizabeth and Fanny, are not excluded.

The final section of the novel, for which Aldington has received most critical acclaim, deals with Winterbourne's time in France and is most obviously autobiographical. It constitutes a vivid and impressive piece of war-writing, and it is most significant that here, the character of the narrator recedes until the narrative becomes in tune with Winterbourne's own consciousness. The bitterness and irony almost entirely disappear, replaced by a pathos that distinctly alters the overall tone of the novel. However, the imbalance remains, and is further heightened by the biographical evidence of Aldington's letters that present his marriage to HD much more sympathetically and in a way that is echoed in *Bid Me to Live*.[53]

Death of a Hero is primarily an anti-war novel, with the additional impulse to emphasise the gap between the soldier and the civilian, almost as a kind of denial of war experience for those who did not fight. For those who did, 'the war will never be over', and this is constantly reaffirmed as Aldington's narrator uses language which is punctuated with war imagery regardless of subject: 'They were walking up Church Street, Kensington, that dismal communication trench which links the support line of Kensington High Street with the front line of Notting Hill Gate.'[54] As Paul Fussell has noted, language itself has been distorted by the war; it pervades consciousness and can never be exhumed.[55]

Cadogan and Craig suggest, 'Richard Aldington's sympathy for the deluded and the exploited soldier has given him a rather jaundiced attitude to those who escaped the horrors of battle'.[56] The result is an attack on the society that allowed the war to happen. He shows no mercy to any of the non-combatant members of that society. His representation of women is particularly hostile, and may have been instrumental in inspiring Vera Brittain to write her autobiography, vehemently articulating an opposing view.

It is here that Aldington's novel is most problematic. The emotional triangle presented by Winterbourne, Elizabeth and Fanny is strikingly similar to the real-life *ménage à trois* of Aldington, HD and Dorothy Yorke. Although Aldington himself claimed that the novel was not autobiographical, the similarities seem too close to be coincidental, especially in the light of the last section, which appears to relate his own front-line experience quite convincingly. He represents the women as heartless and inconsiderate and, significantly, untouched by the war; not a realist representation, but that of a narrator who has 'a vendetta of the dead against the living'.[57] Aldington's love letters to HD written from the trenches suggest that this was not a reproduction of his real view, however this public version of events, even in a fictional form, may have been difficult for those involved to understand.[58]

HD's novel *Bid Me to Live*, with its constant repetition, 'The war will never be over', within the text or in parenthesis, belies Aldington's suggestion that those who remain at home are untouched by the war. Although HD was not involved in any form of war work, retaining civilian status, the war deeply affected her life, her relationships and her writing. It was the war that created her situation, it was responsible for all infidelities, physical and spiritual, and the repercussions would never end. HD's later life indicates the truth of this statement. Emblematised by a series of what Hanscombe and Smyers describe as unorthodox triangle relationships,[59] supported by analysis with Freud, HD's life can be characterised as a pathway for the evolution of a distinct literary style. In her critical Introduction to *Bid Me to Live*, Helen McNeil suggests, '*Bid Me To Live* locates itself in a triangle formed by art, sex, and war'[60] Like the novels considered in the previous section, it rejects patriotic meta-narratives in favour of individual, in this case highly personal, and deeply emotional experience, to create a female modernist novel of startling intensity.

HD's text appears to be a *roman-à-clef*. Her daughter, Perdita Schaffner, suggests, 'The names have been changed. Otherwise, it is straight autobiography, a word-for-word transcript'.[61] But the narrative methods that HD adopts are complex and interesting, making the words live for themselves to create a piece of avant-garde war fiction, as well as being the tools for the relation of a 'straight' autobiography. The opening chapters of the novel are built around an intimate scene, early in the morning as Rafe Ashton, the Aldington character, prepares to return to France leaving Julia

(HD), from whose point of view the story is told, alone in bed. She is emotionally torn by her awareness of the dangers of losing him, both physically and spiritually to another woman, Bella, and literally, permanently as a casualty of war. Time is obsolete, imprisoned by the experience; moments last for hours as Julia's stream of consciousness darts around the issue at hand, blending domestic detail with a myriad of memories. The narrative slides from third person to first, from the conscious to the unconscious and back again, painting a vivid mental picture of Julia's attempts to deal with her emotions:

> She was walking normally, naturally, she was walking out of the mood (paradise) toward the table; she was coming-to from drowning; she was walking out of aether.
> 'Oh, the-time-' she looked at the thing he was looking at; his service wristwatch was spread flat with its leather strap on the table. Its disc was covered with round woven wire, like a tiny basket, bottom side up, or a fencer's mask.
> Time in prison, that time. It ticked merrily away, inside its steel cage.
> 'I can actually hear it ticking.' She had to say something. For she couldn't do this again, she couldn't do this again, she couldn't do this again.[62]

HD's prose is built around the precise images that recall her poetry, but the objectivity is lost in the flood as time and emotion swirl around each vision adding to the atmosphere of confusion. There are contradictions; time is imprisoned in a basket or a cage, yet it is also protected by a mask to repel outward attack. Time, in Julia's consciousness shifts between the past and the present searching for a meaning in the intolerable situation. The atmosphere is dream-like as Julia's body seems to operate independently, 'normally, naturally', while her mind struggles to be free of this powerful, destructively anaesthetising force. Time and reality are out of joint, dislocated in a typically modernist style. The text is constructed around a framework of repetitions; 'I myself', 'the war would never be over', 'she couldn't do this again', which seem to break up Julia's experience into fragments, denying any sense of continuity or cohesion, reinforcing the notion of an uncertain future. Again letters are important as Julia gradually loses the ability to write to her distant husband, unable to find words which still have any meaning for them, as their relationship crumbles in the face of a universal destruction which cannot be articulated. The fragmentation as the scenes and tableaux alter without warning emulates the chaos of her mind and their situation. Thus HD uses the structure of the narrative to establish an environment of despair.

HD's poetic sensibility builds within this, using repeated motifs, specifically an obsessive and continual flower imagery, to create a further aesthetic symbolism. These images, which fill her writing, offer a specifically feminine form of Imagism that colours the tense, heavy atmosphere of the text:

> Roses?
>
> There were roses on the table now, petals fell on teacups. People had been in, then. She could chat about people, Morgan – the boy in the Italian cape – that was it. That brought back visibly (on a thread) beads that were tiny cities, or tiny cities were in her hand like the symbolic cities in the folds of a Pope's robe, painted on a triptych. 'We're painted on a triptych.'[63]

The image of the flowers in decline leads Julia's thoughts on a journey to discover something to say; what to say to a man going back to the front when so much is unspeakable. As is often the case, her thoughts take the form of a succession of tiny images building towards the picture she will ultimately verbalise. HD's modernism blends poetry, myth and aesthetic symbolism in order to find new ways of capturing the sensations evoked by her civilian experience of the war; how it feels to be the one who is left behind.

On another level, it is possible to read HD's flower imagery as a way of filling gaps, to avoid self-censorship, rather like an artistic form of the subtext of silence found in *Not So Quiet* . . . . Similarly, *Death of a Hero* is punctuated with asterisks. Aldington appears to use them to pass over anything that is difficult to express: matters of violence or emotional pain or sometimes sex. Some of HD's flower imagery may be interpreted as a way of solving this problem of articulation. The substitution of a flower holds a certain poignancy even where it may initially appear to signify nothing: 'She did not look at the daffodils. They didn't mean anything. She looked at the daffodils. She said, "Thank you for the daffodils".'[64] There is nothing and there is not nothing between them. HD's retelling of the disintegration of her marriage is much closer to Aldington's letters than to his fictional attempt at exorcism, and her method of telling, more stylistically experimental. Perhaps this gives her the scope to try to express her feelings, which might otherwise be unspeakable, 'that which presents an intellectual and emotional complex in an instant of time'.[65] A type of Imagism operating in prose to achieve the same creative ends.

In one of the most interesting passages in *Bid Me to Live*, HD constructs a collage of images to create an atmosphere of chaos which seems to epitomise her war experience. It is a sequence in which Julia accompanies Vane (Cecil Gray) to the cinema, following an air raid and an unsuccessful dinner. HD presents Julia's experience of the evening as a pastiche, surrounding her unsatisfactory relationship with Vane by fragments of technology (the film), nostalgia (its subject matter, the Italy she visited with Rafe), mythology (her allegorical readings of the film which draw on ancient Greek legend) and the colloquial singing of 'all the soldiers in the world, symbolically . . . packed into this theatre'.[66] The atmosphere builds towards the pitch of hysteria as Julia tries to reconcile the past and the future with an unthinkable present:

> The car swept on. She was dragged forward with the car and the voices rose up in rhythm to the inevitable. The car would swerve, would turn, it swerved, it turned, they swerved, they turned with it, it was dashing to destruction along the edge of a narrow cliff, they were dashing with it. But no, *goodbye Leicester Square*, the car swept on. She edged forward further, her eyes were adjusting, focussing to this scene of danger without. It was danger without. Inside she was clear, the old Greek *katharsis* was at work here, as in the stone-ledged theatre benches of fifth-century Greece; so here, a thousand doomed, the dead were watching destruction, Oedipus or Orestes in a slim car, dashing to destruction.
> *Goodbye Piccadilly.* No, it swerved, it bent, they swerved, they bent with it. The multitude, herself, Vanio, all of them swerved and turned. She was part of this. She swerved and veered with a thousand men in khaki, toward destruction, to the *sweetest girl I know.*[67]

HD uses a series of repetitions to link the cinematic experiences together. Each time she believes in their imminent destruction, fragments of patriotic song struggle through to combat the tide of her despair. Although she perceives the danger to be external, it parallels her interior struggles, the swerving and turning of her emotions as she tries to cope with the complex relationships, distorted by the war, which fill her life. Just as Aldington's narrator expresses sympathy for the fighting men, Julia is attracted to Vane because he has nothing overtly to do with the war; he is a way to try and forget. But her outings with him in London, and this one in particular, remind her that it is impossible to forget; 'the war will never be over', and she is as much involved with it as everyone else. In expressing this, she refutes the allegations of *Death of a Hero* which reproach all those who do not fight. The story as she tells it, is very different. HD's experimental prose allows her to explore the atmosphere of the war, beginning within the female self, permeating outwards to acknowledge a more universal consciousness, illustrating a communion which will taint those who live through it for the rest of their lives.

The other significant relationship of HD's war was with D. H. Lawrence. Lawrence clearly influenced HD as she began to work in prose, involving her in his own work as well as commenting on hers. In *Bid Me to Live*, Frederick (Frederico or Rico) and Elsa (the Lawrences), hounded by the authorities who are suspicious of Elsa's German origins, stay with Julia in her London flat. As Elsa expects to embark on an affair with Vane, so it is anticipated that Julia and Rico will develop a relationship. But he recoils from her physically, electing instead to keep their friendship on a spiritual and intellectual level. This spills over into an internal struggle regarding personal methods of creativity, which forms a distinct subtext in *Bid Me to Live*. Jane Gledhill suggests that Julia's relationship with Rico is not so much about physical or emotional desire, as about the need to discover a new type of creativity with which to articulate her experience:

> She [Julia] longs for him [Rico] to 'bid her to live' so that she can leave behind the objective, non-emotional forms of expression she had learned from Lett Barnes (a shadowy figure representing Ezra Pound), and move into a richer expression of love in life. Lawrence's art encouraged exploration of the emotional life.[68]

Gledhill argues that Julia desires Rico physically because he has become 'the embodiment of his own aesthetic'.[69] If this is the case, his physical rejection of her has further aesthetic symbolism, equating to his simultaneous criticism of her writing for not sticking to what he deems to be an appropriate 'woman-conscious' approach. Julia (HD) goes on to explore the ideas that Rico (Lawrence) gives her for emotional expression, but finally rejects them, turning instead to narrative techniques which have more in common with those developed by other female modernist prose writers such as Dorothy Richardson and Virginia Woolf.

The Julia/Rico relationship is fundamental to *Bid Me to Live*. It is Rico whom Julia is addressing as she struggles to find a place for herself in the creative spectrum. Although tempted by the secret of the emotional intensity of his novels, she becomes disillusioned by his refusal to accept that she can write of male as well as female experience:

> This man-, this woman-theory of Rico's was false, it creaked in the joints. Rico could write elaborately on the woman mood, describe women to their marrow in his writing; but if she turned round, wrote the Orpheus part of her Orpheus-Eurydice sequence, he snapped back, 'Stick to the woman-consciousness, it is the intuitive woman-mood that matters.' He was right about that, of course. But if he could enter, so diabolically, into the feelings of women, why should not she enter into the feelings of men? She understood Rafe [Aldington], really understood that he loved her – that he desired *l'autre*.[70]

HD allows Julia to cling to the idea of Rico, but she cannot find fulfilment in his prose any more than his body. He is a substitute for her husband, with whom she had once found artistic communion, but in the end his creative methods cannot fulfil her purpose any more than Aldington's can. Moving beyond Rico/Lawrence, but incorporating his intensity of emotion along with her Imagism and the other aspects of her literary heredity, she experiments with ideas of artistic androgyny which echo those of Rose Allatini[71] and Virginia Woolf:

> There was one loophole, one might be an artist. Then the danger met the danger, the woman was man-woman, the man was woman-man. But Frederico, for all his acceptance of her verses, had shouted his man-is-man, his woman-is-woman at her; his shrill peacock cry sounded a love-cry, a death-cry for their generation.[72]

Rico is a disappointment because his 'love-cry' is a 'death-cry' and as such he cannot represent an artistic future without gender limitations. Just as she does with some of the work of Richard Aldington, HD responds to and retells the stories and ideas of Lawrence in order to find the most effective way for her to write about her war. Ultimately the intense way that the situation is 'lived' by Julia through the patterns of language which form HD's prose, is more reminiscent of the 'living' of Dorothy Richardson's Miriam Henderson in *Pilgrimage*[73] than of any of Lawrence's characters. HD certainly presents the men in *Bid Me to Live* with much more sympathetic understanding than Aldington does his women, although they are subordinated to the story of herself, her war, her experience. Her narrative may perhaps be defined as 'female', auto-biographical like the letters and diaries of earlier chapters, differing from those of Aldington and Lawrence by the degree of introspection and the personal, intimate nature of her prose, decorated with poetic motifs that are the remnants of her Imagism. But her incorporation of the influences of the men who wrote with her, allows the text to work on a wider, more universally sympathetic level.

HD's prose work, which has its roots in the trauma she suffered in the First World War represents a different kind of modernism, built from the experiences of her own literary past, and those of the men in her life at that time. Rachel Blau DuPlessis sums it up thus:

> HD's subjects and her methods were chosen so she could open up a place for herself in a tradition that may have seemed closed and completed. Indeed, *Bid Me To Live*, a novel set in 1917 and reflecting her early life as a poet, shows how a writer, an HD figure, passed from translating the

'hoarded treasures' of grammarians to 'divination' of the 'inner words' and finally to writing a new coinage as 'she pushed aside her typewriter [from translations and letters to male mentors] and let her pencil and her notebook take her elsewhere'.[74]

At the end of the novel Julia discovers herself, with this pencil and notebook, among the Cornish flowers of her escape. The war seems very far away and finally she locates the emotional space to write the way she chooses to write. Perhaps it is here that HD really begins *Bid Me to Live.*

The fact that it took HD over forty years to prepare this novel for publication, may reflect the difficulty she had in dealing with this traumatic chapter of her life. Unlike Aldington, she did not seem to be able to exorcise it simply by recreating it in a fictional form. Instead she wrote and rewrote for the kind of 'writing cure' that Susan Stanford Friedman suggests. The intimacy of her narrative indicates that she was trying to articulate a painful experience, to which there was no end, just like the war she describes. In order to express her war, and its impact on her life, HD adopts many of the characteristics of a literary modernism initiated by the women prose writers who were her contemporaries, expanding them with the mythic motifs and the poeticism that were the legacy of her Imagist roots. The result is a woman's story constructed of 'living words' of a type quite different to those adopted by Vera Brittain. HD the poet, used to living her life with words, found new ways to adapt them to help her to live her past, her creativity, her war; a female version, a denial of marginality and oblivion.

Vera Brittain's article in the *Manchester Guardian,* printed in November 1929, was a direct response to the spate of 'masculine' war novels and memoirs that had enjoyed success that year. Brittain was concerned that female versions of these and other war stories were being subordinated to a mythology that prioritised masculine experience. To some extent she was right; hence the importance of *Testament of Youth.* But the tales of war had constantly been told and retold by women since the conflict began, and their voices should be given equal standing with those of their men. The shattering of wartime myths of gender and romance in the harsh world of Helen Zenna Smith, HD's poetic search for the articulation of the intimate; these delineate the evolution of new forms, stylistic innovations and new modes of expression; stories told with 'living words' which ensure that the war experience of all women will not be forgotten. In the next chapter I shall pursue the echoes of HD, 'one might be an artist', by examining the way in which the modernist preoccupation with the role of the artist manifests itself in women's war fiction.

Notes

1 Vera Brittain (1929), 'Their Name Liveth', *Manchester Guardian*, 13 November.

2 Siegfried Sassoon (1928), *Memoirs of a Fox-Hunting Man*, in Siegfried Sassoon (1986), *The Complete Memoirs of George Sherston*, London, Faber & Faber (first published 1937); Robert Graves (1973), *Goodbye to All That*, London, Penguin (first published 1929); Erich Maria Remarque (1991), *All Quiet on the Western Front*, London, Picador (first published 1929); Richard Aldington (1929), *Death of a Hero*, London, Chatto & Windus.

3 Pat Barker (1992), *Regeneration*, London, Penguin (first published 1991); Pat Barker (1994), *The Eye in the Door*, London, Penguin (first published 1993); Pat Barker (1995), *The Ghost Road*, London, Viking.

4 Sebastian Faulk (1993), *Birdsong*, London, Hutchinson.

5 Vera Brittain (1992), *Testament of Youth*, London, Virago (first published 1933). *Testament of Youth* was republished by Virago in 1978 complementing a dramatisation for BBC television. It has been in print ever since.

6 See the work of Jane Potter, for example her (1997), '"A Great Purifier": The Great War in Women's Romances and Memoirs 1914–1918', in S. Raitt and T. Tate (eds), *Women's Fiction and the Great War*, Oxford, Oxford University Press.

7 Remarque, *All Quiet on the Western Front*; Evadne Price (Helen Zenna Smith) (1988), *Not So Quiet... Stepdaughters of War*, London, Virago (first published 1930); HD (1984), *Bid Me to Live*, London, Virago (first published 1960).

8 Modris Eksteins (1989), *Rites of Spring*, New York, Bantam Press, p. 276.

9 *Ibid.*, p. 277.

10 Barbara Hardy (1988), 'Introduction' to *Not So Quiet...*, London, Virago, p. 7.

11 Jane Marcus (1989), 'Corpus/Corps/Corpse: Writing the Body in/at War', in H. M. Cooper, A. A. Munich and S. M. Squier (eds), *Arms and the Woman: War, Gender and Literary Representation*, London and Chapel Hill, NC, North Carolina University Press, pp. 124–67.

12 May Sinclair's war novels were all popular and successful, but have all been out of print since first publication so arguably cannot add much to current public perception of the First World War.

13 Marcus, 'Corpus/Corps/Corpse', p. 126.

14 Hardy, 'Introduction', p. 12.

15 Eksteins, *Rites of Spring*, p. 20.

16 *Ibid.*, p. 282.

17 Price, *Not So Quiet...*, pp. 91–2.

18 Eksteins, *Rites of Spring*, p. 294.

19 Hardy, 'Introduction', p. 8.

20 Graves, Sassoon, etc. all discuss the way in which war brings together men from different classes but emphasise an awareness of different accents, responsibilities and civilian backgrounds, suggesting that the war simultaneously breaks down and reinscribes class differences. Remarque is referring to German class structures, which may be slightly different to Britain's.

21 Price, *Not So Quiet...*, pp. 50–1.
22 *Ibid.*, p. 211.
23 *Ibid.*, p. 214–15.
24 Homer (1988), *The Iliad*, Oxford, Oxford University Press (translated by R. Fitzgerald 1974).
25 Price, *Not So Quiet...*, pp. 55–6.
26 *Ibid.*, p. 56.
27 *Ibid.*, pp. 108–9.
28 Eksteins, *Rites of Spring*, p. 288.
29 Price, *Not So Quiet...*, p. 60.
30 *Ibid.*, p. 59.
31 Mary Cadogan and Patricia Craig (1981), *Women and Children First: The Fiction of Two World Wars*, London, Victor Gollancz.
32 Remarque, *All Quiet on the Western Front*, p. 101.
33 Price, *Not So Quiet...*, pp. 173–4.
34 *Ibid.*, p. 126.
35 Marcus, 'Corpus/Corps/Corpse', p. 154.
36 Radclyffe Hall (1994), *The Well of Loneliness*, London, Virago (first published 1928).
37 Marcus, 'Corpus/Corps/Corpse', p. 142.
38 Eksteins, *Rites of Spring*, p. 282.
39 Remarque, *All Quiet on the Western Front*, pp. 51–2.
40 See Paul Fussell (1977), *The Great War and Modern Memory*, Oxford, Oxford University Press. One early exception to this tradition of euphemism is Henri Barbusse's novel *Under Fire*. It is also worth noting that the use of euphemism is not common in later war poetry such as that of Sassoon, Owen and Rosenburg.
41 John Onions (1990), *English Fiction and Drama of the Great War, 1918–39*, London, Macmillan, pp. 54–5.
42 Price, *Not So Quiet...*, p. 44.
43 Eksteins, *Rites of Spring*, p. 293.
44 Marcus, 'Corpus/Corps/Corpse', p. 140.
45 Price, *Not So Quiet...*, p. 98.
46 Marcus, 'Corpus/Corps/Corpse', p. 145.
47 Remarque, *All Quiet on the Western Front*, p. 110.
48 Price, *Not So Quiet...*, p. 167.
49 Jane Gledhill (1993), 'Impersonality and Amnesia: A Response to World War I in the Writings of H.D. and Rebecca West', In Dorothy Goldman (ed.), *Women and World War I: The Written Response*, London, Macmillan, p. 182.
50 Susan Stanford Friedman (1990), 'H.D. (1886–1961)', in Bonnie Kime Scott (ed.), *The Gender of Modernism*, Bloomington and Indianapolis, IN, Indiana University Press, p. 87.
51 Peter E. Firchow (1980), 'Rico and Julia: The HD–DHL Affair Reconsidered',

Journal of Modern Literature, 8 (1), 51–76; D. H. Lawrence (1971), *Aaron's Rod*, London, Heinemann (first published 1923).

52 Richard Aldington (1929), 'Introductory Letter to Halcott Glover', in his *Death of a Hero*, London: Chatto & Windus.

53 Aldington's letters to HD have been collected and published by Caroline Zilboorg (ed.) (1992), *Richard Aldington and H.D.: The Early Years in Letters*, Bloomington and Indianapolis, IN, Indiana University Press. A new edition, also containing *The Later Years in Letters* is due to be published by Manchester University Press in 2001.

54 Aldington, *Death of a Hero*, p. 127.

55 Fussell, *The Great War*.

56 Cadogan and Craig, *Women and Children First*, p. 106.

57 Aldington, *Death of a Hero*, p. 226.

58 Many critics like Peter Fichow have seen the marriage of George Winterbourne and Elizabeth in *Death Of A Hero* as Aldington's bitter representation of his own. However, Caroline Zilboorg has argued against this, suggesting that HD's own version in *Bid Me to Live* is much more accurate. She bases her arguments on the evidence of Aldington's wartime letters to HD which seem to suggest the Rafe/Julia relationship rather than that of the Winterbournes.

59 Gillian Hanscombe and Virginia L. Smyers (1987), *Writing for their Lives: The Modernist Women 1910–1940*, London, Women's Press.

60 Helen McNeil (1984), 'Introduction' to *Bid Me to Live*, London, Virago, p. xiii.

61 Perdita Schaffner (1984), 'Afterword: A Profound Animal' to *Bid Me To Live*, London, Virago, p. 186.

62 HD, *Bid Me to Live*, p. 19.

63 *Ibid.*, p. 25.

64 *Ibid.*, p. 132.

65 Ezra Pound (1972), 'A Few Don'ts by an Imagiste', in Peter Jones (ed.), *Imagist Poetry*, London, Penguin, p. 130.

66 HD, *Bid Me to Live*, pp. 122–3.

67 *Ibid.*, pp. 123–4.

68 Gledhill, 'Impersonality and Amnesia', p. 178.

69 *Ibid.*, p. 181.

70 HD, *Bid Me to Live*, p. 62.

71 Rose Allatini is discussed in Chapter 5.

72 HD, *Bid Me to Live*, p. 136.

73 Dorothy Richardson (1992), *Pilgrimage 1*, London, Virago (first published 1915, 1916, 1917).

74 Rachel Blau DuPlessis (1986), *H.D. The Career of that Struggle*, London, Harvester, p. 19.

5

'Agents of Civilisation'[1]

This is the end of all the arts. Artists will not be allowed to exist except as
agents for the recruiting sergeant. We're dished.[2]

Never was the artist more necessary than now – his freedom of spirit, his
self-assertion, his creative fire . . . the stand of the individual against immen-
sities, a stand always hazardous, becomes a gesture of incredible power and
pride, an attitude of almost impossible heroism.[3]

'One might be an artist.' Perhaps this is the way to deal with the unspeakable experience of the First World War. And by the pursuit of art, rise
above and create beyond the war; becoming an 'agent of civilisation' carrying the torch of culture through the dark days of conflict. It seems to be
no accident that many women writing about war engage with the role of
the artist. This self-conscious consideration of the process of making art
preoccupied so many writers at the beginning of the twentieth century
and is also a significant feature of much modernist writing. As Randall
Stevenson suggests, 'Such frequent and substantial discussion of art and
writing, within the novel, is in one way an extension of the growing debate
in the early twentieth century about the novel *as* art, as a genre with its
own specific formal and structural properties'.[4]

For women, with whom this genre of the novel had already been
identified as a result of the legacy of the nineteenth century, this debate
carried a double-edged significance. The recognition of the novel as art
placed a spotlight on the woman as artist, at once elevating her creative
status, even while it added a different kind of 'otherness' to her female
identity; the artist has the capacity to be as alien to patriarchal convention
as the woman. In modernist art this marginalisation is frequently
acknowledged; however, it is often accompanied by the assertion of a
claim to a kind of spiritual ascendancy – an elitist 'otherness' – the aes-

thetic framework of which can only be really appreciated by those who can move beyond the restrictions of convention. Arguably, it is this emphasis on the significance of the individual artist that made the biggest break from the aesthetic movement of the late nineteenth century that had influenced the birth of modernism. Instead of 'art for art's sake' women writers and artists, female modernists, adopted the creed 'life for art's sake'.[5] And in 1914 life itself was a threatened commodity.

The First World War offered women many practical opportunities to lose their status as 'other' created by the 'separate spheres' ideology of the previous century, allowing them to adopt 'masculine' roles in a society temporarily lacking in men. But many of those women who had assumed the role of artist continued to convey their sense of marginalisation in some of their writings of the war. And in accordance with developing modernisms, the woman, the artist, those outside the accepted boundaries of society, are often given an additional insight within this writing, enabling them to focus on the war in a way which brings a greater clarity of vision regardless of their political affiliations. It is also interesting to consider what happens to the modernist artist in women's fiction when he becomes a combatant and is thrust away from the margins into the centre.

This chapter examines the advocation of the spiritual ascendancy of the artist in the novels of three very different women who were writing during the First World War, May Sinclair, Rose Macaulay and Rose Allatini (writing as A. T. Fitzroy). Their novels are particularly interesting because they were all published during the war, Sinclair's *The Tree of Heaven* in 1917, Macaulay's *Non-Combatants and Others* in 1916 and Allatini's *Despised and Rejected* in 1918.[6] They are all products of an ongoing war culture, appearing much earlier than most of the more famous, radical war texts and those of High Modernism. These writers locate the woman/artist outside the boundaries of convention in a way which enables them to use art to investigate multiple issues within their texts such as social taboos, sexuality, notions of heroism and degeneracy, and, specific to the war, the association between art and pacifism.

A conflict of interests: May Sinclair's *The Tree of Heaven*

May Sinclair was already an extremely successful writer in 1914 as well as a political activist associated with the suffrage campaign. Her links with the development of modernism are strong, not only because of the experimentation in her own writing, but also because of her promotion of many younger writers such as T. S. Eliot, Dorothy Richardson and HD, those recognised architects of modernisms. But Sinclair was also a patriot. She was one of fifty-four British authors, very few of whom were women, who signed the 'Authors' Manifesto', the brainchild of propagandist C. F. G. Masterman, which pledged support for the war.[7] The élitist 'otherness' of the modernist movement seems to have been at odds with the required blanket conformity of patriotism. It is this conflict of interests which forms a framework for the central dialectic of her second war novel *The Tree of Heaven*.

In his essay 'The Women and Men of 1914' James Longenbach examines the links between three primary forces in 1914, the battle for suffrage, the battle for modern art and the battle in the trenches, and identifies that it is precisely these conflicting issues which form the core of Sinclair's novel.[8] For her, each movement creates a separate vortex, drawing in all those whom it touches, and each is distinctly uncomfortable within the Edwardian culture which contains it.

The Tree of Heaven delineates these conflicts through the various members of the Harrison family. As in many war novels, Sinclair begins with a Utopian evocation of the pre-war world in which Anthony and Frances Harrison embody the essence of nineteenth-century security. Anthony, the detached English gentleman with a successful international business, presents a patriarchal symbol of empire. His demure and devoted wife represents a perfect expression of Victorian/Edwardian motherhood, dutifully loving her sons above all things, her husband second, with her daughter and female friends appropriately subordinated to the patriarchal orthodoxy which shapes her life. Yet her dreams, which take root in the pseudo-pastoral world beneath the 'tree of heaven' (an ash tree in their garden), are unconsciously powerful enough to influence a new generation. Consequently, in their turn, Frances's children come to embody these three breakaway movements of the early twentieth century, each rejecting the ideology that ensnares their parents.

Sinclair's own involvement in the modernist movement is reflected in her presentation of this pre-war world as obsolete, and the privileging of her central section, suitably entitled, 'The Vortex'.[9] She focuses on the Harrison children as agents for the modern; Dorothea in the Women's Movement, Michael as a poet and Nicky as an envoy for technological advancement with his interest in mechanisation and his desire to patent the 'Moving Fortress' (the tank).[10] Although, as Longenbach points out, these three are inextricably linked, for the purposes of this chapter it is Michael, the artist, who is the most interesting.

It is through Michael that the conflict in Sinclair's own artistic loyalties is most clearly articulated. It has been suggested that the character Michael Harrison was probably loosely based on the Imagist poet Richard Aldington, whom Sinclair knew well as a result of her association with HD and the Imagist movement in general.[11] Yet it cannot be forgotten that *The Tree of Heaven* works also as a propaganda novel as a result of Sinclair's commitment to the 'Authors' Manifesto', and as such, the portrayal of Michael ultimately functions in opposition to Aldington's own bitter recollections of the war experience recorded in *Death of a Hero*.[12] However, despite the requirement that Michael must eventually collude with the makers of war, his art itself is never really subordinated to the pull of any vortex, and the 'otherness' which creates him is, for most of the novel, lauded as a form of spiritual individuality providing the inspiration for a greater clarity of vision.

From childhood, Michael is represented as separate, different, other, illustrated by his desire to always play alone. Despite narrative suggestions that it is the dreamer in Frances that has helped to shape her eldest son, she is troubled by his childish obscurity:

> There was Michael. She couldn't make him out. He loved them, and showed that he loved them; but it was by caresses, by beautiful words, by rare, extravagant acts of renunciation, inconsistent with his self-will; not by anything solid and continuous. There was a softness in Michael that distressed and a hardness that perplexed her. You could make an impression on Michael – far too easily – and the impression stayed . . . And he had secret ways. He was growing more and more sensitive, more and more wrapped up in Himself.[13]

In the child Michael it is possible to identify many of the characteristics of the adult. His 'otherness' is already prominent and it manifests itself in his mother's awareness of a feminine side of his nature sitting comfortably with the masculine. In his adult self these two blend presenting an oblique version of the artistic androgyny discussed by Virginia Woolf, HD and Rose Allatini. And Michael is already 'wrapped up in Himself', the egoism of the artist endowed with a degree of ambiguous spirituality by Sinclair's capitalisation.

As Michael matures, his identification with the Imagist movement becomes more pronounced. A trip to France introduces him to other poets experimenting in 'live verse', and his mentor Lawrence Stephen introduces him to a Bohemian circle of assorted artists who meet regularly in pre-war London to discuss the state of the arts. The substance of their arguments, which draws upon explosive analysis of the futurist and vorticist movements, is undoubtedly based on Sinclair's own experience of such social gatherings, and incorporates the articulation of ideas, perhaps her own, which could almost form a manifesto for the development of literary modernism:

> He went on to unfold a scheme for restoring vigour to the exhausted language by destroying its articulations. These he declared to be purely arbitrary, therefore fatal to the development of a spontaneous style. By breaking up the rigid ties of syntax, you do more than create new forms of prose moving in perfect freedom, you deliver the creative spirit from its abominable contact with dead ideas. Association, fixed and eternalised by the structure of language, is the tyranny that keeps down the live idea.[14]

Michael is influenced by the arguments he hears at these meetings. And his Imagism borrows more from Sinclair's closer friends. His drifting thoughts, "The pine forest makes itself a sea for the land wind, and the young pine tree is mad for the open sea',[15] are reminiscent of the 'Whirl up, sea – /Whirl your pointed pines,' of HD's 'Oread',[16] reflecting the impact of this modern movement on Sinclair's writing. But while Michael clearly finds this atmosphere of rebellion to be innovatory, he still aspires to an artistic individualism which will be strong enough to preserve his insights beyond the epistemological disputes of his friends: 'He thought of himself going on, free from the whirl of the Vortex, and of his work as enduring; standing clear and hard in the clean air'.[17] Thus singled out, Michael is ready to face the ultimate challenge to modern society: the First World War.

Sinclair's commitment to a pro-war orthodoxy is lived out by the Harrison children in 'Victory', the final part of *The Tree of Heaven*. There is no sense of irony in this title despite the fact that at the time of the novel's publication, the war had been raging for three years with no end in sight. The victory is a spiritual one, belief in the righteousness of the cause, and action to support it, will overcome all evils. Other 'smaller' causes must fall by the wayside. Like Sinclair herself, Dorothea abandons the fight for women's rights to look after Belgian refugees. Reconciled with her fiancé as a result of this shifting political allegiance, she is forced to regret her previous actions as he becomes the novel's first victim of the trenches: 'I could bear it if I hadn't wasted the time we might have had together. All those years – like a fool – over that silly suffrage.'[18]

Nicky, who has become the traditional romantic hero of the novel, immediately joins up and is infected by the 'ecstasy' of the trenches. Sinclair shifts from an omniscient narrator to the voice of Nicky via his letters home as he struggles to convey that 'gorgeous fight-feeling', but being a mechanic rather than a poet, he does not have the linguistic clarity or the spiritual understanding to articulate the experience for the reader adequately. He dies happy, having found fulfilment despite never getting to see his 'moving fortress' in action.

Sinclair's own artistic background dictates that only Michael can possess the spiritual insight to convey what Wilfred Owen described as the 'extraordinary exultation' of war.[19] But Michael, like so many wartime artists, is caught in the clutches of pacifism.[20]

The association of art and pacifism recurs continually in women's writing of the war, and it echoes the modernist links between the privileging of the aesthetic and the rejection of a mechanised mass media culture. Unlike Sinclair's earlier literary hero, James Tasker Jevons, who forfeits his art and jumps at the opportunity to assert his masculinity by joining an ambulance unit in Belgium,[21] Michael fears that the war, as a manifestation of everything that is negative in this culture, will end in the destruction of all the arts; artists will no longer be 'agents of civilisation' but instead 'agents for the recruiting sergeant'. He equates art with religion once more asserting the innate spirituality of the artist:

> It was all very well, but if you happened to have a religion, and your religion was what mattered to you most; if you adored Beauty as the supreme form of Life; if you cared for nothing else; if you lived, impersonally, to make Beauty and to keep it alive, and for no other end, how could you consent to take part in this bloody business? That would be the last betrayal, the most cowardly surrender.[22]

The feminine aspects of Michael's character move to the forefront to reject the 'masculine' militarism which threatens to engulf him at the cost of his art, creating what he perceives to be a new kind of heroism, the heroism of the non-combatant, which is explored both consciously and unconsciously in the writing of many women during the war. It is more heroic for Michael to remain true to his principles than to relinquish his artistic individuality and join the herds on the Western Front. In taking this stand he hints at the degeneracy of a society which can allow such a war to happen. As part of an élite group he must carry the torch of civilisation on behalf of his generation. He tells his mother, 'I *am* doing something. I'm keeping sane, And I'm keeping sanity alive in other people'.[23] Sinclair adopts a role for her artist which embodies an elitist ideology often associated with the modernist movement, heightened by the threatening nature of the war. But this image, although a familiar one in women's war fiction, is problematised in *The Tree of Heaven* by Sinclair's commitment to the patriotic cause.

In order to fulfil its propagandist role, *The Tree of Heaven* can allow for no higher cause than the war itself. The only form of heroism that can be recognised as authentic is that experienced on the field of battle. And there can be no question of degeneracy if the cause is righteous. Consequently, Michael must change his mind, but in order to retain the literary integrity of the artist, his art must not be subordinated. Thus perhaps, Michael comes to embody the conflict of interest that must have complicated Sinclair's own personal beliefs, echoing Dorothea's U-turn over the issue of women's suffrage.

This conflict is difficult to reconcile in Sinclair's text. It is his emotional response to Nicky's death that finally persuades Michael that he, too, must join up. He recognises a patriotic validity in Lawrence Stephen's words, 'Victory – Victory is a state of mind'.[24] But his previous convictions are deliberately infantilised by his realisation that 'he had funked it all the time'.[25] What has already been identified as the heroism of the non-combatant is dismissed; without a uniform, Michael is acknowledged as a coward regardless of his former principles, although in a uniform there is a danger that he may cease to be an individual.

But the salvation of Michael the artist has already been articulated by Nicky in his final letter. Realising his own linguistic inadequacy, he writes of Michael, '*He'd* write a poem about it [that 'gorgeous fight-feeling'] that would make you sit up'.[26] This, of course, is Sinclair's way out. The spiritual exhilaration of the war gives Michael the final inspiration to create a higher art form, thus justifying his own death as part of a cleansing process for mankind.

Michael is liberated even as he is doomed. His change of heart is justified because the experience of war enables him to create the art that he has long sought after, rather than destroying his creativity as he had formerly anticipated. Having finally discovered 'truth', it is suggested that he is able to adapt his art to represent the elation of the war experience accurately, using his modernist skills to articulate the 'real'. Sinclair uses him as a mouthpiece to attack realist representations of the war prompted by Henri Barbusse's *Under Fire*[27] which made a significant impact when it was translated into English in 1917 around the time that she was writing:

Of course we shall be accused of glorifying War and telling lies about it. Well – there's a Frenchman who has told the truth, piling up all the horrors, faithfully, remorselessly, magnificently. But he seems to think people oughtn't to write about this War at all unless they show up the infamy of it, as a deterrent, so that no Government can ever start another one. It's a sort of literary 'frightfulness.' But whom is he trying to frighten?[28]

But unlike Barbusse, Sinclair *is* glorifying the war. As a propagandist, she must do so in order to justify the continuing carnage. Ultimately Sinclair's patriotism forces her to subordinate Michael's modernism to the cause of the war. Admittedly, he is allowed to discover a new creativity as a result of being a combatant, apparently retaining some of the 'otherness' that has marked him throughout the novel. But this is partly achieved as a result of his actually becoming one of a crowd, a crowd which privileges another cause: 'But things you don't do by yourself are a long way the best. Nothing – not even poetry can beat an infantry charge when you're leading it'.[29] The extremity of his U-turn, and the way in which Sinclair fills his letters home not with innovatory prose or poetry, but with conventional romantic rhetoric, actively works to belie his apparent artistic fecundity. He even seems, inadvertently, to articulate this paradox himself:

> It's odd . . . to have gone all your life trying to get reality, trying to get new beauty, trying to get utter satisfaction; to have funked coming out here because you thought it was all obscene ugliness and waste and frustration, and then to come out, and to find what you wanted'.[30]

For the modern reader *The Tree of Heaven* remains problematic. Sinclair seems to be trying to reconcile the war with modernism in a way that does not really work. Michael is less convincing as an artist once he is subsumed by the vortex of the war.[31] The conflict of interests is too strong. Art, it appears, cannot really function when the 'agents of civilisation' take to the battlefield. But the novel is interesting because it can be read across critical boundaries and begins to highlight the important connections between the war and developing modernisms.

As an older writer, needing to promote the righteousness of the cause which so disrupted her civilisation, May Sinclair is not alone in the way that she allows her artist to change his mind. In Edith Wharton's *A Son at the Front*,[32] artist John Campton gradually comes to believe that his son must fight, despite early attempts to keep him out of the conflict. The cause is everything. But at the same time, Wharton acknowledges that war kills art. Campton is unable to paint as long as the fighting continues, and the text is littered with dead and wounded young artists whose talents are crippled or destroyed prematurely.

Claire Tylee suggests, 'It was not until the men returned after the War and Sinclair saw their treatment and the treatment of Germany's starving children that she became disillusioned with her belief in the political and spiritual benefits of war'.[33] May Sinclair's long-term investment in the movements of modern art must have made it very difficult for her to acknowledge the real threat that the war presented to the art she had cultivated. Thus she tries to give her text the best of both worlds. Her postwar understanding may have caused her to question the validity of this endeavour. The conflict of interests at the heart of *The Tree of Heaven* remains difficult to reconcile. The modernist influences are clear, and the concepts articulated form an interesting dialogue for considering the marginalisation and the androgynous potential of the artist at a time when gender roles were being questioned. In the end, however, Sinclair's romantic imagination takes over, patriotism intercedes demanding the comfortable closure of artistic fulfilment and a happy death, and such a narrative structure can only prove inadequate to express the complexity of the relationship between art and war. Perhaps if the patriotism were removed, the relationship might be more fruitful?

A conflict of ideas: Rose Macaulay's *Non-Combatants and Others*

In a world of ambiguity, the certainty that May Sinclair tried to illustrate was an illusion. Rose Macaulay, a younger writer who was touched by the war in different ways, wrote a deeper insecurity into her novel *Non-Combatants and Others* in 1916, a time when it must have felt especially pertinent. After two years of war the expected victories had not materialised and there was no end in sight. Macaulay uses this atmosphere of uncertainty to colour her writing, breaking from literary conventions of security and closure in a way that enabled her to represent the war and the artist without conforming to the inappropriate structures of the nineteenth-century novel. Like Sinclair, Rose Macaulay was already a successful novelist in 1914, but as part of a younger generation, her experience of the war prompted her to use her fiction to record it in a different way. Like *The Tree of Heaven*, *Non-Combatants and Others* has a central focus on the relationship between art and war, but in Macaulay's text there is no real attempt to resolve the problems of the 'otherness' of the artist who cannot conform in a belligerent society.

Macaulay's heroine, Alix Sandomir, is socially marginalised in three different ways: she is an artist, a woman and a cripple, 'a diseased hip-joint as a child . . . had left her right leg slightly contracted'.[34] Thus through Alix, Macaulay is able to address multiple issues of 'otherness' at a time of national crisis. The novel opens to reveal Alix engrossed in the practice of her art to the exclusion of all else, specifically as means of avoiding the necessity to confront the reality of the war that blazes around her. Her cousin accuses her, 'Alix is hopeless; she does nothing but draw and paint. She could earn something on the stage as the Special Star Turn, the Girl who isn't doing her bit'.[35] But for Alix, burying herself in her art provides a shield against the anxieties of being a non-combatant for whom 'a war is poor fun'[36] since she cannot be physically involved, yet she must still deal with letters from the front, 'like bullets and bits of shrapnel crashing into her world'.[37]

Alix's art helps her to retain her individualism in a world of crowds, but ultimately it cannot protect her from the vortex of the war that whirls ever nearer. Like Michael Harrison she identifies this threat to her creativity, but she is less certain of her own spiritual ascendancy, perhaps because of her alternative status as a disabled woman, and therefore is less able to combat it successfully. It is this interior conflict which forms the core of Macaulay's novel. Her representation of her heroine highlights the danger for the artist, but unlike Michael, Alix cannot attain artistic fulfilment by going 'over the top'. Instead, the possible alternative courses of action that are open to her are explored as the novel develops.

Macaulay uses her novel to represent many viewpoints, many different and often conflicting ideas, both combatant and non-combatant, with a detachment that reflects the confusion and ambiguity of the time.[38] These multiple voices add a further dimension to the text as a work of art, endorsing Bakhtin's notion that the novel becomes a polyphonic genre which operates beyond the level of authorial control: 'each character's speech possesses its own belief system, since each is the speech of another in another's language; thus it may also refract authorial intentions and consequently may to a certain degree constitute a second language for the author'.[39] The complexities of the early twentieth century seem to provide an appropriate backdrop for this reading. The uncertainty of *Non-Combatants and Others* is embellished by these multiple layers of possible meanings which are given additional credibility by the lack of authorial intervention. Thus the novel engages in some modernist narrative experiments, acquiring for itself the elevated status which it then bestows onto the artist. This polyphony can also be identified in both *The Tree of Heaven* and Rose Allatini's *Despised and Rejected*. Despite attempts by these two women to assert authorial control with a view to foregrounding certain political ideas, their texts still contain multiple independent voices that present many possible readings regardless of potential propagandist intentions.

Non-Combatants and Others contains little propaganda. Alix operates to some extent as a kind of sponge to soak up these multiple ideas which permeate the text, although she has difficulty identifying a suitable role for herself which can contain her innate rejection of the war. Thus she cocoons herself within her art. This protective shield is first cracked when her wounded cousin John Orme returns home to convalesce. Her sleep is disturbed by his 'crying, sobbing, moaning, like a little child, like a man on the rack'.[40] whilst in the throes of a nightmare. The impact of this experience on her particularly sensitive constitution has severe repercussions for her art: 'Alix, seeing her friends in scattered bits, seeing worse than that, seeing what John had seen and mentioned with tears, turned the greenish pallor of pale, ageing cheese, and dropped her head in her hands. Painting was off for that morning. Painting and war don't go together.'[41] Like Woolf's Lily Briscoe, Alix fails in her struggle to paint a world in which she can find no valid place. She is exiled by her 'otherness' which is inflated by the war, until she can find her own way to channel her artistic energy and create for herself some kind of vision.

Alix's neurasthenia operates on more than one level. As well as highlighting her spiritual sensitivity and her artistic isolation, it also provides a link with her eighteen-year-old soldier brother, Paul, which in turn raises questions about the significance of gender in this war.[42] Paul is the only member of the Sandomir family who is playing the traditional 'heroic' role on the Western Front, and news of his death as reported by Alix's ignorant relations, is bathed in the traditional romantic rhetoric of war; 'The poor dear boy has died doing his duty and serving his country . . . a noble end dearie . . . not a wasted life'.[43] Their patriotic words seem displaced and unreal to Alix. They provide more voices to add to the overall confusion.

But Macaulay's book has no real place for romantic convention. She exposes it as an illusion that blankets a bitter reality. The psychological bond between Alix and Paul is reinforced when Alix inadvertently discovers that Paul committed suicide, an archetypal 'cowards' death.[44] He is emasculated by the desire he shares with his sister, the need to escape from the vortex of the war that has engulfed him. Traditional notions of 'heroism', which will later be deconstructed in much war fiction, are already presented as meaningless in this early novel. Paul is a victim, very young and innocent, and his physical affiliation to Alix, in terms of their shared neurasthenic responses, allows their two identities to blend providing the reader with an empathetic view of his anguish. This blending also endows the Sandomir character with a degree of androgyny that reinforces this isolation against the backdrop of the war.

It seems likely that Rose Macaulay drew on her own personal experiences when constructing *Non-Combatants and Others*. She herself was a victim of the kind of instability that afflicts the Sandomirs, suffering from depression after the murder of her brother in 1909, with a further breakdown in 1919. She was also very distressed by the death, in 1915, of Rupert Brooke who was a close family friend. It is likely that he was the basis for her character Basil Doye, Alix's fellow artist and the man whom she loves, who is likewise artistically silenced by a wound in the hand which will prevent him from ever drawing again.

Macaulay's self-conscious analysis of the role of the artist is not restricted to Alix and her friends. She also joins in the modernist debate about the process of writing itself, and its status as an art form. Journalist Nicholas Sandomir, Alix's other brother exempt from military service on the grounds of poor health, is used as a spokesman to criticise the effect of the war on literature, articulating within the novel a kind of meta-fictional commentary on the status of art in relation to the war and politics.[45] As with some of Michael Harrison's monologues, his arguments serve to detach art from the war; but he also disassociates art from the kind of romantic rhetoric in which Sinclair takes ultimate refuge:

> It's extraordinary, the stream of – of the heroic and epic, isn't that it – that pours forth daily. The war seems to have given an unhealthy stimulus to hundreds of minds and thousands of pens . . . The first-rate people, both the combatants and non-combatants, are too much disgusted, too upset, to do first-rate work.[46]

Is this then 'the end of all the arts'? Sandomir's arguments have the double-edged effect of reinforcing Alix's personal isolation at the same time as they intimate that those who oppose the war occupy a higher cultural and intellectual plain.

'Who was it who said the other day that the writers to whom war is glamorous aren't as a rule the ones who produce anything fit to call literature. War's an insanity; and insane things, purely destructive, wasteful, hideous, brutal, ridiculous things, aren't what makes art.'[47] This elevation of the aesthetic beyond the dimensions of war echoes the early artistic/pacifist arguments of *The Tree of Heaven*, and again insinuates that there is a sinister degree of degeneracy in the common world. But Macaulay does not allow these ideas to be conquered in the same way that Sinclair does. In this novel, art does not enter into the vortex of war even if it cannot thrive outside it, because war always destroys art. Alix, as the representative artist, must find other ways to survive in order that her art might live on in the next era of peace. One escape route that she investigates is that of religion.

Susan M. Squier argues of Macaulay, 'Though she was a part of the milieu of literary modernism, she still felt a distance from modernist concerns and tone, a result of her religious preoccupation'.[48] This may be an accurate evaluation of her personal beliefs, but in the context of this novel at least, Macaulay appears to remain ambivalent. She presents the religious aspects of the novel from the same detached, non-committed point of view that dominates throughout, and allows the narrative to be permeated by a polyphony of different and oppositional clerical voices, none of which is privileged over the others. This suggests an affinity with modernist reassessment despite, or perhaps because of her interest in religious matters. Macaulay's engagement with religion in *Non-Combatants and Others* is reminiscent not only of other female modernists, but also of the experiences of Stephen Dedalus in Joyce's *A Portrait of the Artist as a Young Man*[49] in the analytical and interrogatory style of her discourse:

> They believed in God: but Alix could have no use for the Violette God.[50] Mrs Frampton's God was the Almighty, an omnipotent Being who governed all things in gross and in detail, including the weather (though the connection here was mysteriously vague). A God of crops and sun and rain, who spoke in the thunder; a truly pagan God (though Mrs Frampton would not have cared for the word), of chastisements and arbitrary mercies, who was capable of wrecking ships and causing wars, in order to punish and improve people. The God of the 'act of God' in the shipping regulations. A God who could, and would, unless for wise purposes he chose otherwise, keep men and women physically safe, protect them from battle, murder, and sudden death. An anthropomorphic God, in the semblance, for some strange reason known only to the human race, of a man. A God who was somehow responsible for the war. A God who ordered men's estates so that there should be a wholesome economic inequality among them.[51]

Alix investigates two branches of religion when her art fails her. The high Anglicanism of her cousin Kate, (considered above), offers security in ritual, but she has trouble applying the words of the sermon to the every day experiences of women and non-combatants. It seems to represent the kind of tyranny responsible for the perpetuation of the war rather than a way of dealing with the experience spiritually.

Alternatively there is West, the radical Anglican cleric who shares rooms with her brother Nicholas, and who, despite his church's support for the conflict, advocates that everyone should fight against the war, 'by whatever means we each have at our command'.[52] West's religion does not offer Alix any answers which can provide an adequate substitute for her art. However, he does operate in the text as a precursor to the pacifist voice that has already been linked with the spiritual ascendancy of the artist. This pacifist voice materialises in the final section of the novel in the form of Alix's mother, the indomitable Daphne Sandomir.

Like the artist, the woman and the cripple, the pacifist in the First World War lived on the margins of society, often unwelcome as a result of his or her conscious rejection of the militarist orthodoxy on which society depended in order to sustain the war effort. Thus Sinclair's Michael Harrison becomes an embarrassment to his family when he refuses to enlist. Yet Macaulay's Daphne Sandomir is no marginal figure, nor is she in any way negative. An independent and political woman, she provides a distinct break with the domestic heroines of the past. Daphne is given centre stage to present the arguments for socialism and the peace movement, picking up the pacifist trends articulated in other women's war novels such as Mary Agnes Hamilton's *Dead Yesterday* (1916).[53] Macaulay allows Daphne's family to criticise her views so that the impression of dialogism is retained, but the dynamism of her personality, to some extent, precludes their disapproval as she sweeps Alix along in her wake to search for other recruits, with powerful oration:

> Ignoring: that's always been the curse of this world. We shut our eyes to things – poverty, and injustice, and vice, and cruelty, and sweating, and slums, and the tendencies which make war, and we feed ourselves on batter, and so go on from day to day getting fatter – and so the evils too go from day to day getting fatter, till they get so corpulent and heavy that when we do open our eyes at last, because we have to, they can scarcely be moved at all. It's sheer criminal selfishness and laziness and stupidity . . . It's those three we've got to fight. We've got to replace them by hard working, hard living, and hard thinking. And the last must come first. We've got to *think*, and make everyone think.[54]

Alix analyses the pacifist meetings that she attends with her mother in the same way that she contemplates her excursions into religion. Her decision to join the movement surprises her brother, who is used to sharing her isolation, but it gives her a direction in which to channel her creative energy until the climate is again right for art:

> As I can't be fighting in the war, I've got to be fighting against it. Otherwise its like a ghastly nightmare, swallowing one up. This society of mother's mayn't be doing much, but it's *trying* to fight war; it's working against it in the best ways it can think of. So I shall join it.[55]

To some extent, Alix has to relinquish her individuality in order to retain it. Like Michael Harrison she chooses to become one of a group, but in order to preserve the sanity which is essential to her art. As a pacifist she remains peripheral, and the 'otherness' which is necessary to make her art innovatory is protected. Macaulay herself, in the creation of a work which so clearly highlights the problematic nature of the war for many people, colludes in the foregrounding of the novel as a piece of modernist art, breaking with the more orthodox conventions of the past. The war does not necessarily stifle modernisms; it can produce them as a way of articulating the experience.

Claire Tylee, in her assessment of *Non-Combatants and Others* accepts its 'unVictorian' tendencies; however she also argues that by 'alternating between cynicism and religiosity, Rose Macaulay found no new mental framework, no new literary language, to replace the old ones from which she was now alienated'.[56] I would argue that she finds a female modernist language of uncertainty, ambiguity and defamiliarisation. It is precisely because she offers no definitive answers that Macaulay takes her novel convincingly into the area of literary modernisms. Whereas May Sinclair's characters discuss modernist techniques in her narrative, but ultimately reject them for a more conventional romantic form, Rose Macaulay adopts new modes of writing to bring an ambiguity to her text in keeping with the literary experiments of the age and the uncertain atmosphere of the time. It is her examination of the role of the unconventional artist, that crucial modernist figure, which enables her to do this so effectively.

Macaulay investigates and illustrates the effect of the war on art and the artist both through the multiple voices of her characters and an ambivalent narrative voice. The polyphonic nature of her novel operates to diminish the role of this omniscient narrator, as she experiments with the prose form. She makes no claim to any overriding literary, political or teleological insight. She asks the questions, but it is up to the reader to seek further to find the answers.

Art, pacifism, sexuality: Rose Allatini's *Despised and Rejected*

There is none of Macaulay's ambiguity in Rose Allatini's *Despised and Rejected*, a novel, written under the asexual pseudonym A. T. Fitzroy, which details the struggles of conscientious objectors and clearly advocates the pacifist cause. Allatini's literary rebellion is consolidated in the way in which she addresses issues that can be identified as common themes in the literary modernisms of women. Motifs of 'otherness', gender roles, sexuality and sexual taboos create the substance of her pacifist argument, doubtless all adding to the circumstances which caused the novel to be banned within six months of its publication.

This novel, even more than the two previously examined, passionately insists upon the spiritual ascendancy of the artist, and the need for art to survive the war in the interests of all civilisation. At the same time, it expounds a philosophy of androgyny as the way forward in both art and society if humankind is to avoid falling prey to the social devolution threatened by the war. At times Allatini's arguments seem to resemble those of Mabel St Clair Stobart in *The Flaming Sword*,[57] but her emphasis does not take the form of an essentialist claim for the primacy of women and motherhood. Nor is she content with the ideas of HD in *Bid Me to Live*,[58] or of Virginia Woolf in *A Room of One's Own*: 'It is fatal to be a man or woman pure and simple; one must be woman-manly or man-womanly.'[59] Instead Allatini gives her ideas of androgyny a physical manifestation in the form of male and female homosexuals. Her concepts are not without their flaws, but her novel engages with radical modernisms that were undoubtedly created by the apocalyptic presence of the First World War.

However, it was not officially because of the sexually deviant nature of its content that *Despised and Rejected* was withdrawn in October 1918. The original publisher, C. W. Daniel was prosecuted under the Defence Regulations because the book was 'likely to prejudice the recruiting of persons to serve in His Majesty's Forces, and their training and discipline'.[60] The threat to the patriotic cause was made especially dangerous by the highlighting of a number of marginal groups, among them artists, who stand out against the masses in a way which suggests a kind of spiritual superiority. It is their union through pacifism that gives most substance to this élitism. The unorthodox bravery of their stand against the dictates of militarism undermines the traditional notions of heroism with which they refuse to comply when they will not enlist. And, this time, the courage of the objecting pacifist is not subordinated to that of the trench soldier. Instead the soldier is represented as a misguided victim, lacking the individual initiative to stand up for his own rights in the face of a degenerate patriarchy.

By centralising marginal groups within her text, Allatini seems to be using her art to articulate the modernist message of aesthetic élitism. But she uses the shape of the traditional romance novel to disguise this voice, and consequently the novel received some sympathy from contemporary reviewers. The *Times Literary Supplement* said:

A well-written novel – evidently the work of a woman – on the subject of pacifism and of abnormality in the affections. The author's sympathy is plainly with the pacifists; and her plea for a more tolerant recognition of the fact that some people are, not of choice but by nature, abnormal in their affections is open and bold enough to rob the book of unpleasant suggestion. As a frank and sympathetic study of certain types of mind and character, it is of interest; but it is not to be recommended for general reading.[61]

Thus, although *Despised and Rejected* was not universally condemned, as a piece of art it was marginalised in the same way as its subjects. However, to the modern reader, it offers a new way of looking at the implications of the representation of the artist in women's fiction of the First World War.

For the central character, Dennis Blackwood, the struggle to come to terms with his homosexuality is inextricably linked to his own artistic creativity; he is a musician. Rose Allatini was herself a student of music who married a composer, Cyril Scott. After their separation in 1941, Allatini spent the rest of her life living with a woman, Melanie Mills, in Rye. It is possible to imagine then, that Dennis's inner conflicts are not without foundation in Allatini's own experience. Dennis learns first to accept the 'otherness' of his status as a musician, before the traumas of the war force him to confront the 'otherness' of his sexuality, and all are brought together in his ultimate artistic expression, 'a great symphonic poem, "War"';[62] a marriage of war and modernist art.

This musical theme is picked up again in later war fiction. In Mary Agnes Hamilton's *Special Providence* in 1930,[63] Jean Claviger is a pianist who uses her music as a way to discover feeling and expression as the events of the war threaten to overwhelm her. Similarly Jinnie Gardiner, the heroine of Ruth Holland's 1932 novel *The Lost Generation*, is a violinist who thinks of the war in musical terms, 'The war months were dragging on like a terrible insistent tune, repeated over and over again, nagging louder and louder. Everyone was taut, strained, unnatural, trembling on the verge of hysteria'.[64] Richard Aldington applies the same metaphor to the front line in *Death Of A Hero*: 'CRASH! Like an orchestra at the signal of a baton the thousands of guns north and south opened up.'[65]

But in conceiving of Dennis's composition 'War', Allatini is pre-empting this usage and the 'great symphonic poem' extends the metaphor to encompass all aspects of the conflict, including the pacifist fight against it. It also includes all the emotional anxiety that is bound up with Dennis's gradual admission of his own homosexuality. Like Stephen Gordon in Radclyffe Hall's *The Well of Loneliness*,[66] Dennis finds real love when he is forced to confront the war directly. The isolation of his status as a pacifist prevents this pleasure from being more than a fleeting one, but it inspires him to reach new artistic heights with his musical compositions. Art, pacifism and sexuality are all bound up together in one creative wall of sound.

In keeping with the modernist undertones of the text, Dennis's music breaks with tradition as he instinctively experiments with the concepts of the avant-garde to create a new art for a new generation. Allatini hints at this distancing from convention in her opening pages, although the implications are again blurred by the recurring pastoral idyll of the 1914 summer setting, and the adolescent voice of his younger brother, "'Well it *is* mouldy," insisted the boy, "there's no tune in it, however hard you listen for one".'[67] In fact, Dennis uses his music to try to present a genuine polyphony, attempting to articulate within it the many voices of those oppressed by the war:

> The voice of each he would transfuse into his music. He would make himself the medium through which their individuality, their thoughts, their dreams, their yearnings should be expressed. His brain teemed with the new bold harmonies into which they would be orchestrated. This symphony of his should be as international as art itself; as international as the heart of the man who, seeing beyond hedges and frontiers and class-distinctions, claims the whole world as his 'country', and claims kinship with all people who walk upon the face of it.[68]

So Allatini's socialist/pacifist ideas are bound inextricably within an artistic metaphor. It is only those with a creative gift who can find the voice to speak for the inarticulate masses and give form to the radical ideas of those marginalised by society. Dennis's brainchild is a new opera based on Hans Andersen's fairy tale, 'Karen and the Red Shoes', for which he desires 'an entirely modern impressionistic setting'.[69] The theme of the opera also provides a chilling metaphor which runs throughout the novel, connecting the production of art with intense suffering, which again emphasises the painful isolation of the artist in wartime. As Dennis asserts, 'I'd got to be [a] musician, even if it did mean being different and being lonely. I knew I'd got to suffer, and by suffering – create'.[70]

With the coming of the war Dennis refuses to enlist, to the horror of his family. But the presence of the war around him and his fear that Alan, the man whom he secretly loves, will take the path of conventional heroism, drive him on to create a modernist music which conveys all the anguish of the military cataclysm: 'Deeper and deeper into the crazy depths of the nightmare – nightmare set to his own horrible music, filled with strange faces, figures, voices; and almost like a futurist picture, with bits of streets, buildings, bridges, where he had caught a glimpse of this one, and that'.[71] Dennis's fragmented consciousness reflects the modern artistic atmosphere of the time. This, together with the continual narrative emphasis on his peculiarity, his 'otherness', presents him as a kind of physical embodiment of the modernisms in the arts that opposed the First World War.

As I have already suggested, some of the more radical aspects of *Despised and Rejected* are initially disguised by a pretence that the novel will comply with a more traditional romantic form, in contrast to *The Tree of Heaven* which uses this form to supersede the modernist innovations which are inappropriate to its message.[72] Dennis spends a lot of time trying to forget Alan and, instead, to fall in love with the beautiful and vivacious Antoinette de Courcy in order to retain some degree of sexual 'normality'. But his attraction to her is born of a sense of recognition; he believes that she, too, is attracted to members of her own sex. With the reintroduction of Alan into his life as the danger of conscription mounts, he is unable to live a lie and breaks off their relationship. Not, however, until Antoinette has herself fallen in love with him, a phenomenon that he explains by suggesting that it is the woman in him that attracts her while 'masculine' men leave her cold.

Antoinette keeps up the pretence of a conventional romance plot even when she knows it is hopeless, preventing the possibility of any satisfying romantic closure for the novel. But her clandestine character, which Dennis reveals to her, belies the image of the traditional heroine that she superficially presents. These two go to a costume party, a masquerade in a world on the brink of war. But while the other guests attempt to disguise their identity, Antoinette and Dennis inadvertently reveal theirs. He, arriving late, has no costume, yet the implications are that he is masquerading when he appears to conform to the conventional image of an ordinary man. Antoinette is a bacchante, betraying the decadent nature that prevents her from recognising any immorality in her desire to give herself to Dennis, or to cultivate homosexual relationships. Yet together they stand out against the carnivalesque atmosphere of the party as emblems of sanity, made different from those who surround them by the spiritual superiority of the few.

The 'few', the representatives of the minority groups who make up the pacifist underground, are all given voice in Allatini's text creating a vocal polyphony similar to that found in *Non-Combatants and Others*. *Despised and Rejected* links pacifism to many marginalised groups including socialists, Jews and the Irish, as well as artists and homosexuals, although most of those who meet with Dennis and Antoinette are nominally artistic as well.[73] They meet in a café which is literally under ground, and the constant vision of 'the legs and feet of the passers-by; legs and feet without bodies and heads, continually passing and passing'[74] is reminiscent of the human fragments of those conventionally crippled by the war in the world above ground.[75] But the pacifists too are crippled by the war in ways which highlight a different kind of heroism, the heroism of the estranged.

Gradually, one by one, the conscientious objectors are called up, appeal and, in most cases, are condemned to hard labour in prison, the only alternative to combatant or non-combatant service. The hardships of prison life are presented as a parallel to experience in the trenches, involving a similar danger of crippling injury and death. Indeed, it is suggested that the objector may require more courage than the soldier, since by defying social convention he will have to confront his 'otherness', and literally relinquish the rights to citizenship.[76] In *Most Dangerous Women*, Ann Wiltsher reports: 'Many conscientious objectors were forced to live in filthy, dark and cramped conditions with inadequate food; they were beaten up, and mentally and physically tortured. Many had their health permanently ruined and some committed suicide.'[77]

This is precisely the treatment that Dennis is forced to watch Alan receive as he himself waits for his own arrest after a final appeal. Both men seem to demonstrate a kind of existential heroism that separates them from their more conventional contemporaries.[78] Ultimately, it is essential that they stand up for the principles which will preserve their art and prove them to be 'agents of civilisation' indeed.

Harriet Monroe used her periodical, *Poetry*, to speak out for the importance of the artist during the crisis for civilisation presented by the war:

> Never was the artist more necessary than now – his freedom of spirit, his self-assertion, his creative fire. When the whole world is in the melting pot, when civilisation is to be reminted and no one can tell what stamp its face and reverse will bear . . . then the stand of the individual against immensities, a stand always hazardous, becomes a gesture of incredible power and pride, an attitude of almost impossible heroism.[79]

Monroe identifies the heroism of objectors publicly (she is commenting in general terms). Such heroism is represented here by Dennis and Alan. Indeed she suggests that this bravery is just one more example of the spiritual ascendancy of these individuals. In this assertion Monroe parallels the voice of reason in Allatini's novel, the crippled writer Neil Barnaby.

The ringleader of the café pacifists, he is himself exempt from military service because of his severe physical deformity, and consequently presents a stable pillar to which the others may cling until one by one they lose their appeals or their own personal battles against the war. Barnaby articulates the novel's aesthetic meta-commentary that echoes Monroe's doctrine and forms Allatini's central anti-war theme:

> it's the sacred duty of everyone who's got the gift of creation to try and keep it intact. When the war is over we shall be grateful to those who through the long night of destruction have kept alight the torch of art and intellect. That's rendering a greater service to mankind than putting your life at the disposal of the war-machine.[80]

This is presumably what Harriet Monroe means when she writes of the artist as 'an advance agent of civilisation which means wisdom, forbearance, humour, joy in life and magnanimity in death'[81] Allatini, like some of her contemporary modernist theorists, is advocating the élitism of the artist; a condition which is magnified by the threat of the war.

The identification between this aesthetic elitism and the conscientious objectors serves to highlight for the reader a real danger of the war for art which May Sinclair tries to disguise. Again it is Barnaby who speaks out in another of the staged political set pieces which Allatini uses to break with traditional narrative forms and ensure that her message is heard:[82]

> But it doesn't seem to strike people that shutting up some of these C.O.s in prison is deliberate, wilful murder of brains that are fine, sensitive instruments which might have brought some lasting beauty, some lasting wonder into the world. These men might be rendering far greater service to their country by following their natural bent than by doing navvies' work or performing silly brutalising tasks in prison.[83]

Just as the war stifles Alix Sandomir's art, so it destroys Dennis's ability as a composer; his hands are ruined for the piano by his hard labour, breaking stones in a quarry. Alan, a potential socialist leader, is crippled by torture and ill health.

But as Barnaby delivers his final monologue in a cafe empty of all but Antoinette, he moves beyond physicality to analyse this artistic primacy on a more spiritual level. His is not the religious spirituality of Sinclair and Macaulay, but a plea for an atheistic androgyny that will liberate humankind from the degenerate state into which it has fallen. Like Mabel St Clair Stobart, Barnaby argues that the patriarchal, masculine principles of government which have controlled society for so long, must have failed if such a war as this has been allowed to take place. However it is not woman who must lead the way forward in Barnaby's version, but some other being, a product of a perfect evolution which blends the sexes to create a new harmony. Barnaby's crippled body and overt wisdom render him effectively sexless and an appropriate spokesman for an 'advance guard of a more enlightened civilisation', 'who stand mid-way between the extremes of the two sexes'.[84] The advance guard are the homosexual community but this is no longer about physical sexuality; the homoeroticism detailed earlier in the novel gives way to Allatini's climax of spiritual hope, what evolution may yet produce:

> the human soul complete in itself, perfectly balanced, not limited by the psychological bounds of one sex, but combining the power and the intellect of the one with the subtlety and intuition of the other; a dual nature, possessing the extended range, the attributes of both sides, and therefore loving and beloved of both alike.[85]

Rose Allatini may lack the literary sophistication of Virginia Woolf, but it should be remembered that this text pre-dates *A Room of One's Own* by over ten years, and her arguments are born from a preoccupation with the injustice of the First World War rather than with the nature and process of women's writing. Samuel Hynes argues:

> Rose Allatini saw them [pacifism and homosexuality] as somehow connected, two aspects of a better civilisation that the future might bring. It was a strange prediction to make at such a time, but a comprehensible one, if you stop to think about it: Masculinity in 1918 was manifested in two ways – in heterosexuality, and in war. Allatini's hero stood against both and was punished. But perhaps the future, the world-after-the-war, would be more liberal, and more peaceable.[86]

Equally, *Despised and Rejected* does not present so coherent a pacifist diatribe as Woolf's *Three Guineas*.[87] The war is too close, too immediate. There is not enough time for such a reasoned argument and there are too many other related causes to consider. Nevertheless there can be no doubt about the overriding political message of the text. The blurring of gender in Allatini's novel presents new ways of looking at such politics as well as at the spiritual elevation of the artist, both as an emerging pattern in the development of modernisms in women's writing, and as a response to the destruction of civilisation threatened by the First World War.

In *Modernist Fiction* Randall Stevenson suggests, 'Art and artists begin to figure centrally in modernist fiction because apparently they, almost alone, offered a possibility of dealing with or escaping from the futile and anarchic history their authors surveyed'.[88] The First World War brought this anarchic history firmly and frighteningly into the present. Responding to that threat, May Sinclair, Rose Macaulay and Rose Allatini used their novels to examine the 'otherness' of the artist by identifying the marginalisation of creative groups during a time of national crisis. All three consider the hypothesis that, as 'agents of civilisation', artists need to use their aesthetic enlightenment to fight against that crisis, which manifests itself in militarism, and threatens to engulf the whole of society. Sinclair is unable to follow the argument through. Her patriotism gets the last word as Michael Harrison blends with the crowd and any creative inspiration is quenched along with his life on the Western Front. Rose Macaulay stays with the message of the importance of the artist, but is unable to provide any answers. The war is too much of a powerful force, leaving Alix Sandomir floundering against the tide, hoping that pacifist action may help her to survive, but by no means certain. Allatini's text is more radical with its dissenting blend of art, sex and politics as Dennis Blackwood attempts to convey a myriad of different emotions through his turbulent music.

To some extent *Despised and Rejected* began to embody the very art that war-torn society was attempting to displace when it was banned in 1918. Yet as Claire Tylee points out, it is not just Allatini who has been marginalised, but so many of the women who were actively writing during the First World War; 'In 1930 Cyril Falls failed to list either Mary Hamilton's *Dead Yesterday*, or Rose Macaulay's *Non-Combatants and Others*, or Rose Allatini's *Despised and Rejected* in his annotated *War Books: A Critical Guide*'.[89] May Sinclair's *The Tree of Heaven* has been out of print since the end of the war. The rediscovery of these novels, and their contributions to the debate on the status of art and the process of its creation during such cataclysmic years, combats their earlier marginalisation. Critical attention to examine the way in which they provide important new ways of looking at links between the First World War and the development of literary modernisms in the work of women writers is long overdue. This chapter has begun to redress the balance. In the final chapter I shall look at the work of women who used other modernisms to re-create their own experiences of the war and its aftermath in their fiction.

Notes

1 Harriet Monroe (1987), from *Poetry* (March 1917), quoted in Gillian Hanscombe and Virginia L. Smyers (eds), *Writing for their Lives: The Modernist Women 1910–1940*, London, Women's Press, p. 155.
2 May Sinclair (1917), *The Tree of Heaven*, London, Cassell, p. 253.

3 Harriet Monroe, 'Poet's Circular' originally quoted in Daniel Cahill (1973), *Harriet Monroe*, New York, Twayne, p. 356, in turn quoted here by Hanscombe and Smyers (eds), *Writing for their Lives*, p. 160.
4 Randall Stevenson (1992), *Modernist Fiction: An Introduction*, London, Harvester Wheatsheaf, p. 156.
5 Hanscombe and Smyers (eds), *Writing for their Lives*.
6 Rose Macaulay (1986), *Non-Combatants and Others*, London, Methuen (first published 1916); Rose Allatini (A. T. Fitzroy) (1988), *Despised and Rejected*, London, GMP (first published 1918).
7 For more detailed information of C. F. G. Masterman and the 'Authors' Manifesto' see Samuel Hynes (1990), *A War Imagined*, London, Bodley Head, p. 26; Peter Buitenhuis (1987), *The Great War of Words: Literature as Propaganda 1914–18 and After*, London, B. T. Batsford.
8 James Longenbach (1989), 'The Women and Men of 1914', in Helen M. Cooper, Adrienne A. Munich and Susan M. Squier (eds), *Arms and the Woman: War, Gender and Literary Representation*, Chapel Hill, NC, and London, University of North Carolina Press.
9 May Sinclair's use of the term 'vortex' may have been influenced by Wyndham Lewis's coining of the word in his (1914), *BLAST. The Review of the Great English Vortex, Volume 1* (reproduced in Peter Faulkner (ed.) (1986), *A Modernist Reader: Modernism in England 1910–1930*, London, B. T. Batsford), which presented a manifesto for the Vorticist movement. Fundamental was the notion of 'an art of Individuals'. Its message can be applied to each of the Harrison children in different ways.
10 The tank was developed as a weapon during the First World War and first appeared on the Somme on 15 September 1916. This early form was very primitive and had a limited effect on the battle. For a detailed discussion of the history and symbolism of the tank see Trudi Tate (1998), *Modernism, History and the First World War*, Manchester, Manchester University Press.
11 Claire M. Tylee (1990), *The Great War and Women's Consciousness*, London, Macmillan, p. 132.
12 Richard Aldington (1929), *Death of a Hero*, London, Chatto & Windus.
13 Sinclair, *Tree of Heaven*, p. 39.
14 *Ibid.*, p. 214.
15 *Ibid.*, p. 166.
16 HD (1972), 'Oread', in Peter Jones (ed.), *Imagist Poetry*, London, Penguin.
17 Sinclair, *Tree of Heaven*, p. 216.
18 *Ibid.*, p. 276.
19 Paul Fussell (1977), *The Great War and Modern Memory*, Oxford, Oxford University Press, p. 271
20 Most contemporary propaganda novels presented pacifism as a negative force. The objector was often drawn as a coward or very misguided. A good

example may be found in the character of Julian, the politically naïve pacifist in Elizabeth Robins's (1919) novel, *The Messenger*, London, Hodder & Stoughton. Sinclair's 'conflict of interests' prevents her from presenting Michael Harrison in quite such a simplistic way.

21 May Sinclair (1916), *Tasker Jevons*, London, Hutchinson. The character of James Tasker Jevons was reputedly based on H. G. Wells.
22 Sinclair, *Tree of Heaven*, p. 288.
23 *Ibid.*, p. 285.
24 *Ibid.*, p. 337.
25 *Ibid.*
26 *Ibid.*, p. 324.
27 Henri Barbusse (1974), *Under Fire*, London, J. M. Dent (first published 1917).
28 Sinclair, *Tree of Heaven*, p. 348.
29 *Ibid.*, p. 345.
30 *Ibid.*, p. 349.
31 Unlike Michael Harrison, Richard Aldington, upon whom Sinclair's character was reputedly based, found it very difficult to write poetry in the trenches, raising questions about her representation.
32 Edith Wharton (1923), *A Son at the Front*, London, Macmillan.
33 Tylee, *The Great War*, p. 133.
34 Macaulay, *Non-Combatants*, p. 4.
35 *Ibid.*, pp. 6–7.
36 Rose Macaulay (1915), 'Many Sisters to Many Brothers': 'Oh it's you that have the luck, out there in blood and muck:/You were born beneath a kindly star;/All we dreamt, I and you, you can really go and do,/And I can't, the way things are./In a trench you are sitting, while I am knitting/A hopeless sock that never gets done./Well, here's luck, my dear – you've got it no fear;/But for me . . . a war is poor fun.' Reproduced in Catherine Reilly (ed.) (1992), *Scars Upon My Heart*, London, Virago, p. xxxv.
37 Macaulay, *Non-Combatants*, p. 9. The anxiety regarding a lack of personal role in the war that Macaulay expresses in her early war poetry and in *Non-Combatants and Others* is also common in contemporary women's war fiction. For another good example see Romer Wilson (1919), *If All These Young Men*, London, Methuen.
38 Macaulay also addresses many of the same issues, albeit much more briefly, in her later novel (1923), *Told by an Idiot*, London, W. Collins.
39 M. M. Bakhtin (1981), *The Dialogic Imagination*, ed. M. Holquist, trans. M. Holquist and C. Emerson Austin, TX, University of Texas Press, p. 315.
40 Macaulay, *Non-Combatants*, p. 18.
41 *Ibid.*, p. 21.
42 For more on the neurasthenia associated with this war, often labelled as 'shell shock' or 'hysteria', see discussion in Chapter 6 of this volume; Elaine

Showalter (1987), *The Female Malady*, London, Virago, ch. 7; Tate, *Modernism*, ch. 1; Joanna Bourke (1996), *Dismembering the Male: Men's Bodies, Britain and the First World War*, London, Reaktion Books.

43 Macaulay, *Non-Combatants*, p. 69.

44 Hynes, *A War Imagined*, p. 126, believes this to be the first appearance of such an event in fiction. Later it becomes much more common. For example, see Aldington *Death of a Hero*; Vera Brittain (1936), *Honourable Estate*, London, Victor Gollancz.

45 Hynes, *A War Imagined*, p. 129, has commented thus on Sandomir's speech: 'It is an important passage in the book; it is also important in the larger context of English wartime culture. For it asserts that the war is not an event in history but a *gap*, an annihilation of pre-war reality, and that neither art nor life can simply resume the old continuities when the war ends. This is of course a primary tenet of post-war Modernism; it is worth noting that it emerged during the war years, and in the works of writers like H.G. Wells and Rose Macaulay who were not Modernists in the usual sense of the term.'

46 Macaulay, *Non-Combatants*, p. 45.

47 *Ibid.*

48 Susan M Squier (1990), 'Rose Macaulay', in Bonnie Kime Scott (ed.), *The Gender of Modernism*, Bloomington and Indianapolis, IN, Indiana University Press, p. 253.

49 James Joyce (1965), *Portrait of the Artist as a Young Man*, London, Penguin (first published 1916).

50 'Violette' is the home of Mrs Emily Frampton, Alix's cousin by marriage, and her two daughters with whom Alix lives for a time. Theirs is the first branch of religion that Alix investigates, quickly finding it unsatisfactory.

51 Macaulay, *Non-Combatants*, p. 105.

52 *Ibid.*, p. 144.

53 Mary Agnes Hamilton (1916), *Dead Yesterday*, London, Duckworth.

54 Macaulay, *Non-Combatants*, pp. 162–3.

55 *Ibid.*, p. 185.

56 Tylee, *The Great War*, p. 118.

57 Mary St Clair Stobart (1916), *The Flaming Sword in Serbia and Elsewhere*, London, Hodder & Stoughton.

58 HD (1984), *Bid Me to Live*, London, Virago (first published 1960).

59 Virginia Woolf (1990), *A Room of One's Own*, London, Grafton (first published 1929), p. 99.

60 A line from the Defence Regulations quoted in Jonathan Cutbill (1988), 'Introduction', *Despised and Rejected*, London, GMP (first published 1918).

61 *Times Literary Supplement*, quoted in Cutbill, 'Introduction'.

62 Allatini, *Despised and Rejected*, p. 317.

63 Mary Agnes Hamilton (1930), *Special Providence*, London, George Allen & Unwin.

64 Ruth Holland (1932), *The Lost Generation*, London, Victor Gollancz, p. 137.
65 Aldington, *Death of a Hero*, p. 435.
66 Radclyffe Hall (1994), *The Well of Loneliness*, London, Virago (first published 1928).
67 Allatini, *Despised and Rejected*, p. 14.
68 *Ibid.*, p. 200.
69 *Ibid.*, p. 78.
70 *Ibid.*, p. 83.
71 *Ibid.*, p. 160.
72 Sinclair, *Tree of Heaven*.
73 Another contemporary novel which focuses on the problems of minority groups during the war is G. B. Stern's (1919), *Children of No Man's Land*, London, Duckworth. The novel concentrates on the lives of the Marcus family who are German Jews living in London during the First World War. In addition see Samuel Hynes on links between pacifism and homosexuality which grew out of the wartime interest in Oscar Wilde within certain artistic groups and the subsequent the Pemberton-Billing trial (Hynes, *A War Imagined*, ch. 11).
74 Allatini, *Despised and Rejected*, p. 204.
75 Tylee, *The Great War*, p. 126; Sharon Ouditt (1994), *Fighting Forces, Writing Women*, London, Routledge, p. 156.
76 Convicted conscientious objectors forfeited their rights to citizenship in that they were removed from the electoral roll for several years after the end of the war. An excellent modern fictional account of experience of conscientious objectors can be found in Pat Barker's novel (1993), *The Eye in the Door*, London, Penguin.
77 Ann Wiltsher (1985), *Most Dangerous Women*, London, Pandora, p. 146.
78 See discussion of theories of heroism in John Onions (1990), *English Fiction and Drama of the Great War*, London, Macmillan.
79 Monroe, 'Poet's Circular', p.160.
80 Allatini, *Despised and Rejected*, p. 242.
81 Monroe, from *Poetry*, p. 155.
82 Ouditt, *Fighting Forces*, p.156.
83 Allatini, *Despised and Rejected*, p. 343.
84 *Ibid.*, p. 348.
85 *Ibid.*, p. 349.
86 Hynes, *A War Imagined*, p. 234.
87 Virginia Woolf (1992), *A Room of One's Own* and *Three Guineas*. Oxford and New York, Oxford University Press (first published 1929 and 1938 respectively).
88 Stevenson, *Modernist Fiction*, p. 163.
89 Tylee, *The Great War*, p. 128.

6

Happy foreigners: female modernisms

'Yet you will be happy without me,' he said suddenly . . .
'You've some solace, some treasure of your own.' . . .
'You're a happy foreigner!'[1]

Fanny, the heroine of Enid Bagnold's 1920 novel *The Happy Foreigner* achieves her state of bliss in the face of adversity because she is independent enough to retain her identity in an alien land. There is nothing on the battlefields of post-war France that can shake the confident autonomy with which she conducts herself, secure in her own sense of her identity, status and role. To some extent the war is responsible. Fanny is of the generation of women who have lived through the worst and survived. Now she can apply her own personal talents in a society that has grown ready for her. She precipitates a simple analogy. During and after the war, women writers of Fanny's generation were able to consolidate the experience of the conflict, both direct and indirect, as a focus for the development of experimental narrative techniques; female modernisms.

Randall Stevenson argues that women were extremely important in the development of modernist writing, 'Uneasiness with ordinary language and consequent readiness to reject conventional forms of representation almost forced women writers, in the early twentieth century, into the position . . . at the centre of modernist innovation and stylistic experiment.'[2] Their status as women makes them metaphoric foreigners in the male-dominated literary landscape, searching for new ways to express their experience and identity. Recent feminist scholarship has pointed out that many women did so through the creation of their own modernisms, connected with, yet different from, those of Eliot, Pound, Joyce and Lawrence.[3] Like Fanny, they have survived despite historical marginalisation, and their fictional representations of their wartime experience can provide a valuable interface between the writing of war and the literary innovations of the period.

This chapter draws together many of the ideas investigated earlier in this book. As we have already seen, Enid Bagnold saw service on the battlefield of the hospital ward. In 1918–19 she took a different path, one which led her into the 'forbidden zone' of the battlefields of France, no longer forbidden in the wake of a stagnant peace. She uses *The Happy Foreigner*, a fictional account of her experiences, to explore the notion of a woman's success in this distinctly male territory. Although it is not a modernist novel in the usually accepted sense, Bagnold uses the interaction between the war and womanhood both thematically and structurally to create a modernism of her own. In *The Return of the Soldier* Rebecca West focuses on the home front, illustrating another kind of battlefield through the neurasthenia of her soldier hero Chris Baldry.[4] Her experience as a journalist no doubt serves her well as she explores the interface between the war, politics and contemporary medical discourse through the 'foreign' 'feminine' responses of a modernist narrator. Unlike Bagnold, and to some extent West, Katherine Mansfield took no active role in the war. But like HD, it affected her very deeply, most directly through the death of her beloved brother in October 1915. Her journal is littered with references to the war; many, particularly those that surround her loss, are very painful. Others, however, suggest excitement. For Mansfield, too, entered the forbidden zone of the war both physically and intellectually, and this is reflected in the experimentation of some of her fiction.

'I have broken the silence': Katherine Mansfield's war

Four months after the death of her brother 'Chummie',[5] Katherine Mansfield managed to begin writing again. The story was called 'The Aloe', an early version of 'Prelude', one of her most elegiac and beautiful works, and one for which she has received much critical acclaim. It deals, not with the war, but with memories of the New Zealand childhood that she shared with her brother. She wrote it for him:

> I have broken the silence. It took long. Did I fail you when I sat reading? Oh bear with me a little. I will be better. I will do *all*, all that we would wish. Love, I will not fail . . . Now I will come quite close to you, take your hand, and we shall tell this story to each other.[6]

The depth of her grief is indicated by her personal and intimate rejection of all other aspects of her life:

Dearest heart, I know you are there, and I live with you, and I will write for you. Other people are near, but they are not close to me. To you only do I belong, just as *you* belong to me . . . You know I can never be Jack's lover again.[7] You have me. You're in my flesh as well as in my soul. I will give Jack my 'surplus' love, but to you I give my deepest love. Jack is no more than . . . anybody might be.[8]

Mansfield and her brother had discussed her writing the stories of their past during his army training in England before his embarkation for France. Devastated and possibly suicidal after his death, Mansfield determined that she would live only to fulfil this wish. It was a creative process triggered by the war that demonstrates the essence of Mansfield's modernism. The fragmented, stream of consciousness narratives of 'Prelude', fragile and delicate, built around the 'ordinary' the 'everyday' and the 'feminine', epitomise the style and form of the Mansfield story. From within the harmony of the setting she implies the unspeakable, the tragedy of the lost.

Her chosen genre, the short story, is a frequently marginalised form which has been identified by feminist critics as a primary tool of many of the pioneers of female modernisms.[9] Although criticised as being a minor art form by many of Mansfield's contemporaries, T. S. Eliot among them,[10] the short story, the fragment often dealing with peripheral members of society, is ideally suited both as a forum for narrative experiments, and as is demonstrated in much writing of the period, as a vehicle for articulating the experience of war.[11]

Mansfield's writing suggests an interest in the self, and the construction of the self through the ordinary and domestic processes of living which can be identified in her journal entries concerning her duty to her brother's memory. But it is a structure that is echoed across the wider spectrum of her work. Judy Simons suggests:

> Katherine Mansfield's search for a unified identity is both a central theme of her personal writing and one which informs her fiction, as she experimented with different 'voices' and filtered episodes from her own life through a variety of literary perspectives in order to catch the 'truth' of experience.[12]

This preoccupation with identity can be illustrated through much of her writing, and the way in which it aids her construction of the experience of the war is particularly interesting. In 'The Fly' (1922) the central character, the boss, a man unable to come to terms with the loss of his son in the war, becomes fascinated by the struggles of a fly which has fallen into his ink pot.[13] He admires its courage, yet he covers it with more ink whenever it manages to break free. On the one hand the fly represents the boss's son, destroyed by an older generation who forced him to return again and again to war. But the complexity of the story comes in the examination of the boss's own psyche, as he both admires and identifies with the fly and yet continues to torture it until it dies. The conflict seriously complicates notions of 'truth' as the two irreconcilable sides of the boss's self fail to find an equilibrium, making the outcome of the story uncomfortable.

Other war stories show a similar interest in constructions of identity. 'Late at Night' (1917) presents the reader with the thoughts of a woman, seated alone by her fire on a dark and wintry Sunday evening.[14] Through her stream of consciousness as she peruses a letter from a soldier, she reveals a great deal about her personality, ironically more than she appears to be aware of herself. The way that she reads (or perhaps misreads) the letter as a covert rejection of her advances, indicates her own lack of self-worth, leading on to her negative assessment of her life and achievements. Her disillusionment may be seen as symptomatic of both the experience of the woman and of the war. The melancholy development of the narrative, the fragmentation and dislocation of the woman's thoughts, help to present a vivid picture of discontented selfhood that seems particularly symbolic in 1917 and to Mansfield herself in her state of grief.

In 'Two Tuppenny Ones, Please' (1917), which takes the form of a one-sided dialogue, a lady gossips with a silent friend as they take a bus-ride through wartime London.[15] Again this dialogue reveals much of the character of the lady as she chatters on topics from the loss of her cars to the war effort, (hence the need to use the bus), to fashion and Bridge. The voice presented in this story is quite different from those found in 'The Fly' and 'Late at Night', illustrating Mansfield's ability to view the war from multiple perspectives which are then translated through her writing. None of these vignettes from the home front seem intent on capturing the sympathy of the reader. Instead they attempt to suggest the different selves, the different 'truths', which make up the universal experience of the First World War, an event which caused her so much pain.

But Mansfield used her personal experience of the war to direct her fiction in other ways too. Her 1915 story, 'An Indiscreet Journey', displays a contagious excitement generated by the war, as well as a more solemn overview drawn through the interaction of the characters.[16] 'An Indiscreet Journey' was based on her own clandestine visit to a lover in the forbidden zone of France in February 1915, before the death of her brother devastated her life, and provides a fine example of how subject and style may blend in the short story, presenting a valuable modernist literary fragment.

Mansfield's story is divided into three parts. The narrator is a young woman defying the military authorities to spend time with her lover, 'the little corporal' in a French town close to the front line.[17] The sexual implications of the journey are not made explicit in the first section. The reader is not whole-heartedly invited to collude in their conspiracy. We, like the military police at every station, are told only that she is to visit her aunt and uncle. Yet the narrative is filled with hints of her indiscretion from the echoing words of her bitter old concierge ('You will never get there . . . Never! Never!'[18]), to her discomfort when cross-examined about her motive for the journey by a woman on the train. Suspicions are confirmed at the conclusion of the first section when the narrator and her lover are locked together in a white room, specially chosen for her, and she euphemistically tells us, 'And she opened the door of the white room and shut it upon us. Down went the suitcase, the postman's bag, the *Matin*. I threw my passport up into the air, and the little corporal caught it'.[19] The passport as a metaphor for selfhood, seems particularly appropriate after the red tape through which she has had to pass in order to keep the appointment.

Mansfield's *Journal* describes this encounter in some detail, much of which parallels the early part of the story. 'M. le Colonel' with his heavy Egyptian cigarette and his 'pebble eyes' appears there as a similar menace with 'eyes like two grey stones'.[20] The forbidden cab is 'fed' with her suitcase and his postbag ' both doors flapping and banging'[21] as they fly towards their private room; those 'fools of doors'[22] which jeopardise his position in the story where 'Policemen are as thick as violets'.[23] The fictional 'white room' is 'a most extraordinary room furnished with a bed, a wax apple and an immense flowery clock'.[24]

The prevailing sense in Mansfield's personal recollections of the adventure is one of laughter: 'The whole affair seemed somehow so ridiculous, and at the same time so utterly natural. There was nothing to do but laugh.'[25] 'The act of love seemed somehow incidental, we talked so much.'[26] Removed from the private and placed within the public sphere of fiction the sexual situation has other implications and there is little sense of laughter in 'An Indiscreet Journey'.

The euphoria of the sexual liaison is, in itself, a radical presentation, engaging with modernist interest in issues surrounding sexuality. The dangerous influence of the war on both of the lovers seems to heighten the sensuality of their liaison. That neither the narrator nor 'the little

corporal' are named implies an emphasis on the impersonality of the relationship at odds with the apparent romance of the meeting in adverse
conditions. Although this relationship has a history, they recollect
Montmartre, this is not about elopement, marriage and closure.[27] It is a
sexual adventure such as Jacob Flanders is allowed to enjoy with Florinda,
but it is more radical in its representation of female rather than male
sexual experience. It is equal to the sexual frankness of Helen Zenna
Smith's *Not So Quiet...*[28] which allows women the same needs and desires
as men, particularly in a wartime situation. Mansfield's heroine performs
a sexual role similar to many of the women, not wives, in La Motte's evaluation. However, she is in control of her own destiny and in no way a
victim. The overall texture of the narrative reinforces the vagueness of her
relationship with the little corporal. In the second section the narrator
waits, alone, in a café for her friend; in the third, they drink with two other
soldiers. The fragments of experience, each with a very different atmosphere are juxtaposed to great effect.

In her *Journal*, Mansfield describes this meeting with her lover. It
occurs in 1915, and as a young Frenchman, he is inevitably in the army.
Consequently she must venture into 'the zone of the armies and not
allowed to women',[29] which adds excitement to a passion that is already
illicit. But the war intrudes. It surrounds them physically:

> The soldiers laughed and slapped each other. They tramped about in their
> heavy boots. The women looked after them, and the old man stood humbly
> waiting for someone to attend him, his cap in his hands, as if he knew that
> the life he represented in his torn jacket, with his basket of fish – his peaceful
> occupation – did not exist any more and had no right to thrust itself here.[30]

And it insinuates itself metaphorically: 'Beside me on the chair is a thick
leather belt and his sword . . . The sword, the big ugly sword, but not
between us, lying in a chair.'[31] However, the war does not part them, the
fragility of their affair is enough to do that. They love and lose in spite of
the war. Unlike that in the *Journal*, 'An Indiscreet Journey' is the story of
an experience induced by and enhanced by the war. The war itself is an
almost invisible backdrop, shaping the situation from without, rather as
it does for faded opera singer Miss Ada Moss, out of synchronisation with
the modern world in Mansfield's 'Pictures'.[32]

Giving a context to Mansfield's explorations into notions of selfhood,
Judy Simons argues:

> The enquiry into the concept of self was a crucial feature of literary mod-
> ernism and in Katherine Mansfield's work in particular we see it used to

challenge traditional stereotypical notions of women, while at the same time struggling to define and to resolve the confusions of femininity as they affected her own turbulent psyche.[33]

Unlike the less fortunate Ada Moss who struggles with her identity, or Virginia in 'Late at Night' who is uncomfortable with her own situation and psyche, the narrator of 'An Indiscreet Journey', so closely related to Mansfield herself, is very much in tune with her world and her position in it. A modernist heroine, she refuses to comply with feminine stereotypes that do seem to cause much of the confusion in the other stories. She blends in despite her alien status; she is a female observer, trespassing in a male world, resembling the narrator of Borden's 'Enfant de Malheur'. Her gender emphasises the ephemeral nature of the narrator's voice, making her distant from the action inside the café, even while she penetrates it. She reports minute details but does not participate.

> Madame came through the kitchen door, nodded to me and took her seat behind the table, her plump hands folded on the red book. *Ping* went the door. A handful of soldiers came in, took off their coats and began to play cards, chaffing and poking fun at the pretty waiting-boy, who threw up his little round head, rubbed his thick fringe out of his eyes and cheeked them back in his broken voice . . .
>
> *Ping* went the door again. Two more men came in. They sat at the table nearest Madame, and she leaned to them with a birdlike movement, her head on one side. Oh, they had a grievance! The Lieutenant was a fool – nosing about – springing out at them – and they'd only been sewing on buttons.[34]

Passing through the male war zone she captures its atmosphere distinctly, partly through the relation of her own experience in the first section as she fights to reach her destination, but mostly through her observation of others. The narrator as watcher is particularly pronounced in the second part of the story, an example of which is quoted above, when she sits and observes the life of the café as it grows busier while she awaits the arrival of her lover. She illustrates the relationship between the 'Madame' and her clientele, as they exude a kind of superficial good humour to hold off the battlefield. There is a distinct sense of living for the moment because, for these people, there may not be a tomorrow. This is conveyed through the 'ping' of the door, the laughter and the teasing. It is a man's world, yet one presided over by another female observer, 'Madame' who listens but never intervenes. Like the narrator, she only watches. Perhaps this is the role of women in this part of the forbidden zone, even those who have a legitimate place there.

There is a touch of the surreal here. Assorted soldiers arrive and are waited on by the adolescent boy suggesting chronological order but still, as in so much modernist writing, time is obscure:

> And years passed. Perhaps the war is long since over – there is no village outside at all – the streets are quiet under the grass. I have an idea this is the sort of thing one will do on the very last day of all – sit in an empty cafe and listen to a clock ticking until –[35]

This kind of temporal confusion is reminiscent of Virginia Woolf. In fact Clare Hanson argues that Woolf was influenced by both Mansfield's creative prose and her criticism of Woolf's own. Woolf recorded in her diary that Mansfield's work was 'the only writing I have ever been jealous of'.[36] Hanson suggests that Mansfield's direct criticism of the conventional form of *Night and Day* led Woolf to re-evaluate her style resulting eventually in *Jacob's Room*.[37] Certainly *An Indiscreet Journey* provides a good illustration of how Mansfield's writing may have fed the experimental development of Woolf's work. The above quotation evokes the continual striking clocks and temporal questioning of *Mrs Dalloway*. And the flaneur-like narrator of *Jacob's Room*, reconstructing a male world from the alien position of the female, resembles Mansfield's narrator/protagonist here when she steps outside of the action.

Action is an ironic term when applied to this story. Nothing really happens. In the final section the narrator and the corporal, drinking with the two other soldiers, break the military curfew to go in search of an exotic blend of whisky. The surreal atmosphere is retained as the alcohol goads them into talking of nothing, at cross-purposes.

> 'Bah, I can't stand whisky,' said the little corporal. 'It's too disgusting the morning after. Do you remember, *ma fille*, the whisky in that little bar at Montmartre?'
>
> '*Souvenir tendre*,' sighed Blackbeard, putting two fingers in the breast of his coat and letting his head fall. He was very drunk.
>
> 'But I know something that you've never tasted,' said the blue-eyed soldier, pointing a finger at me; 'something really good.' . . .
>
> 'What is it called?'
>
> 'Mirabelle!' He rolled the word round his mouth, under his tongue. 'Ah-ha, that's the stuff.'
>
> 'I could eat another mushroom,' said Blackbeard. 'I would like another mushroom very much. I am sure I could eat another mushroom if Mademoiselle gave it to me out of her hand.'[38]

Mansfield injects her text with the spirit of decadence; disregard for authority and a sense of living only for the present blend like a ghostly premonition of the ideology of the 1920s. What interests the protagonists is pleasurable sensation combined with a nostalgia for a world that no longer exists. Language itself becomes a pleasure when they have the time to appreciate it, 'He rolled the word around his mouth, under his tongue', as though it, too, may be consumed and enjoyed. The atmosphere of sensuality is laced with sexual implications when the narrator is addressed directly, 'But I know something you've never tasted, . . . something really good' again reminding the reader of her clandestine purpose in this world of men. The narrative is constructed of both English and French giving it a dialogism beyond the single voice of the narrator. She becomes the mediator, through whom the unconnected experiences of a group of individuals are disseminated. It is the war that has given her the space to do this effectively. Filtered through the unusual gaze of a woman's perception, Mansfield's modernist narrative techniques create an altered atmosphere, one of female modernism. It is as though Mansfield/the narrator is the happy foreigner, granted a vision of a male world.

Mansfield's use of language was criticised in her own time for being too 'feminine' because of its preoccupation with domestic or female images. Among her critics was T. S. Eliot who suggested, 'our satisfaction recognises the skill with which the author has handled perfectly the *minimum material*'.[39] It is the lack of interest in quasi-scientific theories of symbolism which differentiates her from Eliot and provides the essence of the innovation of her language. This extract from an early journal illustrates Mansfield's aesthetic belief:

> The partisans of analysis describe minutely the state of the soul; the secret motive of every action as being of far greater importance than the action itself. The partisans of objectivity – give us the result of this evolution sans describing the secret processes. They describe the state of the soul through the slightest gesture – i.e. realise flesh covered bones – which is the artist's method for me – in as much as art seems to me *pure vision* – I am indeed a partisan of objectivity–[40]

It is certainly a 'partisan of objectivity' who has created the narrator of 'An Indiscreet Journey' and the watching 'Madame'. The way that Mansfield translates this definition into the employment of language in her stories is rather like the implementation of Ezra Pound's Imagism without the theorising, or the 'literary Impressionism' of Ford Madox Ford.[41] Indeed the 'impression' created by some of Mansfield's prose is not dissimilar to Ford's style in *Parade's End*. As a 'partisan of objectivity' she fills her text with images that convey impressions with 'the slightest gesture'. 'An Indiscreet Journey' is fleshed out by the aesthetic techniques of the

Imagists, modified, or perhaps feminised, to comply with Mansfield's own experimental prose style. 'I ran down the echoing stairs – strange they sounded, like a piano flicked by a sleepy housemaid';[42] 'Slowly, slowly she sipped a sentence';[43] 'Through it the drip-drip of the wine from the table on to the floor. It looked very strange dropping so slowly, as though the table were crying'.[44] Through her images Mansfield adds further dimensions to her text, introducing other languages which build the dialogism, endowing each minimal event recorded by the narrator with layers of unexpected significance.

'An Indiscreet Journey' is unusual in Mansfield's work in that it places the narrator directly in a war situation, although the atmosphere of chaos propounded by the war is perceptible in many of her stories of the period. And there is a sense of anarchy inspired by the implied amorality of the narrator which reinforces the notion that the war could be a dangerously liberating experience for women. This is tempered by the symbols of innocence which accompany her, the white room, the bunch of violets on the café table; this is not a fallen woman, but an adventurous one. Perhaps it is possible to use this as a metaphor for literary development, allowing that Mansfield's experiences may have influenced the stylistics of her writing regardless of subject matter, creating adventures in literary form. Mansfield was not simply a modernist, but a female modernist, subtly altering the characteristics of male modernisms to suit her female perspective. The presence of the war as both a direct and an indirect experience added to that perspective.

Mansfield was perhaps more fortunate than other women in that she managed to get close enough to the front line for it to colour the experience she presented in her fiction. But as I have suggested, it is perhaps surprising how many women did manage to become deeply involved with the war and experience it close up, and how many of them chose to write about it. At the same time, however, it would be wrong to suggest that those women who remained at home were not able to use their less direct or different experience of the war to feed their fiction, adopting similar modernist techniques and feminising them accordingly. It was not necessary to go to France to produce experimental writing that took the war as its subject; the invasion of the war into domestic England could be just as effective.

Rebecca West: psychoanalysing the home front

The Return of the Soldier, published in 1918, was Rebecca West's first novel, although she was already established as a journalist. The novel, which takes place almost entirely in the domestic sphere of Baldry Court, has often been criticised for being a 'woman's novel', too 'feminine', dealing primarily with sentiment and emotion; not the type of fiction expected from a writer whose socialist/feminist views were well known, nor the type that has generally been read as modernist. As Suzanne Clark suggests in *Sentimental Modernism,* 'Modernist criticism located women's writing within the obscenity of sentimentality'.[45] As Clark's repudiation of such criticism suggests, it does not do justice to women's writing to so dismiss it. West's text provides a good example of how the 'woman's novel' can be innovatory despite being 'sentimental', by foregrounding a number of modernist narrative experiments in a particularly successful way. It also engages with contemporary theories on psychiatry, suggesting Freudian psychoanalysis, through the medium of the war, ubiquitous although distant from this domestic setting. The war is used as a focus around which social, political and psychological debates may be built; debates which might appear foreign in a traditional 'woman's' novel'. It is not necessary to visit the Western Front in order to feel the effects and to use them for literary creation.

In fact it is West's use of the 'woman's novel' format which enables her to approach these issues and experiments from a different angle. Her narrator is a very conventional woman, feminine, but not feminist in outlook, forced to confront ideas foreign to her sphere of experience. Consequently West's modernist experiments are unexpected; they transform the expected romance into a complex debate built around issues of contemporary significance. She uses primarily 'female' experience, not usually associated with innovation, to tell a modernist war story, forcing the reader to confront issues and ideas which are too powerful to be enveloped by sentiment. West may be seen as a 'happy foreigner', carving out a new territory for a 'woman's novel' with a difference.

West herself claimed that *The Return of the Soldier* was 'complete in my mind in the middle of 1915 and complete in typescript, except for a few corrections, not very much later'.[46] The story had two origins. The first was an article in a medical journal from before the war in which a doctor described how an elderly factory hand had fallen down stairs and suffered from the delusion that he was a boy of twenty. As a result of the accident he forgot his wife and demanded to see his former sweetheart. The second was an ex-landlady of West's who made a great impression and seemed to fall into place as the sweetheart.[47]

In *The Return of the Soldier*, West blends these two sources placing them in a wartime setting. She uses the shell shock of Chris Baldry, the soldier of the title, as the cause of his amnesia. Thus the war acts as a catalyst, bringing turmoil to the domestic lives of everyone at Baldry Court. When he returns to his luxurious home, Chris has completely forgotten the life that he led there with his beautiful doll-like wife Kitty and his devoted cousin Jenny, the narrator of the novel. Instead he remembers only the girl he loved fifteen years earlier, the innkeeper's daughter on Monkey Island. The previous harmonious existence at Baldry Court operates as a metonym for the upper-class Edwardian society responsible for, and effectively destroyed by the First World War. In his shell-shocked state Chris has rejected this society. He lives in a Utopian classless world embodied in the allegorical figure of his working-class sweetheart Margaret Allington. These two inhabit a new world within the pastoral idyll of the Baldry Court gardens, while Jenny alone debates the question; should Chris be 'cured' and sent back to face metaphoric death in an archaic society represented by literal death in the trenches, or be allowed to remain in a world which makes him happy.

Claire Tylee argues of *The Return of the Soldier,* 'With the outcome of the story, Chris's return to his manifestly empty marriage, the book finally appears to endorse Jenny's views and the snobbery and vanity that destroyed Chris's inner peace'.[48] But this view fails to address the way in which West structures her narrative to explore the developing perceptions and psychological growth of her narrator. The story is related entirely through the consciousness of Jenny. Her narrative forms a kind of *bildungsroman* moving from childlike romance to an adult reality as she travels from her initial position of material bigotry to one of enlightened self-awareness. As Margaret Diane Stetz argues: 'Clearly the plot of *The Return of the Soldier* centers upon this change in the narrator's values and is, therefore, of a philosophical character. Through Jenny's emotional and intellectual struggles, we are led to a mature understanding of what modern life demands of us.'[49]

West herself stated, 'I had been obliged to tell the story in the first person, in the character of Chris's cousin Jenny, in order that I could the more vividly compare and contrast the effect Margaret produced on Chris's household with the effect she produced on Chris'.[50] This she does successfully, but Jenny's status as a peripheral member of the household, locked in by her unrequited love for Chris, adds a further dimension to the narrative. As she watches Margaret Allington, now Grey, enter and take over their lives she is forced to re-examine her own past and present position. Gradually she learns to locate herself in their history: 'I remember it well because my surprise that he passed me without seeing me had made me perceive for the first time that he had never seen me at all save in the most cursory fashion; on the eye of his mind, I realised thenceforward, I had hardly impinged'.[51] And accordingly to acknowledge her place in the present, 'A sharp movement of Kitty's body confirmed my deep, old suspicion that she hated me'.[52] But even as Jenny's existence is stultified by understanding, Margaret, once beautiful, now jaded, brings her a communion which enables her to realise a different worth. Both doomed by the prospect of Chris's return to 'health', their final embrace symbolises this change, 'We kissed, not as women, but as lovers do; I think we embraced that part of Chris the other had absorbed by her love'.[53] Through Margaret, Jenny re-examines her own identity. Her views may be endorsed, but they are actually too fluid to be as easily categorised as Tylee suggests.

Jenny's extreme emotional involvement in the events of the story, despite her marginalisation, makes her a somewhat precarious narrator. She allows the reader to see her own development; how the overt snobbery of her early views of Margaret, that 'dowd', is superseded by her understanding of the latter's innate maternal and spiritual qualities. This at times lends the text the atmosphere of a confessional, creating an impression, perhaps illusion, of authenticity. Jenny records the history of Margaret and Chris, as they supposedly related it to her, he the tale of their romance, she the futile misunderstanding that led to their parting. But the stream of consciousness nature of the narrative identifies Jenny as a modernist narrator and leads to questions about her reliability. 'I have lived so long with the story which he told me that I cannot now remember his shy phrases. But this is how I have visualized his meeting with love on his secret island. I think it is the truth.'[54] But whose 'truth' does she tell? The other voices that creep into this text are held captive within Jenny's subjective vision. Influenced by the literary experiments of Henry James, West omits crucial scenes, allowing them to be perceived only through Jenny's peripheral gaze. The emotional impact of Chris's reunion with Margaret, and later his sad reawakening when Margaret reveals to him the memory that can cure him, are conveyed entirely through the responses of Jenny, and her shadow Kitty, both excluded from the scenes. Like Mansfield's heroine of 'An Indiscreet Journey', Jenny too is an observer, but she is much more voyeuristic and the images that she presents are filtered through her consciousness to a degree that it becomes impossible to decipher the 'truth'.

As Sharon Ouditt suggests of Chris, 'Paradoxically, the world he occupies in his insanity is saner than the real world.'[55] It is this sense of the hyper-real that colours much of Jenny's narrative; her interpretation becomes more real than the 'truth'. The war triggers a chain of events that enables Jenny to psychoanalyse herself through the text, searching the past for a way to understand the present. The result is a psychological study of a woman, by a woman. The innovatory nature of this analysis, as Jenny learns to understand herself by thinking back through the others around her and her interaction with them, makes the narrative much more complicated than might be expected from the structures of a traditional 'woman's novel'. Jenny's conventional attitudes, which reflect the feminine ideologies of the nineteenth century, gradually develop and adapt to incorporate the innovations and changes of the situation, the war, the twentieth century, even though her material position remains the same. West's narrative is modernist, but it is female modernist in the way that it represents such changes through the perception of the woman, and Jenny's secondary status is emphasised by her position on the margins of the action. By acknowledging that this perspective is as valid as that of the male, West is able to offer a feminist alternative to more masculine modernisms.

It is the psychiatrist Gilbert Anderson, called in by Kitty and Jenny as a last resort, who finally prescribes the formula that will enable Chris to 'return' to his present life and responsibilities:

> There's a deep self in one, the essential self, that has its wishes. And if those wishes are suppressed by the superficial self – the self that makes, as you say, efforts and usually makes them with the sole idea of putting up a good show before the neighbours – it takes its revenge. Into the house of conduct erected by the superficial self it sends an obsession . . . The point is, Mr Baldry's obsession is that he can't remember the latter years of his life . . . what's the suppressed wish of which it's the manifestation?[56]

Accordingly, it is Margaret who can give substance to the formula by identifying that Chris must be reminded of his dead son if he is to 'return': 'She continued without joy. "I know how you could bring him back. A memory so strong that it would recall everything else – in spite of his discontent." . . . "Remind him of the boy,"'.[57] So collectively they conspire for his 'cure' by appealing to his unconscious in a Freudian manner. In fact West rejected links between psychoanalysis and her novel, suggesting that the new science only achieved prominence after her work had been written and that it was too complicated for authentic inclusion. She also argued that the psychoanalyst was 'an unimportant device' in the plot.[58] However, it is difficult to ignore the coincidence of the topicality of the debate during the First World War and the idea that Rebecca West was interested in the problems of amnesia and psychological dislocation.[59]

There has been much subsequent critical and fictional discussion of the treatments for shell shock. In *The Female Malady,* Elaine Showalter examines various methods, from the physical tortures of Dr Lewis Yelland[60] to the psychoanalytic techniques of W. H. R. Rivers.[61] Although the psychological strategies of Rivers appear to be much less directly harmful than those of his contemporary, Showalter's analysis of Rivers's treatment of Siegfried Sassoon at Craiglockhart in 1917 still gives the sense that most 'cures' for shell shock were intrinsically problematic. A question mark remains as to whether or not Sassoon had been correctly diagnosed, and Rivers's success in persuading him to withdraw his anti-war protest was extremely convenient for the military authorities. Showalter also suggests that Septimus Warren Smith, the shell-shock victim in Virginia Woolf's *Mrs Dalloway* 'perhaps owes something of his name, his appearance, and his war experience to Sassoon'.[62]

The treatment of Septimus Warren Smith is again very traumatic. His mental suffering at the hands of his doctors, Holmes and Sir William Bradshaw, ultimately sends him 'over the top, straight on to the bayonet-like railings'.[63] These veterans, feminised in the clutches of a war-induced 'madness', are as much at the mercy of their physicians as the female hysterics of the nineteenth century, and the consequences are often equally as damaging. Gilbert Anderson, who appears to resemble Rivers, and Margaret Grey collude (against her better judgement) to 'cure' Chris by returning to him the painful knowledge of the death of his infant son by showing him the dead child's jersey and toy ball. Like Septimus Warren Smith, he too will face the bayonets and the possibility of death as a result of this treatment. Samuel Hynes identifies the problems with this conclusion:

> *Cured* is a bitterly ironic word here; and so is *soldier.* A decent man has been cured of happiness and peace, which can have no place in a world at war; his cure is something that has been done to him, against his will, in order to return him to the reality of suffering and perhaps death.[64]

As a result the ending of the novel is deeply ambiguous and unsettling. West denies her readers the comfortable closure which might be expected of a 'woman's novel'. The fact that she engages with such debates in *The Return of the Soldier* moves the novel far beyond the implied simplicity of such a label, and she deserves recognition for the thematic intricacies of her text.

West also uses the psychoanalytic links in her novel to engage with other contemporary debates. Jenny's unconscious life is almost as apparent to the reader as her conscious one, glimpsed primarily through the relation of her dreams. Interpretation of these dreams can suggest interesting comments on the state of society, the country and the war.

> Of late I had had bad dreams about him. By night I saw Chris running across the brown rottenness of No Man's Land, starting back here because he trod upon a hand, not even looking there because of the awfulness of an unburied head, and not till my dream was packed full of horror did I see him pitch forward on his knees as he reached safety – if it was that.[65]

At first safety appears to be a trench. Later, as he runs across the no man's land of his lawn, safety is found in Margaret's arms. When he has been 'returned' to 'reality' at the end of the novel, he once again traverses his alien garden but this time Jenny has become aware that he will find no safe haven to protect him. He is condemned by society to the Western Front. In other dreams, Jenny imagines Chris visualising Margaret, 'transfigured in the light of eternity',[66] in contrast with herself and Kitty who walk unchanged, 'for we are as we are and there is nothing more to us. The whole truth about us lies in our material seeming'.[67] West uses the dreams to express Jenny's inner questioning of her own significance, and her place in a changing world. Thus she uses Jenny's unconscious to transcribe social and political messages.

The ideas articulated in these dreams highlight West's representation of the insubstantial nature of a society controlled by a class whose dominant ideology is built around material values. The class of Jenny and Kitty is obsolete, a classless Utopian future represented by Chris and Margaret, although equally impossible, is the best way forward. The war has brought this outmoded Edwardian world to a watershed causing Jenny to lament, 'No one weeps for this shattering of our world'.[68] Chris is sent back to France 'Every inch a soldier'[69] to assist with its destruction. As the reader interprets Jenny's dreams so West's political messages are revealed. Arguably then, West harnesses Freudian ideas of the unconscious within her text in order to create an arena for political debates, in this instance, one built around her socialist beliefs.

In her essay 'Impersonality and Amnesia: A Response to World War 1 in the Writing of H.D. and Rebecca West', Jane Gledhill identifies a connection between the aesthetic techniques of the Imagist poets and the prose writing of West in *The Return of the Soldier*. Gledhill points out that the novel has been read as 'a fictional exposition of the Freudian wish. It is innovative in style and technique and uses images to elucidate the states of mind of the main characters'.[70] Later she suggests 'Psychotherapists often use images as a means of explaining mental and emotional states'.[71]

West's adoption of patterns similar to those of Imagism, do indeed give an insight into the unconscious minds of the characters. As in the work of Katherine Mansfield, domestic images appropriate to the situation are used to convey a range of emotional responses. Margaret represents 'a spreading stain on the fabric of our life',[72] capturing in an instant the full implications of her arrival at Baldry Court. She watches Chris gesticulating about his private thoughts, 'like a housewife watching a saucepan of milk lest it should boil over'.[73] And the language of the narrator gives away as much about her own state of mind as it does about the characters whom she illustrates. Margaret herself is described by Jenny thus:

> The bones of her cheap stays clicked as she moved. Well, she was not so bad. Her body was long and round and shapely and with a noble squareness of the shoulders; her fair hair curled diffidently about a good brow; her grey eyes, though they were remote, as if anything worth looking at in her life had kept a long way off, were full of tenderness; and though she was slender there was something about her of the wholesome endearing heaviness of the draught-ox or the big trusted dog. Yet she was bad enough. She was repulsively furred with neglect and poverty, as even a good glove that has dropped down behind a bed in a hotel and has lain undisturbed for a day or two is repulsive when the chambermaid retrieves it from the dust and fluff.[74]

Jenny's 'not so bad' is still noticeably unflattering. Margaret is a draught-ox or a dog, rather than a fellow human being. Her greatest crime is that she sounds and she looks working class and therefore lacking in confidence and unable to keep herself in good condition. The final image of the glove speaks volumes about both Margaret and Jenny, the perception of the latter placing both women firmly in separate social categories.

Later in the novel Jenny comes to see Margaret in another light, as an instinctive mother figure who carries the healing powers to give Chris perfect happiness; to save him from himself. In this mood Jenny presents Margaret very differently, allowing a new kind of beauty to belie her shoddy appearance. Here she comes upon Margaret and Chris sitting in the gardens at Baldry Court:

> What she had done in leading him into this quiet magic circle out of our life, out of the splendid house which was not so much a house as a vast piece of space partitioned off from the universe and decorated partly for beauty and partly to make our privacy more insolent, out of the garden where the flowers took thought as to how they should grow and the wood made

formal as a pillared aisle by forestry, may be judged from my anguish in being left there alone. Indeed she had been generous to us all, for at her touch our lives had at last fallen into a pattern; she was the sober thread whose interweaving with our scattered magnificences had somehow achieved the design that otherwise would not appear. Perhaps even her dinginess was a part of her generosity, for in order to fit into the pattern one sometimes has to forgo something of one's individual beauty. That is why women like us do not wear such obviously lovely dresses as cocottes, but clothe them-selves in garments that by their slight neglect of the possibilities of beauty declare that there are such things as thrift and restraint and care for the future.[75]

What is particularly interesting about this passage is the way it suggests that Jenny has come to identify herself with Margaret. Her tone is quite different now. She recognises the emptiness of her home in comparison to the fullness of the wilder part of the garden. Natural beauty takes precedence over the cosmetic, and domestic values are prioritised over the more artificial concerns of appearance and luxury. Again she adopts a domestic image to describe the force of Margaret, 'the sober thread . . . interweaving with our scattered magnificences'. It is as though she has come to believe that before Margaret none of them had any real purpose. Their shared dinginess becomes an emblem of this new-found knowledge and Jenny is forced to join the couple resting on the blanket because she can no longer bear to be excluded from their harmony.

Suzanne Clark has suggested, 'The modernist revolution turned away from ordinary language and everyday life. This disconnection from social consequence, from history, has everything to do with the gendering of intellectuality'.[76] Indeed, West's use of domestic imagery and her representation of Margaret as a figure of profound maternal symbolism, do operate to feminise the text in a way which is not usually accepted as a modernism. But it can be read as modernist nonetheless. The application of domestic Imagism here, in the work of Katherine Mansfield and in the flower imagery of HD, represents a kind of female Imagism, subtly different to the rigid masculinity of Pound's verse. Like the war metaphors used to describe Chris, these images allow West to build clearer psychological pictures of her characters, as well as adding to the process of psychoanalysing her narrator, creating a 'poetic fiction which draws from the ideas about writing poetry that were most original at that time'.[77] But it takes these ideas a step further onto a new level of creativity. Female Imagism is a female modernism, different, but as valuable as the male equivalent.

That West should have been influenced by the Imagists seems entirely reasonable. She knew Ezra Pound, T. S. Eliot and HD, and particularly admired Richard Aldington. She also wrote 'an introduction of "imagisme," incorporating material from *Poetry* magazine, to preface Pound's poetry in the August 15, 1913, issue of the *New Freewoman*'.[78] That she wrote prose not poetry ensures her exclusion from their ranks. But as with Katherine Mansfield, the adoption of Imagist aesthetic ideas for use in the writing of prose fiction adds a new and innovatory dimension to her work, particularly effective in the process of attempting to articulate the experience of the war.[79]

West's use of language, together with her narrative experiments and inclusion of contemporary theoretical issues, all operate to illustrate the modernist nature of her writing. But it is a modernism from a female perspective, perhaps not consciously acknowledged in her own time. She herself believed in her own alienation. Bonnie Kime Scott writes that, 'Despite her appreciation of their work, West expressed feelings of marginality to canonized modernists'.[80] However, this may only be perceived as negative if we consider this canon to be impregnable. If we break it down and acknowledge the multiple modernisms produced by contemporary artists, it is easy to recognise the value of *The Return of the Soldier*. Other novels are less effective. Her 1930 commission, *War Nurse: The True Story of a Woman Who Lived, Loved and Suffered on the Western Front*,[81] which West published anonymously, is much less successful despite its subject matter. Her literary longevity, and her diversity, does mean that she is impossible to categorise within any single literary movement. She was, perhaps, a 'happy foreigner' embracing different techniques as it suited her, reinforcing the notion that female modernisms were very diverse and that the war had a part to play in such creativity

The Happy Foreigner: Enid Bagnold and the post-war woman

Enid Bagnold is perhaps the most marginalised of the writers considered in this chapter. She is remembered chiefly for *National Velvet* and a handful of plays and children's stories, but few have identified the innovatory nature of some of her early work. She achieved instant notoriety in 1918 with the publication of *A Diary without Dates*.[82] With the subsequent loss of her job at the Royal Herbert Hospital, Bagnold was left to look for some alternative kind of war work. She found it in the autumn of the armistice when she was persuaded by Prince Antoine Bibesco to become a driver for the French army. From November 1918 until the following summer she worked as a FANY, writing long letters home to her mother recording every detail of her experience. The intention was to use them as the basis of a new book. The result was *The Happy Foreigner*.

Stylistically *The Happy Foreigner* is very different from *A Diary without Dates*. Although it is, to some extent, based on Bagnold's personal experience, it is a work of fiction. On the surface it is an apparently conventional romance between a driver Fanny (FANY), the 'happy foreigner' of the title, and Julien Chatel a captain in the French army. Gone is the first person narrative, gone the staccato sentences and clinical atmosphere which helped to earn *A Diary without Dates* such radical acclaim. At first sight Fanny appears to be much more the traditional heroine of a 'woman's novel' lost to the austere 'reality' which makes the *Diary* such an uncomfortable read. But closer analysis reveals that there is much more to Bagnold's later book. She again breaks with narrative conventions, but in different ways, and it is possible to locate many connections between this and the other female modernist war texts examined here. One of the aspects of the novel that makes it interesting in an alternative way, is the focus on a woman as a primary character in the process of post-war reconstruction. *The Happy Foreigner* is a war story that begins at the end of the war.

Fanny is extremely important because she represents a woman liberated by the experience of the war; she is the survivor who will move on to better things. It is the personal confidence generated by this survival that separates her from women like Helen Zenna Smith in *Not So Quiet . . .* with whom she shares many of the hardships of driving and army life, although there are no longer any wounded so she is spared the trauma that accompanies them. Like Jenny in *The Return of the Soldier*, Fanny is on a journey of self-discovery, albeit a much more traditional one, here symbolised by her steady acquisition of increased personal space. But although Fanny's journey may appear to be more conventional, her ending is very different from those achieved by most nineteenth-century heroines.

Her first posting at Bar-le-Duc places her in accommodation reminiscent of that which housed Helen Smith or Mary Borden's narrator in 'Moonlight':

> Outside the black hut the jet-black night poured water down. Inside, the eight cubicles held each a woman, a bed, and a hurricane lantern. Fanny, in her paper box, listened to the scratching of a pen next door, then turned her eyes as a new and nearer scratching caught her ear. A bright-eyed rat stared at her through the hole it made in the wall.[83]

After this initial discomfort, her situation gradually improves with each new billet until she finally obtains not just a room of her own but a house of her own by the time she reaches her last posting at Charleville. The fact that it is in a state of decay after having held soldiers of all nationalities for four years matters little to her. Gradually she, the last soldier, rebuilds enough to create her own world, a microcosmic version of post-war reconstruction.

> All day she rummaged in the empty house – finding now a three-legged armchair which she propped up with a stone, now a single Venetian glass scrolled in gold for her tooth glass.
>
> In a small room on the ground floor a beautiful piece of tapestry lay rolled in a dusty corner. Pale birds of tarnished silver flew across its blue ground and on the border were willows and rivers.
>
> It covered her oak bed exactly – and by removing the pillows it looked like a comfortable and venerable divan. The logs on the fire were soon burnt through, and she did not like to ask for more, but leaving her room and wandering up an down the empty house in the long, pale afternoon, she searched for fragments of wood that might serve her.[84]

The derelict and decaying house, another victim of the war, is filled with the possibilities of its own rejuvenation just like the war-torn country. It is Fanny who is creative enough to initiate this recovery, making it her own as she does so. In a sense, Bagnold pre-empts Virginia Woolf's message in *A Room of One's Own*.[85] In her own space Fanny blossoms, not so much artistically, but personally. Even the myth of her romance with Julien Chatel is exposed. She superficially waits for his return and perhaps the consummation of their relationship. But each day that he fails to arrive she understands better how little she needs him; it is as he suggests, she has 'some solace, some treasure' of her own.[86]

The narrative of *The Happy Foreigner* has a disrupted texture, reading rather like a collection of stories, perhaps modernist fragments. Fanny's adventures as she travels through post-war France have only the thread of her romance with Julien as a motif running through them. She is entirely comfortable to be a soldier in a man's world, having only a token pair of silk stockings as a symbol of her femininity during most of her romantic encounters. The only time she abandons her uniform is for an army fancy dress dance, at which she wears a frilled white crinoline hand-painted with blue and green flowers. Her desire to present herself to Julien in this ultra-feminine light may appear emblematic of a need to conform with the social stereotypes of her upbringing in a secure world, rather as Helen Smith tries to remember her coming-out dance to drown the cries of her cargo of wounded. However, Bagnold represents the scene as a romantic fantasy, deliberately out of tune with the real Fanny. The fantasy is effectively shattered when Fanny is asked to sit for her portrait during the evening; to have the triumph of her beauty recorded. The drawing is not a success, 'He had made too many drawings that evening, and any talent he had hung in his mind as wearily as a flag in an airless room'.[87] Fanny's adoption of the trappings of traditional femininity is allowed its moment of glory, but even as she enjoys it, Bagnold reminds us that it is a myth and not an important factor in the construction of her post-war identity.

The ease with which Fanny fits into a man's world again calls to mind Sandra Gilbert's arguments in 'Soldier's Heart: Literary Men, Literary Women, and the Great War', in which she identifies the female invasion of the male domain as intrinsically empowering.[88] Fanny is given the freedom of mobility by her possession of a car. She is responsible for driving many important men of different nationalities, all of whom are persuaded to accept her sex and in time, are even impressed by it. She is a lone woman visiting the *citadelle* beneath the smashed town of Verdun, penetrating right to the heart of a male territory which, a few months earlier before the end of the war, would have been absolutely closed to her.

Fanny is also sexually empowered. As she can drive men unchaperoned, so she can drive her lover, alone, regardless of the time of day. She is prepared to break any rule to see him, crossing an icy river for a clandestine meeting at Chantilly. When she is prevented from returning by bad weather conditions, she seems to enjoy the risk of personal disgrace, fuelled by the excitement of the experience. Again Bagnold tempers romance with reality by emphasising Fanny's extreme physical discomfort as she tries to return to her billet secretly in freezing conditions. But ultimately the spirit of independence supersedes all other experiences, 'Cocks were crowing on the other side – the sun drew faint colours from the ice, the river clattered at the side of the boat, wind twisted and shook her skirt, and stirred her hair. All was forgotten in the glory of the passage of the river'.[89] She shares this spirit with many of the heroines of nineteenth-century fiction. But her location in a fractured, male world of wartime reconstruction and her rejection of femininity and romance, places the novel determinedly in the twentieth century.

Bagnold also seems to engage with the argument that counters Gilbert's, the 'double helix' argument put forward by Margaret and Patrice Higonnet in *Behind the Lines: Gender and the Two World Wars*,[90] again suggesting the complexity of this debate. Although the women drivers have enjoyed a privileged status as members of the forces, as civilian life once more takes precedence over the military so they are moved 'backward', as they recognise that the time to return home is approaching: "'Already,'" said one, "our khaki seems as old-fashioned as a crinoline. A man said to me yesterday: 'It is time mademoiselle bought her dress for the summer!'"[91] Civilians begin to be prioritised in the distribution of rations. The women, like all the allied armies, are no longer important. But Fanny is a modernist heroine who is happy to move on with the times because she knows the times will make space for her. The narrative exudes a distinct sense of living for the present, like an early manifestation of the prevalent ideology of the young in the 1920s which can be found in other female modernist texts: Fanny claims, 'I am old enough – I have learnt again and again – that there is only one joy – the Present; only one Perfection – the Present. If I look into the future it is lost.'[92] But despite Fanny's resolute cry, a product of wartime experience, the novel as a whole looks beyond this, collecting the debris of the past and transposing it into hope for the future in a way which highlights a liberation for women, articulating a future of independent possibilities that ultimately becomes the philosophy of Fanny, and perhaps of Bagnold herself. Thus she prioritises a feminist politics.

It is possible to make a connection between Fanny, and Virginia Woolf's post-war new woman, Lily Briscoe in *To the Lighthouse*.[93] The destruction of the mores of the old society brought about in the 'Time Passes' section of Woolf's novel, releases Lily from the 'feminine' restrictions which stifled her art and thereby, her personal autonomy. Similarly, Fanny is able to evolve as a human being in the space presented to her by the empty battlefields of France. She becomes part of a post-war phenomenon, part of the reconstruction of society on more egalitarian terms envisioned by Rebecca West. She is a 'happy foreigner' not only because she is in France, but also because she traverses no man's land and creates a place for herself within it. While living only for the present she is able to rebuild her hopes for the future as she realises the implications and the possibilities of her own freedom. Having left Julien in the final moments of the novel, knowing she will never see him again, she experiences an ecstatic abandonment as she rides back down the mountain to Charleville:

> She was invincible, inattentive to the voice of absent man, a hard, hollow goddess, a flute for the piping of heaven – composing and chanting unmusical songs, her inner ear fastened upon another melody. And heaven, protecting a creature at that moment so estranged from earth, led her down the wild road, held back the threatening forest branches, brought her, all but standing up at the wheel like a lunatic, safety to the foot of the last hill.[94]

Like Lily Briscoe, as the lighthouse is finally breached, Fanny too has had her vision.

Despite the feeling of euphoria that often penetrates this book, Bagnold does not allow the reader to forget the tragedy of the late war. As Fanny drives across the battlefields there is a distinct emphasis on the modernist preoccupation with the machine. The hideous mechanisation of this war is constantly highlighted, 'Everywhere she saw a wild disregard for life, everywhere she winced before the menace of speed, of weight, of thundering metal'.[95] This is no futurist celebration. It is more like what Daniel Pick describes as 'representations of deranged machinery of war' in *War Machine*.[96] She passes cemetery after cemetery for the mechanical casualties of war. Not cleared away and buried like the bodies of men, they rust in the sunlight, vast metaphorical representations of the destruction of human armies. Broken signposts in the derelict trenches allow the dead to speak from their graves, reluctant to be forgotten, adding multiple voices to the text. Nationality is no object. Wrecked German guns articulate the pain and anger generated by the war:

> The hungry noses of old guns snuffed at the car as it rolled by, guns dragging still upon their flanks the torn cloak of camouflage – small squat guns which stared idly into the air, or with wider mouths still, like petrified dogs for ever baying at the moon – long slim gun which lay along the grass and pushing undergrowth – and one gun which had dipped forward and, fallen upon its knees, howled silenced imprecations at the devil in the centre of the earth.[97]

This is the technology of war that has caused destruction on an unimaginable scale. Created by man to destroy man, Bagnold uses them to express the madness of the past conflict. They are also symbols of the modernity which cuts Fanny off from her Edwardian roots for all time; a schism that cannot be reversed.

But even in this wasteland that was so recently a battlefield she finds the seeds of hope for the future:

> Ahead lay the terrible miles. She seemed to make no gain upon them, and could not alter the face of the horizon, however fast she drove. Iron, brown grass – brown grass and iron, spars of wood, girders, torn railway lines and stones. Even the lorries travelling the road were few and far between. A deep loneliness was settled upon the desert where nothing grew. Yet, suddenly, from a ditch at the side of the road, a child of five stared at her. It had its foot close by a stacked heap of hand grenades; a shawl was wrapped round it and the thin hands held the ends together. What child? Whose? How did it get here, when not a house stood erect for miles and miles – when not a coil of

smoke touched the horizon! Yes, something oozed from the ground! Smoke, blue smoke! Was life stirring like a bulb under this winter ruin, this cemetery of village bones?[98]

Bagnold uses the metaphor of the bulb, of new life, to create the idea of a future despite the scale of the destruction. The presence of the child, pure, innocent and unscathed, works with equal symbolism. The juxtaposition of the image of the child next to the pile of hand grenades effectively reinforces the difference between the past carnage and the future re-growth, even as it highlights the continuing danger of the apparently dormant battlefield. This is a danger that continues today, as eighty years on French and Belgian farmers still discover live shells and ammunition when they plough their fields. In 1919 it is a desert, it is the colour of a desert tinged with an appropriate modernity, 'iron, brown grass – brown grass and iron'. Yet the coil of smoke oozes from the ground almost like some fragile new life form growing despite everything from the subterranean depths. Fanny, the foreigner, discovers that the child belongs to a family that has returned to what was once their village. Like other families they are living in the cellar of their old house; it is all that remains. But it is a start. She donates her hammer to their reconstruction before moving on, thus adding her own stone to the terrible work of rebuilding.

This haunted landscape also contains people from many other counties. Everywhere Fanny meets Americans anxiously awaiting the order to return home. With their money, possessions and good quality rations, it is clear that they represent an affluent future, a new kind of imperialism juxtaposed with the archaic French colonial system which now employs frightened Chinese and Annamite civilians to do the heavy work of reconstruction. The many nationalities add a dialogism to the text which is reinforced by the objectivity of Bagnold's narrative. She refuses to pass judgement, at times adopting a reporter-like style, creating a document which is specifically designed to give space to all viewpoints. The other voices that infiltrate the text engage with political and social debates concerning the state of the post-war world making this a multidimensional novel rather like Rebecca West's.

Like the other stories discussed earlier, Bagnold's narrative structure employs a kind of dialogism. The authorial voice speaks through the consciousness of Fanny and Julien and sometimes other, more minor characters. At times it fades completely, leaving only the spoken dialogue of the protagonists, giving them voices which appear to operate beyond authorial control. Bagnold also allows the narrative to shift, enabling it to

operate on an entirely allegorical level when she assesses the condition of
the post-war world:

> 'Go away!' said France restlessly, pushing at the new nations in her bosom.
> 'It's all done. Go back again!'
>   'Are you an Ally?' said the Allies to each other balefully, their eyes no
> longer lit by battle, but irritable with disillusion – and each told his women
> tales of the other's shortcomings.[99]

The disharmony of this embittered Europe, which reflects the troubled
negotiations at Versailles, to some extent problematises the notion of 'the
happy foreigner'. Fanny's freedom sometimes denies responsibility for
the necessary reconstruction, at times heading dangerously close to the
decadent ideology of a 'lost generation'. Nonetheless, as an individual she
reconstructs her own world and touches the lives of others whom she
passes as they too struggle to rebuild. It is left to Julien, the post-war
industrialist, to rehabilitate society into the new orthodoxies of the twentieth century. There may be something symbolic in Fanny's rejection of
him in favour of the more spiritual and aesthetic pleasures of life. But she,
too, is embarking on a new adventure at the close of the novel; liberated
by the war and by experience, she moves beyond traditional concepts of
marriage and closure to pursue the journey of her personal growth: '"It is
true," she whispered, as she entered the room, "that I am half out of reach
of pain" – and long, in plans for the future, she hung over the embers.'[100]
Julien is a product of the war who fades with demobilisation, proving
him to be no more than a stepping-stone on Fanny's path to personal
reconstruction.

    As with Mansfield and West, it is possible to identify the aesthetic
legacy of contemporary poetic tendencies in Bagnold's text. But Bagnold
does not focus on the domestic as much as the others do. Indeed there is
only a distorted version of the domestic in Fanny's world of cars and
billets. Instead her language tends to operate on a different level, binding
the personal and the emotional to the wider themes of the text: 'they were
old enough to be afraid that the vague happiness that fluttered before
them down the path would not be so beautiful when it was caught'.[101] She
does not adopt the precision of imagism. Instead she creates an atmosphere which evokes the more general sense of freedom experienced by the
survivors of the war; and fear that such a freedom might be ephemeral.

    The war itself takes on a different meaning too. The derelict battlefields,
and there are many in this novel, stretch out like the wasteland that is the
modern world. Verdun, once the emblem of the battle for France and

French identity, stands ironically as an awesome symbol of what human-kind has done to society: 'As they neared it the town began to show its awful frailty – its appearance of preservation was a mockery. Verdun stood upright as by a miracle, a coarse lace of masonry – not one house was whole'.[102] But Fanny's entry into Verdun and into the territory of the battlefields works as a kind of conquest. As the woman is welcomed into the man's world, so a new era begins.

Like *A Diary without Dates*, *The Happy Foreigner* is a politically moti-vated novel instigated by the war which makes it part of a new movement for women writers. Enid Bagnold creates a multi-layered text that is con-cerned with examining the legacy of the war in both positive and nega-tive, personal and public ways. With the war behind her she can assess its impact on the position and experience of women, while to some extent detaching herself from the actual slaughter. She takes a nineteenth-century heroine on a voyage of discovery and places her in a world where nineteenth-century values are obsolete. In her narrative she adopts some of the recognised characteristics of literary modernisms, and adapts them to surround Fanny, creating an old-fashioned heroine, totally moder-nised. Again the war initiates a type of female modernism which deserves recognition in the wider field of literary studies. For too long this novel, like *A Diary without Dates*, has been hidden beneath a disguise con-structed by Bagnold's own, less challenging literary reputation, when she could have been heralded as much more innovatory. Once uncovered, these works can be incorporated effectively into contemporary argu-ments that aim to reveal the variety of modernisms that make up early twentieth-century experimental fiction.

So Fanny, the 'happy foreigner' can act symbolically to represent women writers penetrating the world of men through the medium of the war; the physical world of the battlefield and the literary world of devel-oping modernisms, female modernisms, diverse and fluid rather than hegemonic. For the modernisms of the war cannot be monolithic. In the writing of Woolf, Mansfield and West, as well as Borden, La Motte and Bagnold, it is possible to locate many experiments of different kinds, involving narrative structure, political, social and theoretical debates and different uses of language. For Mansfield, primacy is given to artistic sym-bolism in language and constructions of the self. West is concerned with narrative structure and the psychological. For Bagnold, it is the political and the liberating, with the benefits of hindsight and an optimism for the future. And all such writers prioritise female interpretations of war expe-rience.

It is one thing for these women to be 'happy foreigners' in the wasteland of an armistice, engaging with their own literary experiments, but subordinated to much of the war writing of men and the male modernisms which have always been privileged. But eventually the battlefields must be re-colonised. Like Fanny, women writers must survive their marginalisation and take up their own places in both the history of war writing and that of literary development. The identification by feminist researchers of many previously hidden female modernists, has, in recent years, done a great deal to rewrite these histories. The emphasis on the connection between the war and the development of female literary modernisms endorses this work, foregrounding women whose writing has been overlooked for too long, adding new dimensions to a stage of literary innovation which has many significant repercussions for literature today.

Notes

1 Enid Bagnold (1987), *The Happy Foreigner*, London, Virago (first published 1920), pp. 289–90.

2 Randall Stevenson (1992), *Modernist Fiction: An Introduction*, London, Harvester Wheatsheaf, p. 188.

3 See for example, Bonnie Kime Scott (1990), *The Gender of Modernism*, Bloomington and Indianapolis, IN, Indiana University Press; Suzanne Clark (1991), *Sentimental Modernism: Women Writers and the Revolution of the Word*, Bloomington and Indianapolis, IN, Indiana University Press; Marianne DeKoven (1991), *Rich and Strange: Gender, History, Modernism*, Princeton, NJ, Princeton University Press; Gillian Hanscombe and Virginia L. Smyers (1987), *Writing for their Lives: The Modernist Women 1910–1940*, London, Women's Press.

4 Rebecca West (1987), *The Return of the Soldier*, London, Virago (first published 1918).

5 Leslie Heron Beauchamp, killed in action 7 October 1915 shortly after his first arrival at the front.

6 Katherine Mansfield (1954), *Journal of Katherine Mansfield*, ed. J. M. Murry, London, Constable, p. 97, 15 February 1916.

7 John Middleton Murry, Mansfield's lover whom she married in May 1918.

8 Mansfield (1954), *Journal*, p. 86, 29 October 1915.

9 See Bronte Adams and Trudi Tate (eds) (1991), *That Kind of Woman*, London, Virago; Lynn Knight (ed.) (1993), *Infinite Riches*, London, Virago.

10 T. S. Eliot quoted by Clare Hanson (1990), 'Katherine Mansfield

(1888–1923)', in Bonnie Kime Scott (ed.), *The Gender of Modernism*, Bloomington and Indianapolis, IN, Indiana University Press, pp. 298–305.

11 See the recent of anthology of short stories: Trudi Tate (ed.) (1995), *Women, Men and the Great War*, Manchester, Manchester University Press.

12 Judy Simons (1990), *Diaries and Journals of Literary Women from Fanny Burney to Virginia Woolf*, London, Macmillan, p. 149.

13 'The Fly' is reproduced in Trudi Tate (ed.) (1995), *Women, Men and the Great War*, Manchester, Manchester University Press.

14 'Late at Night' is reproduced in Katherine Mansfield (1984), *Collected Stories*, London, Constable.

15 'Two Tuppeny Ones, Please' is reproduced in Katherine Mansfield (1984), *Collected Stories*, London, Constable

16 'An Indiscreet Journey' is reproduced in Katherine Mansfield (1984), *Collected Stories*, London, Constable. Claire Tylee equates it to Joyce's *Dubliners*, which were intended 'to reveal the sordid meanness and materialism of Dublin life' (Claire M. Tylee (1990), *The Great War and Women's Consciousness*, London, Macmillan, p. 89) For a further discussion of this story see *ibid.*, pp. 85–91.

17 'The Little Corporal' was actually Francis Carco, French poet, novelist and journalist whom Mansfield met through John Middleton Murry. Earlier he had given her French lessons in Paris. He was also, perhaps, the model for Raoul Duquette in 'Je Ne Parle Pas Francais'. For further details see Claire Tomalin (1987), *Katherine Mansfield: A Secret Life*, London, Viking.

18 Mansfield, *Collected Stories*, p. 628.

19 *Ibid.*, p. 636.

20 Katherine Mansfield (1927), *Journal of Katherine Mansfield*, ed. J. M. Murry, London, Constable, p. 26.

21 *Ibid.*, p. 27.

22 Mansfield, *Collected Stories*, p. 635.

23 *Ibid.*

24 Mansfield (1954), *Journal*, p. 75.

25 *Ibid.*, p. 77.

26 *Ibid.*, p. 78.

27 The 1927 edition of Mansfield's *Journal* includes the line 'It was like an elopement' (p. 27). Murry excludes this from the more detailed 1954 'definitive edition' of Mansfield's *Journal*, which includes material suggesting the inaccuracy of this statement: 'he does not really love me at all . . . I don't really love him now I know him – but he is so rich and careless – *that* I love' (p. 75).

28 Evadne Price (Helen Zenna Smith) (1988), *Not So Quiet . . . Stepdaughters of War*, London, Virago (first published 1930).

29 Mansfield (1954), *Journal*, p. 74.

30 *Ibid.*, p. 76.

31 *Ibid.*, pp. 75–8.

32 'Pictures' is reproduced in Katherine Mansfield (1962), *Bliss and Other Stories*, London, Penguin (first published 1920).
33 Simons, *Diaries and Journals*, pp. 149–50.
34 Mansfield, *Collected Stories*, p. 638.
35 *Ibid.*
36 Virginia Woolf [*Diaries*, vol. 2, p. 227], quoted in Hanson, 'Katherine Mansfield (1888–1923)', p. 303.
37 Hanson, 'Katherine Mansfield (1888–1923)', pp. 303–4.
38 Mansfield, *Collected Stories*, p. 641.
39 T. S. Eliot, quoted in Clare Hanson (1990), 'Katherine Mansfield (1888–1923)', in Scott (ed.), *The Gender of Modernism*, p. 300.
40 Katherine Mansfield quoted in Scott (ed.), *The Gender of Modernism*, p. 305.
41 Literary Impressionism borrows the term applied to the nineteenth-century school of French painting and was adopted by Ford Madox Ford early in the twentieth century to describe his narrative experiments when he was working with Joseph Conrad. It can be applied to writing which attempts to describe the 'transitory mental impressions' of an observer rather than concentrating on objective description.
42 Mansfield, *Collected Stories*, p. 628.
43 *Ibid.*, p. 629.
44 *Ibid.*, p. 639.
45 Clark, *Sentimental Modernism*, p. 2.
46 Rebecca West (1982), 'On the Return of the Soldier', *Yale University Library Gazette*, 67, p. 67.
47 *Ibid.*
48 Tylee, *The Great War*, p. 144.
49 Margaret Diane Stetz (1987), 'Drinking the Wine of Truth: Philosophical Change in West's The Return of the Soldier', *Arizona Quarterly*, 43 (1), p. 75.
50 West, 'On The Return of the Soldier', p. 68.
51 West, *Return of the Soldier*, p. 109.
52 *Ibid.*, p. 167.
53 *Ibid.*, p. 184.
54 *Ibid.*, p. 71.
55 Sharon Ouditt (1994), *Fighting Forces, Writing Women*, London, Routledge, p. 114.
56 West, *Return of the Soldier*, pp. 163–4.
57 West, *Return of the Soldier*, pp. 168–9.
58 West, 'On The Return of the Soldier', pp. 67–8.
59 G. E. Hutchinson, Prefatory Note to West's 'On The Return of the Soldier': 'Even before the First World War was producing the symptoms of what came to be known as shell shock, it is clear from her letter [On The Return of the Soldier, published in *The Observer*, 24 June, 1928] that Dame Rebecca was interested in the problems of psychological disassociation and amnesia. This

is further shown in a cutting from an unidentified newspaper of September 18, 1911, when she was not yet nineteen, in which there is an evident reference to the researches of Morton Prince on multiple personality.' This cutting was reproduced in the *Yale University Library Gazette* to accompany Rebecca West's letter.

60 Elaine Showalter (ed.) (1993), *Daughters of Decadence*, London, Virago, p. 176.
61 For a fictional interpretation of the war work of Rivers, see Pat Barker's trilogy: (1992), *Regeneration*, London, Penguin (first published 1991); (1994), *The Eye in the Door*, London, Penguin (first published 1993); (1995), *The Ghost Road*, London, Viking.
62 Showalter, *Daughters of Decadence*, p. 192.
63 Ouditt, *Fighting Forces*, p. 197.
64 Samuel Hynes (1990), *A War Imagined*, London, Bodley Head, p. 213.
65 West, *Return of the Soldier*, pp. 13–14.
66 *Ibid.*, p. 137.
67 *Ibid.*
68 *Ibid.*
69 *Ibid.*, p. 188.
70 Jane Gledhill (1993), 'Impersonality and Amnesia: A Response to World War 1 in the Writing of H.D. and Rebecca West', in D. Goldman (ed.), *Women and World War 1: The Written Response*, London, Macmillan, p. 182.
71 *Ibid.*, p. 185.
72 West, *Return of the Soldier*, p. 37.
73 *Ibid.*, p. 129.
74 *Ibid.*, p. 25.
75 *Ibid.*, pp. 145–6.
76 Clark, *Sentimental Modernism*, p. 3.
77 Gledhill, 'Impersonality and Amnesia', p. 185.
78 Scott, *Gender of Modernism*, p. 566.
79 For example e. e. cummings uses Imagist techniques within the narrative of his semi-autobiographical war memoir: e. e. cummings (1922), *The Enormous Room*, New York, Boni & Liseright.
80 Scott, *Gender of Modernism*, p. 568.
81 Rebecca West (Anon) (1930), *War Nurse: The True Story of a Woman Who Lived, Loved, and Suffered on the Western Front*, New York, Cosmopolitan Book Corporation.
82 Enid Bagnold (1978), *A Diary without Dates*, London, Virago (first published 1918).
83 Bagnold, *Happy Foreigner*, p. 11.
84 *Ibid.*, p. 252.
85 Virginia Woolf (1990), *A Room of One's Own*, London, Grafton (first published 1929).

86 Bagnold, *Happy Foreigner*, p. 139.
87 *Ibid.*, p. 252.
88 Sandra Gilbert (1983), 'Soldier's Heart: Literary Men, Literary Women, and the Great War', *Signs*, 8 (3), Spring, pp. 422–50. Gilbert's ideas are discussed in more detail in Chapter 3.
89 Bagnold, *Happy Foreigner*, p. 218.
90 Higonnet, M. R., Jenson, J., Michel, S. and Weitz, M. C. (eds) (1987), *Behind the Lines: Gender and the Two World Wars*, New Haven, CT, and London, Yale University Press. Margaret and Patrice Higonnet's ideas are also discussed in Chapter 3.
91 Bagnold, *Happy Foreigner*, p. 265.
92 *Ibid.*, pp. 183–4.
93 Virginia Woolf (1989), *To the Lighthouse*, London, Grafton (first published 1927).
94 Bagnold, *Happy Foreigner*, p. 291.
95 *Ibid.*, p. 14.
96 Daniel Pick (1993), *War Machine: The Rationalisation of Slaughter in the Modern Age*, New Haven, CT, and London, Yale University Press.
97 Bagnold, *Happy Foreigner*, p. 88.
98 *Ibid.*, p. 226.
99 *Ibid.*, p. 231.
100 *Ibid.*, pp. 291–2.
101 *Ibid.*, p. 58.
102 *Ibid.*, p. 67.

Conclusion:
the aspect of peace[1]

The night of the 10th. The morning of the 11th. The world held its breath.
Eleven o'clock. Sirens, and a crash of bells. The world went mad. The
Armistice was signed.[2]

The day that the Armistice was signed it rained. It was a gloomy, grey
autumn day which, for many observers, seemed to symbolise the cessa-
tion of a nightmare, just as the patriots of 1914 had heralded the beginning of the First World War under sun-drenched August skies. Despite
an expected show of public euphoria, there is almost always a sense of
emptiness or loss which clouds written representations of the end of the
war, as though society was shell shocked, unable to reconcile the past
with the changed world of the future. Many of the diarists who kept such
conscientious records during the early years of the war had abandoned
their pens before 1918. Similarly, the end of the war is not much cele-
brated in published works. There is often an ambiguity to be found in the
emotional responses of the writing, a question mark hanging over what
comes next.

There were a few who managed to shed the war years without apparent difficulty, returning to the pre-war rhetoric of an old ideology. Ethel
Bilborough wrote:

11 November 1918, Monday:

PEACE! The armistice is signed, 'the day' has come at last! and – it is ours!
Every heart is vibrating to the wonderful song of triumph that swells
throughout the Empire this day. The war is over and We have won the war,
& glory honour and victory is ours.[3]

Bilborough's return to notions of honour and glory seems to suggest that
she has come through the war relatively unscathed emotionally. She

makes no attempt to consider what 'peace' and 'victory' actually mean
and her words sit uncomfortably with the reader, particularly since they
are followed by a newspaper clipping informing us that the war has lasted
precisely four years, fourteen weeks and two days, a reminder of the longevity of the suffering. Other diarists reflect the excitement of that day,
recording their involvement in the celebrations as thousands took to the
streets in London. VAD Hilda Craven, originally from Lancashire, was
thrilled to be close enough to London to join in:

> Monday November 11th 1918.
>
> London mad with joy and it was grand to see the lights full on again and
> hear good-hearted cheers – crowds round Buckingham Palace where we
> made for and as luck would have it we only had to wait 20 minutes before
> the King, Queen, Princess Mary and the Duke of Connaught appeared on
> the balcony. Oh it was a grand sight and the crowd seemed to cheer them
> from their very hearts.[4]

Craven focuses on the noise and sincerity of the crowd, caught up in a
patriotic embrace, and was clearly very moved by the experience. But at
the same time she records it as a kind of madness, four years of suppressed
hysteria finally given the appropriate forum to emerge. This hysteria
caused problems for other witnesses. Patricia Hanbury, a teenaged
schoolgirl, after suitably pious celebrations in church ventured into
nearby Maidenhead to observe the festivities of the less sedate. She was
disappointed by what she saw: 'Beyond a few cheers there was nothing
exciting & our rejoicings were rather damped when we came across
several hopelessly drunk Tommies. It seems so sad that getting drunk
should be their way of rejoicing'.[5]

   Hanbury's youthful musings reflect the problematic nature of the
armistice. For many people there was an awful lot to try to forget, and
limited means by which they could achieve the necessary oblivion.
Accounts that are filled with noise, activity and movement, seem
superficial, hiding the emptiness beneath. Most of the other diarists considered in this book greet the end with silence. The experience of the war
overwhelms the immediate aftermath, producing hysteria or disillusionment, or nothing at all. Virginia Woolf wrote, 'We should have done well,
I think, to be satisfied with the aspect of peace'.[6] Her own diary entry
records a nightmarish trip to London, filled with people gone mad, like a
kind of ghastly parody of the public excitement at the outbreak of the
war.[7] For Woolf, who had opposed the war, and hardly alluded to it in her
personal writing, the notion of peace seems to be an illusion, a veil

adopted to disguise the chaos, but too fine to withstand the further conflicts of the post-war world.

This then, is the beginning of the atmosphere of despair, the suggested breeding ground for the great works of High Modernism. As the noise of the bells and sirens faded, it was replaced by a reality filled with the physically and emotionally scarred demobbed, unemployment and poverty. A metaphoric wasteland identified by many in the poetry of T. S. Eliot and the narrative chaos of James Joyce. While many of the male writers who had fought in the trenches, sat silent, waiting to come to terms with the war, these 'modernist masters' took centre stage, finding new ways to represent symbolically the era in which they flourished.

The power of this writing has been long enduring. As the 1920s progressed it was joined by the prose works of the soldier/writers, causing the boom in war literature at the end of the decade. Together they form the twin strands that have come to represent historically the war and post-war years, the literary canons of war and modernism, both of which have been dominated by men.

The purpose of this book has been to add a new strand to the growing movement away from these trends that have directed understanding of the First World War throughout the century; to put forward the argument that the war-writing of men represents only half the picture and that notions of High Modernism exclude much of the important and innovatory literature of the period; that, indeed, it is most useful to read across those critical boundaries and acknowledge the links between the experience of the war and the development of varying modernisms.

To find valuable writing produced during the war itself, it is not necessary to look only to an older generation of male writers, such as H. G. Wells and Arnold Bennett, while waiting for youth to return from the trenches. Women began writing of the war, privately and publicly, on the day that war broke out, and in many cases, they wrote very well. Much of the writing of women like Ethel Bilborough, Eleanora Pemberton and Mabel St Clair Stobart demonstrates a comprehensive knowledge of literary tradition as they fill their pages with literary motifs that reflect their education. They display a clear understanding of how language works, and as the war develops, how the traditional forms of their past gradually cease to be adequate to convey the new and terrible experience of twentieth-century combat.

As Jay Winter has argued, 'Modernists reconfigured conventions; they didn't discard them'.[8] Evidence of this process can even be found in the dairies of ordinary women as they struggle to write about the First World

War. They experiment with different literary styles as they attempt to find one or more which is suitable to articulate what appears to be unspeakable. The result is often a pastiche, which juxtaposes different narrative techniques, giving the text the appearance of being fragmented or impressionistic. Thus, perhaps accidentally, the atmosphere of confusion created by the war is reproduced on the page. Some diaries illustrate this process more effectively than others. The paratactic structure of the tiny diary of Mabel St Clair Stobart with its contrasts of stark realism and expressionistic poetry, punctuated by ellipses, provides a particularly helpful example. Similarly, the 'Base Notes' of Muriel Thompson, which mesh together colourful poetic allusion and the blinding darkness of life in a constant blackout, create an inspired interface between the literary past and the literary future.

These processes can also be found in the more controlled formats of the stories of nurses and ambulance drivers; women reworking conventions, often those associated with women's fiction of the nineteenth-century, to create an atmosphere of anachronism which reinforces the alienation of the war experience. From the contradictory nun-nurses of *A Diary without Dates*, who know everything and yet nothing of the men that they care for, to the enquiries into female sexuality of Mary Borden, to the uncomfortable blend of both feminine and masculine in Helen Zenna Smith, these women produce their own valid modernisms through complex linguistic and structural experiments, in many cases, published too early to have been influenced by the 'modernist masters'. The psychology of despair, propounded by the chaos that followed the armistice, may have done much to inspire the development of acknowledged modernisms. But the war itself played a part in the production of alternative modernisms and these can often be identified as the work of relatively unknown women.[9]

It has also been my purpose to engage with the political modernisms of women writers, many of which were again, symptomatic of the war experience. The direct address of social and sexual taboos is a characteristic strongly associated with the recognised female modernists of the 1920s, manifested in their exiled lives on the margins of Paris society, denial of patriarchal authority and their lesbian politics. But the war initiated an earlier development of these modernisms as women felt obliged to speak out publicly on unorthodox subjects that moved them. The essentialist feminism of Mabel St Clair Stobart in *The Flaming Sword*, the advocacy of extreme pacifism and alternative modes of sexuality by Rose Allatini in *Despised and Rejected*, and the socialist politics of Rebecca

West, expressed through the mechanisms of psychoanalysis in *The Return of the Soldier*, all provide early examples of women using the discourse of war as a forum for revolution. The chronological location of this writing suggests that it was the experience of the war itself, not the desolation of its aftermath that provided the trigger for this alterity.

Although the women examined here have been used as examples of different types of innovation, there are many overlaps. HD, as a writer of letters, could be included in Chapter 1, and as a woman who addresses the role of the artist in wartime through Julia Ashton, could fit equally well into Chapter 5. Mary Borden's female modernist techniques would be appropriate for inclusion in Chapter 6. These overlaps are intentional and operate to reinforce the thread of the central argument. These women are not only interesting individually, but in the way that they each represent a part of a growing movement, one that links the war and the development of female modernisms in a new and exciting way. Their similarities point to a unity of material and focus which is too significant to be over-looked.

What began during the war, continued after it. Those women writing female modernist war texts in the 1920s, 1930s and later, demonstrate a greater degree of literary sophistication than the early or accidental modernists of the diaries, letters and hospital stories. This indicates both the influence of the growing modernist movement on their work, and justifies their incorporation within that culture. But the inclusion of the earlier writing functions to illustrate the way in which the direct experience of the First World War influenced the development of female modernist practice, opening up a pathway for a diverse range of different experimental discourses.

In 1918 the experience of war was replaced by the aspect of peace. International political wrangling continued as the great powers fought each other at Versailles, each hoping for something different from the peace settlement. The harsh treatment of Germany at the hands of the Allies was seen by many as highly dangerous, opening the way for further bloodshed in the future. But some had already spoken out, expressing similar fears. With his sinister prophecies, Rose Allatini's hero Dennis Blackwood appears to be a precursor to the organisers of the League of Nations who feared the worst:

> If the so-called fruits of victory are withheld from them all alike, there's a chance that the people of each nation, seeing the true nature of the war-machine by which they've been driven, will clamour to have it broken up; will protest against the maintenance of great armies and navies for their

mutual destruction. There'll be some chance of an era of real peace – not the sham peace of the lull before the storm, which will exist if the powers can be definitely divided into conquerors and conquered, with the conquered merely biding their time to reverse those titles, and the conquerors ever on the watch to see that they shan't do so. A lasting peace can never be achieved by war, because war only breeds war.[10]

The origins of many of the political modernisms of the inter-war years can also be located in the writing produced in the war. It is part of a developing process which led to the dislocation and displacement of many people, particularly artists and writers in the following decades.

The aspect of peace always remained fragile, and this can be seen in the later work of other modernist women such as Virginia Woolf, HD, Mary Butts and Jean Rhys.[11] Perhaps it represents a second phase in the development of women's twentieth-century experimental writing. It is certainly a psychology of despair that is often associated with modernism, but it would be simplistic to imagine that the history of that psychology did not play a major part in the creative process.[12] This book considers that history, providing exciting documentary evidence of the important relationship between women, the experience of the First World War and the diversity of modernism.

Notes

1 Virginia Woolf (1977), *Diary of Virginia Woolf*, vol 1, *1915–1919*, London, Hogarth Press, p. 216.
2 Irene Rathbone (1988), *We that Were Young*, London, Virago (first published 1932), p. 407.
3 Ethel Bilborough, unpublished diary, Department of Documents, Imperial War Museum.
4 Hilda Craven, unpublished diary, Liddle Collection, Brotherton Library, University of Leeds.
5 Patricia Hanbury, unpublished diary, Liddle Collection, Brotherton Library, University of Leeds.
6 Woolf, *Diary*, vol 1, p. 216.
7 This extract is reproduced in Angela K. Smith (ed.) (2000), *Women's Writing of the First World War: An Anthology*, Manchester, Manchester University Press.
8 Jay Winter (1995), *Sites of Memory Sites of Mourning: The Great War in European Cultural History*, Cambridge, Cambridge University Press, p. 197.
9 I would again emphasise that these arguments could be made equally effectively about the writing of men. It is simply the agenda of this book to consider women's writing.

10 Allatini, R. (A. T. Fitzroy) (1988), *Despised and Rejected*, London, GMP (first published 1918), p. 197.

11 See for example the novels of Virginia Woolf (1992), *Jacob's Room*, Oxford and New York, Oxford University Press (first published 1922) and (1976), *Mrs Dalloway*, London, Grafton (first published 1925); those of Jean Rhys (1930), *After Leaving Mr Mackenzie*, London, Penguin, and (1939) *Good Morning Midnight*, London, Penguin; the short stories of women like Mary Butts, Kay Boyle, Djuna Barnes and HD in Bronte Adams and Trudi Tate (eds) (1991), *That Kind of Woman*, London, Virago.

12 Most important studies of female modernisms focus on the women who wrote through this 'psychology of despair' during the inter-war years, without substantial references to the important literary legacy of the First World War itself. See for example, Shari Benstock (1987), *Women of the Left Bank*, London, Virago; Gillian Hanscombe and Virginia L. Smyers (1987), *Writing for their Lives: The Modernist Women 1910–1940*, London, Women's Press.

Select bibliography

Memoirs and letters held by the Department of Documents, Imperial War Museum

Bilborough, Ethel Mary, unpublished diary, MS.
Brown, Mary Ann, unpublished diary, MS.
Clarke, Mary, unpublished diary, MS.
Kenyon, Winifred, unpublished diary, TS.
Neal, Rosie, unpublished memoir, MS.
Pemberton, Eleanora Blanshard, unpublished letters, TS.
Stobart, Mrs Mabel St Clair, unpublished diary, TS.
Williams, Daisy, 'Adventures in Germany, May–September 1914', MS

Memoirs held by the Liddle Collection, the Brotherton Library, University of Leeds

Craven, Hilda, unpublished diary, MS.
Hanbury, Patricia, unpublished diary, MS.
Macleod, Mary Lillias, unpublished memoir and letters, TS.
Thompson, Muriel, 'Base Notes', unpublished diary, MS.

Primary sources

Aldington, R. (1929), *Death of a Hero*, London, Chatto & Windus.
Allatini, R. (A. T. Fitzroy) (1988), *Despised and Rejected*, London, GMP (first published 1918).
Asquith, C. (1968), *Diaries 1915–18*, London, Hutchinson.
Bagnold, E. (1978), *A Diary without Dates*, London, Virago (first published 1918).
Bagnold, E. (1987), *The Happy Foreigner*, London, Virago (first published 1920).
Barbusse, H. (1974), *Under Fire*, London, J. M. Dent (first published 1917).
Blunden, E. (1978), *Undertones of War*, London, W. Collins (first published 1928).

Borden, M. (1929), *The Forbidden Zone*, London, William Heinemann.

Borden, M. (1931), *Sarah Gay*, London, William Heinemann.

Brittain, V. (1992), *Testament of Youth*, London, Virago (first published 1933).

Brittain, V. (1936), *Honourable Estate*, London, Victor Gollancz.

Brittain, V. (1981), *Chronicle of Youth: War Diary 1913–17*, London, Victor Gollancz.

Cahill, A. F. (ed.) (1993), *First World War Papers of Margaret Fawcett*, Pietermaritzburg, Wyllie Desktop Publishing.

Canfield, D. (1918), *Home Fires In France*, New York, Henry Holt.

Cannan, M. W. (1976), *Grey Ghosts and Voices*, Kineton, Roundwood Press.

Crane, S. (1994), *The Red Badge of Courage*, London, Penguin (first published 1895)

cummings, e. e. (1922), *The Enormous Room*, New York, Boni and Liseright.

Dixon, T. (ed.) (1988), *The Little Grey Partridge: First World War Diary of Ishobel Ross*, Aberdeen, Aberdeen University Press.

Doolittle, H. (HD) (1984), *Bid Me to Live*, London, Virago (first published 1960).

Duhamel, G. (1918), *The New Book of Martyrs*, London, William Heinemann.

Eliot, T. S. (1990), *Selected Poems*, London, Faber & Faber.

Ford, F. M. (1982), *Some Do Not . . .*, London, Penguin (first published 1924).

Ford, F. M. (1982), *No More Parades*, London, Penguin (first published 1925).

Ford, F. M. (1982), *A Man Could Stand Up*, London, Penguin (first published 1926).

Ford, F. M. (1982), *The Last Post*, London, Penguin (first published 1928).

Graves, R. (1973), *Goodbye to All That*, London, Penguin (first published 1929).

Hall, R. (1994), *The Well of Loneliness*, London, Virago (first published 1928).

Hamilton, M. A. (1916), *Dead Yesterday*, London, Duckworth.

Hamilton, M. A. (1930), *Special Providence*, London, George Allen & Unwin.

Holland, R. (1932), *The Lost Generation*, London, Victor Gollancz.

Jones, P. (ed.) (1972), *Imagist Poetry*, London, Penguin.

Kaye-Smith, S. (1918), *Little England*, London, Cassell (first published 1918).

La Motte, E. N. (1916), *Backwash of War*, London, G. P. Puttnam's Sons.

Lawrence, D. H. (1971), *Aaron's Rod*, London, Heinemann (first published 1923).

Lawrence, D. H. (1986), *Women in Love*, London, Penguin (first published 1920).

Macaulay, R. (1923), *Told by an Idiot*, London, W. Collins.

Macaulay, R. (1986), *Non-Combatants and Others*, London, Methuen (first published 1916).

Mansfield, K. (1927), *Journal of Katherine Mansfield*, ed. J. M. Murry, London, Constable.

Mansfield, K. (1954), *Journal of Katherine Mansfield*, ed. J. M. Murry, London, Constable.

Mansfield, K. (1962), *Bliss and Other Stories*, London, Penguin (first published 1920).

Mansfield, K. (1984), *Collected Stories*, London, Constable.

Price, E. (Helen Zenna Smith) (1988), *Not So Quiet . . . Stepdaughters of War*, London, Virago (first published 1930).

Rathbone, I. (1988), *We that Were Young*, London, Virago (first published 1932).

Reilly, C. (ed.) (1992), *Scars upon my Heart*, London, Virago.

Remarque, E. M. (1991), *All Quiet on the Western Front*, London, Picador (first published 1929).

Richardson, D. (1992), *Pilgrimage 1*, London, Virago (first published 1915, 1916, 1917).

Robins, E. (1919), *The Messenger*, London, Hodder & Stoughton.

Sandes, F. (1916), *An English Woman-Sergeant in the Serbian Army*, London, New York and Toronto, Hodder & Stoughton.

Sandes, F. (1927), *The Autobiography of a Woman Soldier. A Brief Record of Adventures with the Serbian Army 1916–1919*, London, H. F. & G. Witherby.

Sassoon, S. (1986), *The Complete Memoirs of George Sherston*, London, Faber & Faber (first published 1937).

Sinclair, M. (1915), *A Journal of Impressions in Belgium*, London, Hutchinson.

Sinclair, M. (1916), *Tasker Jevons*, London, Hutchinson.

Sinclair, M. (1917), *The Tree of Heaven*, London, Cassell.

Sinclair, M. (1920), *The Romantic*, London, W. Collins.

Stern, G. B. (1919), *Children of No Man's Land*, London, Duckworth.

Stobart, M. St C. (1913), *War and Women*, London, G. Bell.

Stobart, M. St C. (1916), *The Flaming Sword in Serbia and Elsewhere*, London, Hodder & Stoughton.

Tate, T. (ed.) (1995), *Women, Men and the Great War*, Manchester, Manchester University Press.

T'Serclaes, Baroness de, and Chisholm, M. (1916), *The Cellar House at Pervyse: A Tale of Uncommon Things from the Journals and Letters of the Baroness de T'Serclaes and Mairi Chisholm*, London, A. & C. Black.

West, R. (Anon) (1930), *War Nurse: The True Story of a Woman Who Lived, Loved, and Suffered on the Western Front*, New York, Cosmopolitan Book Corporation.

West, R. (1987), *The Return of the Soldier*, London, Virago (first published 1918).

Wharton, E. (1923), *A Son at the Front*, London, Macmillan.

Wilson, R. (1919), *If All These Young Men*, London, Methuen.

Woolf, V. (1976), *Mrs Dalloway*, London, Grafton (first published 1925).

Woolf, V. (1977), *Diary of Virginia Woolf*, vol. 1, *1915–1919*, London, Hogarth Press.

Woolf, V. (1989), *To the Lighthouse*, London, Grafton (first published 1927).

Woolf, V. (1990), *A Room of One's Own*, London, Grafton (first published 1929).

Woolf, V. (1992), *Jacob's Room*, Oxford and New York, Oxford University Press (first published 1922).

Woolf, V. (1992), *A Room of One's Own* and *Three Guineas*, Oxford and New York, Oxford University Press (first published 1929 and 1938 respectively).

Secondary sources

Adams, B. and Tate, T. (eds) (1991), *That Kind of Woman*, London, Virago.

Bagnold, E. (1985), *Enid Bagnold's Autobiography*, London, Century (first published 1969).

Bakhtin, M. M. (1981), *The Dialogic Imagination*, ed. M. Holquist, trans. M. Holquist and C. Emerson Austin, TX, University of Texas Press.

Barker, P. (1992), *Regeneration*, London, Penguin (first published 1991).

Barker, P. (1994), *The Eye in the Door*, London, Penguin (first published 1993).

Barker, P. (1995), *The Ghost Road*, London, Viking.

Beauman, N. (1983), *A Very Great Profession*, London, Virago.

Benstock, S. (1987), *Women of the Left Bank*, London, Virago.

Benstock, S. (ed.) (1988), *The Private Self: Theory and Practice of Women's Autobiographical Writings*, London, Routledge.

Bergonzi, B. (1980), *Heroes' Twilight*, London, Macmillan.

Blodgett, H. (1988), *Centuries of Female Days: Englishwomen's Private Diaries*. New Brunswick, NJ, Rutgers University Press.

Bourke, J. (1996), *Dismembering the Male: Men's Bodies, Britain and the Great War*, London, Reaktion Books.

Brittain, V. (1929), 'Their Name Liveth', *Manchester Guardian*, 13 November.

Buitenhuis, P. (1987), *The Great War of Words: Literature as Propaganda 1914–18 and After*, London, B. T. Batsford.

Cadogan, M. and Craig, P. (1981), *Women and Children First: The Fiction of Two World Wars*, London, Victor Gollancz.

Cahill, A. F. (ed.) (1999), *Between the Lines: Letters and Diaries from Elsie Inglis's Russian Unit*, Bishop Auckland, Pentland Press.

Cardinal, A., Goldman, D. and Hattaway, J. (1999), *Women's Writing on the First World War*, Oxford, Oxford University Press.

Cecil, H. and Liddle, P. H. (eds) (1996), *Facing Armageddon: The First World War Experienced*, London, Leo Cooper.

Clark, S. (1991), *Sentimental Modernism: Women Writers and the Revolution of the Word*, Bloomington and Indianapolis, IN, Indiana University Press.

Cooke, M. and Woollacott, A. (eds) (1993), *Gendering War Talk*, Princeton, NJ, Princeton University Press.

Cooper, H. M., Munich, A. A. and Squier, S. M. (eds) (1989), *Arms and the Woman*, Chapel Hill, NC, and London, University of North Carolina Press.

DeKoven, M. (1991), *Rich and Strange: Gender, History, Modernism*, Princeton, NJ, Princeton University Press.

DuPlessis, R. B. (1986), *H.D. The Career of that Struggle*, London, Harvester.

Eksteins, M. (1989), *Rites of Spring: The Great War and the Birth of the Modern Age*, New York, Bantam Press.

Faulkner, P. (ed.) (1986), *A Modernist Reader: Modernism in England 1910–1930*. London, B. T. Batsford.

Ferguson, N. (1998), *The Pity of War*, London, Allen Lane.

Figes, E. (1994), *Women's Letters in Wartime 1450–1945*, London, Pandora.

Firchow, P. E. (1980), 'Rico and Julia: The Hilda Doolittle–D. H. Lawrence Affair Reconsidered', *Journal of Modern Literature*, 8 (1), 51–76.

Florence, M. S., Marshall, C. and Ogden, C. K. (1987), *Militarism versus Feminism*, London, Virago (first published 1915).

Fussell, P. (1977), *The Great War and Modern Memory*, Oxford, Oxford University Press.

Garner, L. (1984), *Stepping Stones to Women's Liberty*, London, Heinemann Educational.

Gilbert, S. M. (1983), 'Soldier's Heart: Literary Men, Literary Women, and the Great War', *Signs*, 8 (3), Spring, 422–50.

Gilbert, S. M. and Gubar, S. (1988), *No Man's Land: The War of the Words*, New Haven, CT, and London, Yale University Press.

Gilbert, S. M. and Gubar, S. (1994), *No Man's Land: Letters from the Front*, New Haven, CT, and London, Yale University Press.

Goldman, D. (ed.) (1993), *Women and World War 1: The Written Response*, London, Macmillan.

Hanley, L. (1991), *Writing War: Fiction, Gender and Memory*, Amherst, MA, University of Massachusetts Press.

Hanscombe, G. and Smyers, V. L. (1987), *Writing for their Lives: The Modernist Women 1910-1940*, London, Women's Press.

Hardy, B. (1988), 'Introduction' to *Not So Quiet . . . Stepdaughters of War*, London, Virago.

Higonnet, M. (1993), 'Not So Quiet in No Woman's Land', in M. Cooke and A. Woollacott, (eds), *Gendering War Talk*, Princeton, NJ, Princeton University Press.

Higonnet, M. (1999), *Lines of Fire: Women Writers of World War 1*, New York, Penguin.

Higonnet, M. R., Jenson, J., Michel, S. and Weitz, M. C. (eds) (1987), *Behind the Lines: Gender and the Two World Wars*, New Haven, CT, and London, Yale University Press.

Hogan, R. (1991), 'Engendered Autobiographies: The Diary as a Feminine Form', *Prose Studies*, 14 (2), September, 95–107.

Holton, S. S. (1986), *Feminism and Democracy: Women's Suffrage and Reform Politics in Britain 1900–1918*, Cambridge, Cambridge University Press.

Homer (1988), *The Iliad*, Oxford, Oxford University Press (translated by R. Fitzgerald 1974).

Huston, N. (1986), 'The Matrix of War: Mothers and Heroes', in S. R. Suleiman (ed.), *The Female Body in Western Culture*, Cambridge, MA, Harvard University Press.

Hynes, S. (1990), *A War Imagined*, London, Bodley Head.

Jelinek, E. (1980), *Women's Autobiography*, Bloomington and Indianapolis, IN, Indiana University Press.

Joyce, J. (1965), *Portrait of the Artist as a Young Man*, London, Penguin (first published 1916).

Joyce, J. (1986), *Ulysses*, London, Penguin (first published 1922).

Knight, L. (ed.) (1993), *Infinite Riches*, London, Virago.

Leed, E. J. (1981), *No Man's Land: Combat and Identity in World War 1*, Cambridge, Cambridge University Press.

Light, A. (1991), *Forever England*, London, Routledge.

Lumley, J. (ed.) (1993), *Forces Sweethearts*, London, Imperial War Museum.

Marcus, J. (ed.) (1983), *The Young Rebecca: Writings of Rebecca West 1911–17*, London, Virago.

Marcus, J. (1989), 'The Asylums of Antaeus: Women, War and Madness – Is there a Feminist Fetishism?', in H. Veeser (ed.), *The New Historicism*, London, Routledge, pp. 132–51.

Masters, J. (1970), *Fourteen Eighteen*, London, Corgi Books.

Nichols, P. (1995), *Modernisms: A Literary Guide*, London, Macmillan.

Onions, J. (1990), *English Fiction and Drama of the Great War, 1918-39*, London, Macmillan.

Ouditt, S. (1994), *Fighting Forces, Writing Women*, London, Routledge.

Ouditt, S. (1999), *Women Writers of the First World War – An Annotated Bibliography*, London, Routledge.

Parfitt, G. (1988), *Fiction of the First World War: A Study*, London, Faber & Faber.

Pick, D. (1993), *War Machine*, New Haven, CT, and London, Yale University Press.

Playne, C. E. (1925), *The Neuroses of the Nations*, London, George Allen & Unwin.

Playne, C. E. (1931), *Society at War 1914–16* London, George Allen & Unwin.

Playne, C. E. (1933), *Britain Holds on 1917, 1918*, London, George Allen & Unwin.

Raitt, S. and Tate, T. (eds) (1997), *Women's Fiction and the Great War*, Oxford, Clarendon Press.

Samuel, R. (ed.) (1989), *Patriotism*, vol. 1, London, Routledge.

Scott, B. K. (ed.) (1990), *The Gender of Modernism*, Bloomington and Indianapolis, IN, Indiana University Press.

Sebba, A. (1986), *Enid Bagnold: The Authorised Biography*, London, Weidenfield & Nicholson.

Sebba, A. (1994), *Battling for News*, London, Hodder & Stoughton.

Segal, L. (1987), *Is the Future Female*, London, Virago.

Showalter, E. (1987), *The Female Malady*, London, Virago.

Showalter, E. (ed.) (1993), *Daughters of Decadence*, London, Virago.

Simons, J. (1990), *Diaries and Journals of Literary Women from Fanny Burney to Virginia Woolf*, London, Macmillan.

Smith, A. K. (2000) *Women's Writing of the First World War: An Anthology*, Manchester: Manchester University Press.

Stanley, L. (1992), *The Auto/biographical I*, Manchester, Manchester University Press.

Stetz, M. D. (1987), 'Drinking the Wine of Truth: Philosophical Change in West's *The Return of the Soldier*', *Arizona Quarterly*, 43 (1), 63–78.

Stevenson, R. (1992), *Modernist Fiction: An Introduction*, London, Harvester Wheatsheaf.

Strachey, R. (1989), *The Cause*, London, Virago (first published 1928).

Summers, A. (1988), *Angels and Citizens: British Women as Military Nurses 1854–1914*, London, Routledge.

Tate, T. (1998), *Modernism, History and First World War*, Manchester, Manchester University Press.

Tennyson, A. (1994), *The Works of Alfred Lord Tennyson*, Ware, Wordsworth Editions.

Tomalin, C. (1987), *Katherine Mansfield: A Secret Life*, London, Viking.

Tylee, C. M. (1990), *The Great War and Women's Consciousness*, London, Macmillan.

Tylee, C. M. (1999), *War Plays by Women*, London, Routledge.

Vansittart, P. (1998), *Voices From the Great War*, London, Pimlico.

West, R. (1982), 'On The Return of the Soldier', *Yale University Gazette*, 67, 66–71.

Wheelwright, J. (1989), *Amazons and Military Maids*, London, Pandora.

Wiltsher, A. (1985), *Most Dangerous Women*, London, Pandora.

Winter, J. (1988), *The Experience of World War 1*, London, Guild.

Winter, J. (1995), *Sites of Memory Sites of Mourning: The Great War in European Cultural History*, Cambridge, Cambridge University Press.

Woolf, V. (1966), *Collected Essays*, vol. 2, London, Hogarth Press (first published 1925).

Zilboorg, C. (ed.) (1992), *Richard Aldington and H.D.: The Early Years in Letters*. Bloomington and Indianapolis, IN, Indiana University Press.

Further reading

Aldrich, M. (1918), *On The Edge of the War Zone*, London, Constable.

Auerbach, N. (1979), *Communities of Women: An Idea in Fiction*, Cambridge, MA, Harvard University Press.

Balfour, F. (1918), *Dr Elsie Inglis*, London, Hodder & Stoughton.

Beer, G. (1970), *The Romance*, London, Methuen.

Boll, T. M. (1973), *Miss May Sinclair: Novelist*, London, Associated University Presses.

Bracco, R. M. (1993), *Merchants of Hope: British Middlebrow Writers of the First World War 1919–39*, Providence, RI, Oxford, Berg.

Braybon, G. and Summerfield, P. (1987), *Out of the Cage: Women's Experiences in Two World Wars*, London, Pandora.

Cahill, A. F. (1994), 'From Sitting Still to Making History: Elsie Inglis's Russian Unit 1916–1917', paper given at the Annual Conference of the Women's History Network, University of Natal, South Africa.

Canfield, D. (1930), *The Deepening Stream*, London and Toronto, Jonathan Cape.

Cannan, M. W. (1934), *The Lonely Generation*, London, Hutchinson.

Cather, W. (1987), *One of Ours*, London, Virago (first published 1922).

Cecil, H. (1995), *The Flower of Battle: British Fiction Writers of the First World War*, London, Secker & Warburg.

Condell, D. and Liddiard, J. (eds) (1987), *Working for Victory*, London, Routledge.

Coppard, G. (1969), *With a Machine Gun at Cambrai*, London, Imperial War Museum.

Cork, R. (1994), *A Bitter Truth: Avant-Garde Art and the Great War*, New Haven, CT, and London, Yale University Press.

Delafield, E. M. (1918), *The War-Workers*. London, William Heinemann.

DuPlessis, R. B. (1985), *Writing Beyond the Ending*, Bloomington and Indianapolis, IN, Indiana University Press.

DuPlessis, R. B. (1990), *The Pink Guitar*, New York and London, Routledge.

Elliott, B. and Wallace, J.-A. (1994), *Women Writers and Artists: Modernist (im)positionings*, London, Routledge.

Elshtain, J. B. (1987), *Women and War*, London, Harvester.

Firda, R. (1993), *All Quiet on the Western Front: Literary Analysis and Cultural Context*, New York, Twayne.

Gilbert, S. M. and Gubar, S. (1984), *The Madwoman in the Attic*, New Haven, CT, and London, Yale University Press.

Griffin, G. (1994), *Difference in View: Women and Modernism*, London, Taylor & Francis.

Hamilton, C. (1917), *Senlis*, London, W. Collins.

Hamilton, C. (1919), *William an Englishman*, London, Skeffington.

Hamilton, P. (1978), *Three Years or the Duration: The Memoirs of a Munition Worker 1914-1918*, London, Peter Owen.

Haste, C. (1992), *Rules of Desire. Sex in Britain: World War 1 to the Present*, London, Chatto & Windus.

Hemingway, E. (1988), *A Farewell to Arms*, London, Guild (first published 1929).

Hill, S. (1985), *Strange Meeting*, Bath, Chivers Press (first published 1971).

Hirschkop, K. and Shepherd, D. (eds) (1989), *Bakhtin and Cultural Theory*, Manchester, Manchester University Press.

Holtby, W. (1981), *The Crowded Street*, London, Virago (first published 1924).

Ingram, A. and Broe, M. L. (eds) (1989), *Women's Writing in Exile*, London and Chapel Hill, NC, University of North Carolina Press.

Ingram, A. and Patai, D. (eds) (1993), *Redisovering Forgotten Radicals: British Women Writers 1889–1939*. London and Chapel Hill, NC, University of North Carolina Press.

Jameson, F. (1983), *The Political Unconscious*, London, Methuen.

Jardine, A. A. (1985), *Gynesis: Configurations of Woman and Modernity*, London, Cornell University Press.

Joannou, M. (1995), 'Gender, Militancy and Wartime', in J. Swindells (ed.), *The Uses of Autobiography*, London, Taylor & Francis.

Joannou, M. (1995), *'Ladies, Please Don't Smash These Windows': Women's Writing, Feminist Consciousness and Social Change 1918–38*, Providence, RI, and Oxford, Berg.

Jones, N. and Ward, L. (eds) (1991), *The Forgotten Army*, Beverly, CA, Highgate Publications.

Khan, N. (1988), *Women's Poetry of the First World War*, London, Havester Wheatsheaf.

Kristeva, J. (1986), *The Kisteva Reader*, ed. T. Moi, London, Blackwell.

Lawrence, D. H. (1955), *Kangeroo*, London, William Heinemann (first published 1923).

Levenback, K. L. (1999), *Virginia Woolf and the Great War*, New York, Syracuse University Press.

Lewis, P. W. (1967), *Blasting and Bombardiering*, London, Calder and Boyars (first published 1937).

Liddington, J. and Norris, J. (1978), *One Hand Tied behind Us: The Rise of the Women's Suffrage Movement*, London, Virago.

Liddle, P. (1994), *The Worst Ordeal: Britons at Home and Abroad 1914–1918*, London, Leo Cooper.

MacDonald, L. (1978), *They Called It Passchendaele*, London, Penguin.

MacDonald, L. (1980), *The Roses of No Man's Land*, London, Penguin.

Macdonald, S., Holden, P. and Ardener, S. (eds) (1987), *Images of Women in Peace and War*, London, Macmillan.

Manning, F. (1990), *The Middle Parts of Fortune*, London, Penguin (first published 1930 as *Her Privates We*).

Marcus, J. (ed.) (1985), *New Feminist Essays on Virginia Woolf*, London, Macmillan.

Miller, J. E. (1994), *Rebel Women: Feminism, Modernism and the Edwardian Novel*, London, Virago.

Millet, K. (1977), *Sexual Politics*, London, Virago.

Moers, E. (1986), *Literary Women*, London, Women's Press.

Moi, T. (1993), *Sexual Textual Politics*, London, Routledge.

Pankhurst, E. S. (1987), *The Home Front*, London, Hutchinson (first published 1932).

Read, H. (1930), *In Retreat*, London, Faber & Faber.

Sherriff, R. C. (1929), *Journey's End*, London, Victor Gollancz.

Showalter, E. (1982), *A Literature of their Own*, London, Virago.

Showalter, E. (1992), *Sexual Anarchy: Gender and Culture at the Fin de Siecle*, London, Virago.

Showalter, E. (ed.) (1992), *The New Feminist Criticism*, London, Virago.

Silkin, J. (1981), *The Penguin Book of First World War Poetry*, London, Penguin.

Smith, J. (ed.) (1992), *Femmes de Siecle*, London, Chatto & Windus.

Smith, S. (1987), *The Poetics of Women's Autobiography: Marginality and the Fictions of Self-Representation*, Bloomington and Indianapolis, IN, Indiana University Press.

Spender, D. (ed.) (1983), *Feminist Theorists*, London, Women's Press.

Stubbs, P. (1979), *Women and Fiction*, London, Harvester Wheatsheaf.

Thomas, H. (1972), *As It Was and World without End*, London, Faber & Faber (first published 1926 and 1931 respectively).

Trotter, D. (1993), *The English Novel in History 1895-1920*, London, Routledge.

Tylee, C. M. (1988), '"Maleness Run Riot": The Great War and Women's Resistance to Militarism', *Women's Studies International Forum*, 11 (3), 199–210.

Von Arnim, E. (1917), *Christine*, London, Macmillan.

Waugh, P. (1992), *Practising Postmodernism Reading Modernism*, London, Edward Arnold.

Wheeler, K. (1994), *'Modernist' Women Writers and Narrative Art*, London, Macmillan.

Wussow, H. (1988), 'The Nightmare of History: The Great War and the Work of Virginia Woolf and D. H. Lawrence', PhD thesis, Oxford University.

Zegger, H. D. (1976), *May Sinclair*, Boston, Twayne.

Index

'n.' refers to a note on the page indicated.

Printed in the United Kingdom
by Lightning Source UK Ltd.
118039UK00001B/420